DEFENSIVE FLYING

DEFENSIVE FLYING

FLYING

Edited by Norbert Slepyan

Prologue by Max Karant

An **AOPA** Book

AN ELEANOR FRIEDE BOOK

Macmillan Publishing Company · New York
Collier Macmillan Publishers · London

Macmillan Publishing Company
866 Third Avenue, New York, N.Y. 10022
Collier Macmillan Canada, Inc.

Library of Congress Cataloging-in-Publication Data
Defensive flying.
"An AOPA book."
"An Eleanor Friede book."
Includes index.
1. Aeronautics—Safety measures.   2. Airplanes—
Piloting.   I. Slepyan, Norbert.
TL553.5.D44   1986   629.132'52'0289   86-14719
ISBN 0-02-611520-4

Macmillan books are available at special discounts for bulk purchases for sales promo-
tions, premiums, fund-raising, or educational use. For details, contact:

Special Sales Director
Macmillan Publishing Company
866 Third Avenue
New York, N.Y. 10022

10 9 8 7 6 5 4 3 2 1

Designed by Jack Meserole

Printed in the United States of America

CONTENTS

ACKNOWLEDGMENTS   vii

EDITOR'S INTRODUCTION   *by Norbert Slepyan*   ix

PROLOGUE   "Fear"   *by Max Karant*   xiii

Part One   MIDAIR AVOIDANCE

1   The Friendly Little Airport   3

2   Seeing to Avoid   28

3   Living with the Green Demon   51

4   Under Control   67

5   "6241 Yankee . . ."   91

Part Two   SURFACE CONFLICTS

6   How Clear to Land?   107

7   Roughing It   121

8   Getting Up and Around   142

Part Three   PRECARIOUS PARTNERSHIPS

9 Accidental Sabotage   165

10 Fuel Mismanagement   190

11 Briefing Obscured?   214

Part Four   QUESTIONS OF COMMAND

12 En Route Decisions   233

13 Command and the Real World   250

14 Left Seat, Right Seat   274

15 Pilot Impairment   300

INDEX   327

ACKNOWLEDGMENTS

From the pages of AOPA Pilot, the following contributors are acknowledged with thanks:

Stephan P. Barnicle
Bruce Barton
Edward E. Beatty
Don Bragg
Randolph S. Diuguid
Carole K. Dundas
James W. Dunn
Larry J. Duthie
Robert W. Ehrlich
Larry F. Ferguson
James S. Forney
James B. Freed
Kevin Garrison
Edward J. Gauss
J. H. Grosslight
Lee Gruenfeld
Joel Hamm
Philip Handelman
Thomas A. Horne
Denny Komes
William P. Krieter
Mark M. Lacagnina
Terry T. Lankford
Russell S. Lawton
William Lipsky

Roger S. Macomber
Richard H. Mansfield
Robert P. Mark
David G. Martin
Ray Martin
Rick H. Martin
Charles W. Mellon
Herman L. Meltzer
J. Jefferson Miller
Dave Minion
William E. Moore
Anton S. Nesse
James J. Newell
Steve Nieman
Phil Van Ostrand
Eugene Roberts
Robert M. Ross
Roger Rozell
Tony Shideler
Mary F. Silitch
Mark R. Twombly
Robert T. Warner
Alfred L. Wolf
John S. Yodice

For pilots, there are two kinds of instruction. One is the formal sort, which is regulated by the Federal Aviation Administration, overseen by an army of certified instructors, and peopled by eager students intent on getting licenses, ratings, and the knowledge the various curricula have to offer.

The other kind is the school of hard knocks. Its curriculum is regulated by circumstance. Its instructors are pilots who have survived and are willing to talk or write about flights in which things did not go right. The students are pilots of all levels of experience who are willing to learn from others' triumphs and failures.

Hard-knocks instructors have much to offer. They can confirm formally taught procedures and techniques and also point up stressfully discovered, lifesaving responses to crises. Their wisdom includes hard-found tricks of the trade that may augment what the curricula contain. Their lessons are offered not from the lofty position of the Instructor indoctrinating the lowly Student, but with the more convincing authority of tough candor tinged with painful embarrassment.

Formal instructors tend to say, "Do what the FARs and I say to do. Do what I show you to do." In the school of hard knocks, our colleague/teachers say, "Understand what I admit doing or failing to do, and do *not* follow that example."

Defensive Flying is about flight as pilots experience it. Like its predecessor, *Crises in the Cockpit,* it is an instruction manual from the school of hard knocks. Drawn in a revised form from *AOPA Pilot* magazine, its pages contain National Transportation

ix

Safety Board reports about the hardest knocks, when aircraft crashed and pilots and passengers died or were hurt. More important, it contains pilots' vivid narrations of hazardous experiences, as related in the magazine's popular feature, "Never Again." It also provides instruction by the *AOPA Pilot* staff. These contributions have been gathered and organized to provide insights into such areas as collision avoidance, operations at airports, dangers in fuel management and aircraft maintenance, potential hazards in working with ATC and Flight Service, and critical problems of command.

The greatest difference between formal aviation instruction and hard-knocks lessons is the latter's insistence that pilots maintain a heightened awareness of the reliability gap. Flying is a complex world of powers and responsibilities and doesn't permit complacency over procedures and working relationships. The lessons point out why one cannot always rely on things going right if rules and procedures are followed robotically by unthinking pilots and their ground support. We must be defensive in our approach, anticipating and being ready to respond to the errors of others, just as we try to avoid making errors of our own.

Defensive flying, like defensive driving, calls for alertness without paranoia. Because aviation is a high-cooperation endeavor, defensive flying does not tolerate hostility, but it does demand a realistic recognition of human weakness, and the adoption of tactics for self-protection.

On the ramp and in the cockpit, wariness and respect are saving graces. They must be kept in proper balance and maintained constantly. We respect our fellow pilots as well as the controllers, mechanics, and FSS briefers who are charged with helping to make our flights as safe as possible. But we must also be wary of their fallibility. "Other" pilots do forget their responsibilities or fall short in skill and good sense. Controllers, briefers, and other ground personnel do steer us wrong in various ways. In short, people we rely on can fail to do their jobs—even as we can fail to do ours. Knowing this calls for the kind of fear Max Karant describes in the prologue to this book—a healthy respect for the possibility of things going wrong, but without the paralyzing effects of panic or hysteria.

Defensive flying, above all, means knowing and respecting our mutual responsibilities, under the dominant stipulation that the pilot-in-command is always accountable for the safety of the flight, from before the hour when he rolls the machine out of the hangar until he rolls it back in.

This emphasis by no means intends to diminish the sheer fun of flying. In fact, conscientious pilots will find in these recommendations little, if anything, that will cramp their style, as long as their style is configured to having fun without incurring grief. The instruction does, however, take into account that the evolution of general aviation and the problems that have accompanied it have led to new traffic, weather and technological considerations that pilots must incorporate into their command methods and decisions.

It is a pleasure for AOPA to make available to the general pilot community what has essentially been the "property" of AOPA members. The "Never Again" narrators have presented their experiences with honesty, humility, and generosity. The *Pilot* staff writers have provided much the same kind of service. They are active pilots who, like their readers, have seen things go wrong from time to time. They may not tell war stories in these pages, but their advice comes as much from years of hands-on experience as from textbooks. All of the contributions have worked in service to the trust that we are all together in trying to make flight ever safer and ever more the fulfilling adventure and instrument it is meant to be.

Together we enjoy flying's delights and suffer some losses. Behind this book is the belief that we best prevent such losses together, honestly and generously as sharers of the skies.

NORBERT SLEPYAN

Fear

Any pilot who says he's *not* fundamentally afraid of airplanes is either a liar or a fool. If he's honest about his innermost feelings, he'll be a lot less likely to end up a statistic. Unfortunately, far too many pilots stick their macho chests out and tell the world they know all about that particular set of circumstances—so what the hell!

There are many kinds of fear—but they are gradations of the same thing. Many psychiatrists say that fear is a health self-preservation emotion.

I've experienced many gradations of fear and am not ashamed to admit it. That is why I've been flying for well over 30 years and nearly 10,000 hours and am still going. Many people confuse fear with panic. These things are different, and not many pilots who panic survive. I fear panic.

Panic is the extreme. It's uncontrollable terror. The only things that might possibly save you in that state are the design of the airplane you're in, its flight characteristics—if you let go of it—or luck.

Having been in on the birth of the AOPA's Air Safety Foundation and many of its programs, I've had the rewarding opportunity to see pilots coping with everything from nervousness to panic.

In the few times I've come close to it, I couldn't even tell you what two and two equalled. A lot of guys who have admitted to experiencing panic say the same thing. Not many pilots live to confess a bout with panic. Fortunately for me, I have. Once, I got so much ice while flying on instruments over the

Alleghenies that my plane was pushed below the minimum en route altitude. It was winter, but I was sweating. Then I remembered what a wise old instructor had warned me of years before: When you feel *that* coming on, slap yourself, yell, jump up and down—anything to get your thoughts back on a logical track. I did, and immediately told Center my predicament and asked where the nearest radar approach control facility was. Center said Charleston, West Virginia. I envisioned that wild terrain.

Soon Center handed me over to Charleston Approach, and it was clear Charleston had been warned that I sounded shaken. When Approach acknowledged radar contact, I told him I was 2,000 feet below the MEA at full throttle and asked where the nearest dangerous obstructions were. He calmly told me there was a ridge 20 miles south and that it should be no problem to me.

I managed to reduce the panic to apprehension and nervousness and was thinking fairly clearly. I blessed that Canadian bush pilot friend of mine who told me how to burnish the leading edges of my props and spray them with silicone to keep the ice off (it worked like a charm). I told the controller to give me *very* gentle turns onto the ILS for fear of stalling (he'd already figured that out), and I broke out of the freezing rain just above 1,000 feet agl—at full throttle. Slowing down, I chose what seemed to be the safest combination of gear and flaps, then landed going like a bat out of hell. I still sweat over it.

Panic approached at Santiago, Chile, too. It was solid IFR, and I found I'd filed for an airport that wasn't there! It was a new terminal; the approach plate was published, complete with frequencies. But in the air, a Chilean pilot told me the airport wasn't there yet. I was low on fuel and in the Andes—the kind of country that's not conducive to bluffing. I'd been told the radio aids at the old airport were out of service. Frantically I began tuning around the VOR receiver. Suddenly, I received a station that was the VOR on the old airport. I told the tower I had it, and he casually said, "Okay, go ahead and use it."

They're very casual and informal down there in South America—another worry.

I set up a VOR approach and frantically kept tuning the ADF to nearby beacons on either side of the approach. My inbound track matched what I had on the approach chart for the old airport. A hole opened in the heavy rain clouds, and in the hole was the end of Runway 03—a sight I'll never forget. I'm not an aerobatic pilot, but I was that day. I went into that hole like a performer at the National Air Races, leveled off over the runway number, and touched down—only to see a line squall obliterating the other end of the runway, moving toward me. I didn't give a damn at that point; my wheels were solid on the ground.

This is the kind of experience that can kill people. In normal, everyday flying, I experience nervousness, some apprehension, and worry. Will I hit a bird? Will an engine quit, and where would I land? (Any grass strip—or a SAC base would suit me then.) Is some other plane, like an airliner, coming up my rear, where I can't see him? I stay on radar for protection. Is that little trouble with the gear likely to keep it from extending? I've got a theory with my plane: My major concern is to keep fuel flowing to the engines and get the wheels down. Everything else may be difficult, but not a crisis.

I'm *always* apprehensive about the National Weather Service, either VFR or IFR. No matter what they tell you, you must be prepared for the opposite and the worst. That icing in the mountains was a morning flight, and those experts didn't know a thing about that weather or its hazards. When a DC-3 corporation pilot (who landed after me) and I told them in some rather nonregulation language after we got on the ground, these were their first pireps. Meteorologists have told me it was CAVU from Washington to Philadelphia—and I've run into a squall line 20 miles northeast of Washington. No explanation, just a shrug. My instrument rating is my life insurance.

Playing the role of the sage, I'd tell *any* pilot to prepare himself for some level of fear whenever he flies. That preparation will help to alleviate some of the problem. Once you're in the air, stand by with the controllers in the centers and towers, no matter whether you're VFR or IFR. In case of trouble, they can be wonderful helpers.

Have a healthy respect for fear, and don't be ashamed of it. Used properly, it can keep you alive.

MAX KARANT

Part One
MIDAIR AVOIDANCE

1
The Friendly Little Airport

What pilot has not at some time watched in alarm as a fellow pilot's aircraft streaked close by, seemingly from out of nowhere? Sometimes we have the precious time, sense, and reflexes to keep our craft clear. If not, we may only catch a momentary glimpse of the other plane as it passes or maneuvers to miss us. When we get our breath back after dodging such a bullet, we may reflect that a difference of only a few seconds, a degree or two of heading or a relatively few feet of altitude could have meant disaster. All too often we can only gratefully and fearfully chalk up our escape to blind luck or Providence.

At such times it becomes unimpressive that every year an average of "only" 30 midair collisions occur in American airspace. At such times, the statistical odds in our favor mean nothing. Death by midair becomes a presence as tangible as the dryness in our throats and the trembling of our hands.

The statistics carry both comfort and threat. From 1973 to 1982, for instance, there were 303 midair accidents in the United States, 168 of them fatal. Only one collision in that period involved two airliners; three were between airliners and general aviation airplanes; eight involved general aviation and military planes. All the rest—291 midairs—were between general aviation aircraft. In 1984 there were 592 reported near misses.

Considering that these near-miss incidents came to less than one per 100,000 flights, the odds still seem to be on our side, but it remains sobering to recognize that it has taken great efforts by pilots and air traffic control to keep the numbers low. Millions of dollars' worth of technology and reams of regula-

3

tions over the years testify to the enormity of the task. What is important is not how few or how many collisions occur but that they do happen and that each one represents a failure by the pilots or the system or both.

In essence, the issue comes down to what people in their cockpits can do to fly defensively, observing the fighter pilot's article of faith that the enemy you do not see is the enemy most likely to get you.

How do these friendly bogeys get us? Where are we most likely to encounter them, and how do we allow the lethal contacts to occur? What defenses do we have, and how much of a shield is there in regulated procedures, positive control and the traffic-tracking equipment we tend to take for granted? In this section of *Defensive Flying,* we will examine how collisions occur and how they can be avoided. Special problems are involved, not only at airports, where the traffic is most dense, but en route, especially where inhabitants of the "green demon's" airspace may painfully surprise us.

A National Transportation Safety Board survey of collision accidents provides a typical portrait of the overall problem for general aviation. In one ordinary year, 1979, 25 midairs occurred, of which 14 were fatal to 34 people. All but one involved only general aviation airplanes. While 40 percent of them happened in cruise flight, the same percentage took place in landing patterns, and 72 percent were within five miles of an airport. Only two percent were at night.

A typical midair situation might be this: daylight, good visibility, airspeed below cruise, altitude below 5,000 feet, aircraft near or in the traffic pattern in a *low-density* traffic area. For various reasons, most midairs occur at noncontrolled airports and can happen even when some ATC surveillance is at work.

Lessons from a Midair

An accident that took place recently, in August 1984, has revealed several ways in which lapses by pilots and the system can encourage a catastrophe.

This collision—between a Wings West Beech 99 and a single-engine Rockwell Commander—happened near San Luis Obispo, California. It was a beautiful morning: 15,000 scattered, 15 miles visibility, only a whisper of wind.

The Rockwell, with two pilots on board, was out of the Paso Robles airport. One pilot was highly experienced and, according to students who flew with him, an instructor who was given to insisting, "Keep your eyes out of the cockpit." The other crewman was a retired Navy pilot. He held a commercial ticket and an instrument rating, with about 2,500 hours of military flight time. He was being checked out in the Commander.

Shortly before 11 a.m., local time, the Commander called for airport advisories from the Paso Robles Flight Service Station and then departed for the San Luis Obispo Airport (SBP). The Los Angeles Center computer recorded its flightpath down the 196-degree radial of the Pas Robles VOR to an inbound track that generally coincided with the San Luis Obispo localizer.

At about 11:15 a.m., the Unicom operator at SBP heard the aircraft call, "Inbound, approach, Dobra." Less than a minute later, he heard the sharp, high-pitched *crack* that must have been the midair collision. The crash occurred at 3,400 feet msl, approximately eight miles northwest of SBP and about one mile northwest of Dobra Intersection.

The Beech 99 was operating as a regularly scheduled Wings West Airlines commuter flight. That day, the airplane and its crew had already been from SBP to Los Angeles and Santa Maria and back to SBP. It was now destined for San Francisco. The flight left the gate at SBP at 11:10 with 13 passengers and a flight crew of two. Because the weather was good, the crew opted to depart VFR and to pick up an IFR clearance en route.

Los Angeles Center maintains a canned IFR SBP–San Francisco flight plan, which consists of a Crepe One SID to Crepe Intersection, direct Big Sur Vortac, direct San Francisco, at 8,000 feet. For a Runway 29 takeoff, the SID calls for a climb via the SBP localizer on a northwest, 290-degree course to Crepe.

The flight departed Runway 29. Neither the Wings West flight follower nor the Unicom operator later recalled hearing any radio transmissions from the Beech as it taxied out and before it took off. However, a pilot who took off just prior to the Beech did hear it announce over Unicom, "Departing Runway 29 straight out."

Once airborne, Wings West called Los Angeles Center for its IFR clearance. After radio contact was established, Center assigned the flight a transponder code and reported radar contact six miles northwest of SBP. The controller asked for an altitude report, and the response was "three-thousand-one-hundred climbing." The controller then cleared the flight to the San Francisco airport, as filed, and to climb to and maintain 7,000 feet; he provided the current altimeter setting.

During the postcrash investigation the controller said that a few seconds after Wings West's readback, at about five miles northwest of where he first observed the beacon target, he lost radar contact. He attempted to reestablish radar and radio contact, but to no avail. The two aircraft had collided virtually head-on. There were no survivors.

Failure to Watch

According to the NTSB's calculations, which were based on head-on target size, at best the Rockwell would have had 23 seconds to avoid the collision after sighting the Beech. The Beech would have had 17 seconds. There were four pilots up front in the two craft—men who were highly experienced, safety-conscious, and especially knowledgeable about the need to look for other traffic—and, although the time was short, each pilot apparently had the ability to observe the approaching traffic and avoid the conflict. Yet not one of them did. Clearly, a momentary relaxation of see-and-avoid vigilance can lead to a midair.

An accompanying lesson is that it can be a tragic mistake to rely too much on radar advisories from ATC. Wings West was in radio and radar contact with Center. The center's computer, which records and stores target information, showed the Rockwell transponder target merging with Wings West, but the Beech was never warned of conflicting traffic.

Four controllers should have been in a position to spot the merging targets but later reported seeing none near Wings West: the controller handling Wings West, who was being given a radar certification check (he said that he had seen no other traffic in Wings West's vicinity when he formally established radar contact with the flight, 22 seconds before the collision, or thereafter, until the target went into "coast," meaning when a target is lost or weak, after the collision); the fully qualified controller monitoring him, a man fully experienced at that position; another controller who was working the data position right next to the other controllers and checking the scope from time to time; and a first-line supervisor who was observing the performance of the controller being checked. In its consideration of the causes, the NTSB noted as an underlying factor the shortness of the time that was available to the controllers to detect and appraise the radar data and to issue a safety advisory.

This should be warning enough for pilots against a common tendency to relax their outside scan when they are under radar control or assume that potential traffic is being watched.

Noncontrolled Confusion

The NTSB's analysis of this midair focused heavily on operations near uncontrolled airports. The board said that the probable cause of the accident was the failure of the pilots to follow the recommended communications and traffic advisory practices for noncontrolled airports contained in the *Airman's Information Manual.*

According to the *AIM,* "it is essential that pilots be aware of and look for other traffic and exchange traffic information when approaching or departing an uncontrolled airport." For those airports that have a Unicom facility, it recommends that pilots "call about 10 miles from the airport and state your aircraft identification, type of aircraft, altitude, location relative to the airport, and request wind information and runway in use; report on downwind, base, and/or final approach as appropriate; and report clearing the runway." It recommends that outbound aircraft advise traffic of their departures by broadcasting the name of the airport, aircraft type and call sign, and the departure runway.

SBP has a 122.8 MHz Unicom frequency. There is evidence that Wings West announced its departure on Runway 29 "straight out" and the Rockwell called "inbound approaching Dobra" on the same Unicom frequency. Yet they probably did not hear each other. At about the time of the Rockwell's call, Wings West was some five miles from the airport calling Center for its clearance and was probably not on Unicom to hear the Rockwell's position report. The NTSB criticized their failure to abide by the *AIM*'s recommendation to monitor the airport's common traffic advisory frequency (SBP's Unicom) until ten miles from the airport. The board also cited the airline's requirement that its pilots always monitor the company frequency. Had one pilot continued to monitor Unicom while the other talked to Center, they might have known that the Rockwell was approaching from ahead and might have been able to see and avoid it.

The board guessed that, because of the route it had taken, the Rockwell was conducting a practice instrument approach. Further evidence of this was that the Commander's Number 1 radio receiver, though badly damaged, showed 108.7 MHz, one

MHz below the SBP localizer frequency. Among the *AIM*'s recommended procedures is that "at airports without a tower, pilots wishing to make practice instrument approaches should notify the facility having control jurisdiction of the desired approach as indicated in the approach chart."

A pilot who had often flown with the instructor said that the instructor almost always informed Los Angeles Center of intentions to conduct such approaches. Why he did not do so this time remains a mystery. Had he done so, the Center controller would have known of the Commander's position before he began to handle Wings West and would have been able to call out the traffic to each of the flights.

The NTSB pointed out another important circumstance about this flight: The standard instrument departure and the standard instrument approach at the airport could cause aircraft to fly head-on into each other. Though operating VFR at the time, Wings West was proceeding from SBP's Runway 29 by the Crepe One SID. If the Rockwell was practicing a localizer approach to Runway 11, the two flight paths were directly opposed. The board's subsequent recommendation caused the FAA to include a note on the approach and SID charts, "During VFR conditions, watch for opposing traffic on the localizer." Opposing IFR procedures exist at many airports, and pilots should be alert to them.

Similarly, at noncontrolled airports, pilots descending out of IFR into marginal or imaginary VFR can find themselves—if granted the time to discover it—in conflict with VFR pilots practicing in the pattern or making a sneaky scud-run approach:

• A Swearingen SA-226-TC Merlin corporate airplane with two pilots aboard was conducting a VOR/DME approach to an uncontrolled airport at the end of a small peninsula in Texas. Before crossing the final approach fix, one of the pilots contacted Unicom and requested an airport advisory. The Unicom operator, a certified weather observer, said that the wind was from

140 degrees at eight knots and relayed a pilot report of a 500-foot ceiling and two miles visibility over the airport but "zilch" (zero/zero) over the water.

The pilot of a Grumman AA5A Cheetah (private license, 1,700 total hours) then reported on Unicom that he was turning final for Runway 14. (This was a misstatement; the airplane actually was on a left downwind for the runway.) Unicom advised the Cheetah pilot of the reported weather conditions and that another aircraft was inbound for Runway 14. (The operator assumed, correctly, that the Merlin would terminate its northeasterly approach by circling to land on Runway 14.)

The Cheetah was flying straight-and-level on an extended downwind, and the Merlin was turning onto left base when they collided over the water at about 300 feet.

Both pilots aboard the Merlin were killed as was the pilot of the Cheetah. In addition to citing the pilots' failure to see and avoid, the NTSB determined that inadequate communications by the pilots contributed to the collision. Here, communications, courtesy, and visual contact were all critical defenses.

Concealed Weapons

Most pilots seem to understand that in the air, courtesy and consideration are not merely the marks of ladies and gentlemen but are essential to survival when traffic cops are not around to enforce them. They know that it may take patience to accept the inconveniences of accommodating to others. Still, they also know that cooling it pays.

Sad and even frightening to say, however, the atmosphere around many a friendly little airport is not one of gentility or even of universal common sense or sanity. Some pilots cut other pilots off or devise their own bewildering, instant procedures without regard for what anyone else is doing. A pilot on a prescribed left base may suddenly confront someone on an illegal or at least unethical right base for the same runway, or on glancing to his right may suddenly spy someone barreling in unannounced on a dramatic and no doubt more convenient straight-in. And just as some pilots may widen and elongate a pattern to the breaking point, others may decide to "tighten things up" by turning inside the flow, like line crashers at a movie. And, of course, there are always those scrambling, dashing devils who, like drag racers, squeal onto the active for sneak take-offs just ahead of "slowpokes" on short-short final. These aces are brothers and sisters to, or are even the same folks as, pilots who magically depart the pattern at just the right point to confound custom-abiding arrivals. We won't mention the experts who, according to their own peculiar lights, blithely take off and land with no consideration given to wind, traffic, or right reason.

Though they would deny it, such jockeys in effect use their lightplanes as weapons, often concealed weapons, for they are not apt to inform the traffic of what they are doing, assuming they know what they are doing. Those who do announce often do so peremptorily, cutting themselves in and others out with little or no warning and no awareness or concern that they are fouling things up. Moreover, a stint of pattern watching at a busy uncontrolled airport can demonstrate that it is not simply inexperienced pilots who make such errors. Professional pilots are as guilty of poor airport flying as low-time students.

Add to the outrages of such bozos the difficulties of seeing other aircraft in some conditions—certain of which are created by pilots themselves—and a "friendly" little airport can become a place devoutly to be avoided.

Yet at many noncontrolled fields, corporate Learjets, Citations, King Airs and Conquests share the pattern with a variety of piston-powered aircraft. Helicopters approach from many directions, staying clear of fixed-wing traffic. There, too, gliders operate from grass strips paralleling hard runways, and occasionally a gyrocopter or ultralight may take to the air, keeping to its own world. It is possible for birds of various feathers to flock together if the brains who fly them are not feathered, too.

Pattern Protocol

The shape and procedures of the pattern are among the first things we learn as students, yet familiarity does breed contempt and forgetfulness and can lead pilots literally and dangerously to cut the corners of the pattern rectangle. More important still, jaded pilots may overlook that in VFR flying, the time spent in the traffic pattern is likely to be the busiest time of a flight. There the pilot becomes preoccupied with chores inside the cockpit—completing checklists, setting power, lowering flaps and gear—and may temporarily disregard the primary jobs of steering the airplane and watching for traffic. The best way to handle the workload is to plan in advance and approach pattern flying systematically. And except when conditions dictate otherwise, you should follow that system consistently.

On takeoff, climb straight ahead until you pass the departure end of the runway and are within 300 feet of pattern altitude. Then, unless noise abatement procedures call for a different maneuver, turn 90 degrees to the crosswind leg if you intend to remain in the pattern. To exit the pattern, turn 45 degrees after reaching both the end of the runway and the pattern altitude and hold that course until you are well clear of and above the pattern. A pattern can also be exited via a straight-out departure, if traffic permits. Under most circumstances, do not make a right turn if the pattern is left-handed, for you could fly into an aircraft making a crosswind entry to downwind. However, an instrument departure or ATC instruction could require such a turn, so look carefully.

The FARs do not specify procedures for entering traffic patterns, and there is some debate among pilots about the best methods for doing so. However, the FAA's recommended procedure, as outlined in the *AIM,* is the 45-degree pattern entry. Ideally, you should establish yourself on the 45-degree entry course several miles from the airport. This angle provides an excellent view of other aircraft in the pattern. Your flight path should place you abeam the runway's midpoint as you reach the pattern. Meanwhile, your descent to the airport should have been managed to reach pattern altitude well before pattern entry.

When you approach an airport from the side opposite the downwind leg, it may seem inconvenient to circumnavigate the field by several miles so that you may enter on a 45-degree angle, but it is the safest and most courteous way to arrive in the pattern. Crosswind entries and straight-in approaches are not illegal but are inadvisable when a potential for traffic conflict exists. On an approach along a flight path opposite the downwind leg's direction, give the airport a berth of several miles to avoid downwind traffic. Entering the pattern in a steeply banked turn can obstruct your view and surprise other pilots.

However you enter or depart, activate your landing and recognition lights to alert other pilots to your presence.

The downwind leg should be flown approximately one-half to one mile from the landing runway. The size and speed of the aircraft should determine the pattern width. A number of piston twins and singles cannot fly slowly enough to maintain trail position behind small, slow aircraft. If yours is such a plane, fly a wide pattern to maintain separation. Heavier piston- and turbine-powered aircraft should fly a higher and wider pattern. A wide pattern allows pilots of faster craft to observe slower traffic and safely fit themselves into the traffic flow.

For light aircraft, the pattern altitude is usually 700 to 1,000 feet above the airport elevation. Heavy piston twins and turbine-powered aircraft should fly a 1,500-foot pattern. Uncontrolled airports should be overflown by at least 2,000 feet *above the pattern* to avoid the traffic.

To pilots flying a pattern altitude, other aircraft at the same altitude will appear on or near the horizon. A rule of thumb for selecting a downwind speed is to fly at 1.7 V_{SO} (stall speed in the landing configuration). For most high-performance aircraft, this speed should be below the maximum speed for operating the landing gear. To maintain an adequate distance behind your preceding traffic, it may be necessary to make gentle S-turns or to slow the airplane to its final approach speed (V_{ref})— usually 1.3 V_{SO}—while adding power as required to maintain altitude. If the spacing is still too tight, you can extend the downwind leg after the traffic ahead turns base.

On downwind, complete the landing checklist. The landing gear should be extended by this point. If there is a crosswind, you may have to maintain a crab to avoid drifting too near or far from the runway.

Make a 90-degree turn to base after you have passed abeam the approach end of the runway. Your object is to turn sufficiently far from the end to make a gradual descent to the touchdown point. Many pilots find that a 45-degree bearing to the numbers is a good rule of thumb for beginning the turn.

A crosswind threatening to push you closer to the runway can lead to trouble when you turn final, for it could become a leg-shortening tailwind on base. The turn to final should begin early enough to avoid flying through the extended centerline of the runway. Pilots who find themselves on the wrong side of the centerline sometimes make tight turns in order to double back and line up with the runway. This is the classic prelude to a stall/spin, for when the turn is made, the pilot may cross the controls and haul back on the yoke to compensate for an over-steep bank and a dropping nose. The best defense against such a hazardous combination of errors is to make a coordinated turn to final. To ensure that you will do so in spite of a crosswind factor, fly a wider downwind leg, which will result in a longer base and a shallower, coordinated turn to final. In any case, if you cannot make a normal descent to the runway, initiate a go-around.

In a lightplane, make the turn to final at least one-quarter mile from the runway threshold to provide enough distance to make a steady, stable approach. Final approach should be flown at V_{ref}. If conditions are gusty, compensate by increasing the approach speed by one-half the normal approach speed (for instance, if the wind is 15 knots gusting to 25, increase the approach speed by 5 knots).

Approach-slope aids, such as VASI lights, are extremely helpful, especially for pilots landing at unfamiliar airports, where obstructions may not be readily visible. Maintain a descent profile that stays on or slightly above the glideslope. Low dragged-in approaches are unwise for several reasons. It is easy to overlook obstructions such as wires or branches, especially if you don't really know the airport or the approach is a bit tricky. Low-level engine failures are far more hazardous than high-level ones. Dragged approaches are noisier for the airport's neighbors. Most important for the defensive flier is the danger that another aircraft can accidentally descend upon a plane flying below the normal glidepath. (Turbine and piston aircraft weighing more than 12,500 pounds, when landing on runways equipped with an ILS or a VASI, are required to fly on or above those glideslopes during approaches made VFR.)

Unless they are otherwise indicated by ground markers or are announced as such by Unicom or controllers, all patterns are flown with left-hand turns. High terrain, obstructions or noise-abatement considerations may dictate a right-hand pattern. At some airports, L-shaped markers may surround the windsock, wind tee or tetrahedron to indicate traffic direction. At night, a blinking amber light in the segmented circle or atop a ground structure indicates a right-hand pattern.

Show and Tell

Flying in any congested airspace and especially in noncontrolled busy airspace can be like flying a fighter when you know the enemy is aloft. Your bogey may come at you out of a low-lying sun or out of a background of haze or terrain or simply be too razor thin and small to be noticed when looked at from the front. Like the fighter pilot, we have to scan the sky to detect the intruder.

Few of us fly under dome canopies that facilitate rear vision, and all lightplanes have blind spots, so unlike fighter pilots, we don't try to make ourselves hard to find but, instead, must make ourselves as conspicuous to potential bogeys as possible: We show ourselves to other aircraft, and we tell of our presence among them.

The value of lights at night need hardly be discussed, except to point out that the "old-fashioned" red rotating tail beacon and red and green wingtip lights are nowhere nearly as effective as strobes and other devices, and that it is highly advisable to show one's landing light at least when near any airport and even during cruise, when visibility is not clear and traffic may be nigh.

Many pilots activate their strobes and landing lights even during the daytime, when visibility is good, which makes sense since that is when most midairs occur.

Strobes get other pilots' attention far better than ordinary nav lights. Two other recent additions to the pilot's defenses are the Tel-Tail system and pulse lights. Tel-Tail is a set of exterior lights that illuminate the vertical tail. Depending on the type aircraft, the lights may be installed on the wingtips, engine pylons, or horizontal stabilizer.

Pulse Lights are an aircraft's existing landing, taxi or recognition lights wired to pulse at 40 to 90 cycles per minute. The rewired lights can be operated in the pulsing mode or in their normal steady state. Because the Pulse Light system is wired to an aircraft's forward-facing lights, it does not offer increased protection in situations where aircraft converge from the rear. It may offer greater recognition at a longer distance than convential lights, including strobes. As they pulse on and off in series, the lights look a bit like highway caution lights that endlessly blink back and forth. Whatever one's system, good lighting is a vital defensive asset.

As the San Luis Obispo midair demonstrated, a genuine attempt by endangered pilots to see and be seen can make all the difference. Still, as those pilots headed inbound and outbound along that localizer, the catastrophic effects of self-imposed deafness helped spell their doom. Flying VFR and unguided—and one of them actually unnoticed—by ATC, they were, in effect, their own inadequate controllers.

At any noncontrolled field, all of us in the pattern are like elements of an inclusive traffic controller or airport tower. At the friendly little airport, as at any large controlled one, successful traffic regulation is a combination of recognition, cooperation, and *communication*. When we can't see or be seen, our only salvation may be to hear and he heard.

Why is it that more than half the midairs that plague us take place in VMC, in airspace within five miles of and 1,000 feet above uncontrolled airports? One reason may well be that radio communication at these airports can be a virtual shambles. To understand the magnitude of the problem, listen to any Unicom frequency at any uncontrolled airport. Pilots announce pattern entry without mentioning the airport's name; they fail to give advance notice of their approach to the traffic pattern; they neglect to mention their positions and intentions in the pattern; and many of them indulge in citizen's band (CB) radio slang, social banter, and other extraneous palaver. At times, listening on Unicom yields nothing but ear-blowing squeals as pilots step on each others' attempts to get a word in. A woeful lack of discrete Unicom frequencies is made worse by the indiscretions of those who use them.

Perhaps because our noncontrolled airports' self-regulated, pilot-operated "towers" are so often constructed of babble, many VFR airmen resist the idea, expense, and discipline of maintaining a good radio presence and watch. Many of them cite years of conflict-free flying without radios and insist that since they fly for *fun,* they don't need to emulate the frequency-bound "big boys." They make the point that many pilots become such slaves to radio procedures, instructions, and reports, that they fly with their heads buried in the cockpit, as if headsets were like blankets pulled over their heads. Radios for emergencies, yes, but otherwise. . . .

A letter to *AOPA Pilot* put the case this way: "Airplanes have been around for quite a while now and have been operated very safely without radios. Those of us who fly without radios fly because it is fun; we don't have to get anywhere in particular or do anything important. Some of us spend most of our disposable cash just trying to keep a flying machine in the air. . . . If you haven't tried flying without a radio, don't knock it; it is as safe as the rest of flying. But the ultimate responsibility for safe flying rests with the pilot, not the radio."

There is a kernel of truth in that, since mouths and ears are not meant to be substitutes for eyes in VFR flying. A head buried in the cockpit is an endangered one. Yet how many pilots struck down in midairs have had among their last thoughts sheer surprise at having collided with an airplane they looked for but for some reason did not or could not see?

Party Line Procedures

No regulations govern radio procedures at uncontrolled airports. This is as it should be, since about 16 percent of general aviation aircraft are not equipped with communication radios. Also, unique safety considerations and other factors such as terrain and proximity to other airports may make standardized procedures unworkable for all airports. While radio-less VFR flying at uncontrolled airports can be safe, pilots who have radios and know how to make clear, meaningful reports have an advantage. They can learn the locations and intentions of nearby traffic and keep others informed of their progress in the pattern.

The guidelines for traffic advisory practices at noncontrolled airports can be found in Chapter Four, paragraph 157 of the *AIM* and in *AOPA's Handbook for Pilots*. The proper procedures for participation in the airport party line can be divided into three categories: selecting the correct frequency; announcing your position and/or intentions at the appropriate time and place; and using recommended phraseology.

In an attempt to encourage the use of a common frequency at uncontrolled airports and to clarify the frequency to use, the FAA has established the concept of the common traffic advisory frequency. CTAF is the frequency that should be used for an airport's radio traffic advisories. Unfortunately, these frequencies are not widely publicized. They are published in the FAA's *Airport/Facilities Directory (AFD)* and on instrument approach plates. Established CTAFs are also published in *AOPA's Airports USA*.

Uncontrolled airports can be of several types. One is an airport with a part-time tower. When the tower is closed, its frequency becomes the CTAF. (Check the *AFD*, approach plates, or sectional charts to determine a part-time tower's hours.) In cases where a tower-frequency CTAF is in use and a Unicom is operating on the field, pilots may obtain wind and runway information over the Unicom frequency. It will be necessary to switch back to the CTAF if it is different from the Unicom frequency, once this information has been received.

Another type of uncontrolled airport is one with a flight service station that provides an airport advisory service (AAS) on 123.6 MHz or on some other designated frequency. When the AAS is in operation, FSS specialists provide basic information, such as the wind direction, favored or designated runway, altimeter setting, known traffic (not all traffic in the vicinity may be communicating with the AAS), notices to airmen, airport taxi routes, traffic pattern information, and information concerning instrument approach procedures.

When the AAS is in operation, use this service. When the AAS is off duty, the AAS frequency often is used as the CTAF.

If an airport is served by both a tower and an airport advisory service, and both are closed, a discrete CTAF frequency may be established and should be used for communications. (Again, check published sources for the correct CTAF.)

Most uncontrolled airports have neither tower nor AAS frequencies, but they often have designated Unicom frequencies, usually 122.7, 122.8, or 123.0 MHz. Check sectional charts, instrument approach plates or the *AFD* to determine the proper Unicom frequency. At these uncontrolled airports, the Unicom frequency is the CTAF.

If there is no tower, FSS, or Unicom on the field, the CTAF is 122.9 MHz, which is also known as the multicom frequency. In the past, this frequency was allotted for air-to-air communications, but it degenerated into an airborne variant of CB channel 19. The new frequency for air-to-air communications is 122.75 MHz (it is also set aside for use as Unicom at private-use airports). Apparently many pilots are not aware of this frequency change, and their chattiness has made airport traffic-sorting difficult at some fields. Again, know the purpose of the frequency you are using and use it for that purpose.

FREQUENCIES AND USES

122.700   Uncontrolled airports

122.725   Private airports (not open to the public)

122.750   Private airports (not open to the public)
          and air-to-air communications

122.800   Uncontrolled airports

122.900   Airports with no tower, FSS, or Unicom
          (multicom frequency)

122.950   Airports with control towers

122.975   High altitude

123.000   Uncontrolled airports

123.050   Heliports

123.075   Heliports

To summarize, the CTAF works on a top-down hierarchy, from the tower through the flight service station through Unicom, and then to Multicom. The trick lies in knowing where to look on available charts and flight information documents to find the highest level of service provided at any time. In a recent study, the NASA Aviation Reporting System found that a great number of people who had experienced near collisions in the vicinity of uncontrolled airports had used the proper procedures for traffic advisories, but either their own or the interfering aircraft had been using the wrong CTAF.

The Radio-effective Pilot

What are the proper advisory procedures? In essence, they are practices that create as few surprises as possible, that keep the traffic situation clear for anyone listening to the frequency, and that enable participating pilots to operate without anxiety or irritation.

To listen to most airline pilots as they communicate when things are hectic is to feel you are in the presence of friendly professionals who know what they are doing. Clarity and courtesy—and, of course, knowing what one is doing—are the hallmarks of savvy airmen on any frequency anywhere, from the little airport to the monstrous terminal. Clarity means being effective *and* economical in one's transmissions, allowing more helpful messages to be exchanged as the traffic flows on. Courtesy and consideration create the same results and enable pilots to keep their minds on the business at hand while maintaining an even string. You don't need a Yeager drawl or a basso profundo voice to seem like a professional, but you do need the professional's technique.

Rule number one for the radio-effective pilot is know what you want to find out or report and what you *need* to say to get the job done. Think before you speak, for hemming and hawing are vices of the confused and confusing amateur. Before you key the mike, listen to ensure that you will not transmit simultaneously with another pilot. By listening, you may also learn what runway is in use, what traffic is in the pattern and get wind and altimeter information without needing to ask.

Concise, accurate communication is essential. You want to be quick, even terse, and still be understood. Speaking too fast or in an oral shorthand that only you are likely to comprehend can only confuse others and ultimately waste time. If you frequently have to repeat your messages you are probably doing it wrong.

When you approach a non-tower airport, announce your position and intentions when you are still five to ten miles out. The timing of this first communication depends on how fast you are approaching the field. Give the name of the tower, Unicom service or airport, then report your N-number, location, and intentions, and then make your request—for instance, "Frederick Unicom, Navajo 6273R, ten miles south of the airport, 3,000 feet, inbound for landing, airport advisory, please."

A similar advisory should be made if you are practicing an instrument approach. The usual procedure is to broadcast your position and intentions when you are at the IAF, then at the FAF or outer marker and then, again, when you are on final approach. It is also advisable to report your position when inbound from a procedure turn. You will thus alert approaching and departing pilots as well as others who may be practicing the instrument approach. On a practice IFR approach, plan to break off before the DH or MAP and make a normal entry to the pattern at pattern altitude, unless you are *certain* you can complete the approach without conflicting with traffic. If you plan to execute a missed approach, report your intention, including the direction of your turn, and initiate the maneuver at pattern altitude. When you execute an instrument approach to an uncontrolled airport in actual IMC, report your position for the benefit of VFR traffic, for there may be some, even if the ceiling and visibility are relatively low. During IFR departures at uncontrolled fields, monitor Unicom or CTAF while talking to ATC, including clearance delivery. This will decrease the chance of an IFR departure blocking a taxiway or runway or creating a conflict in the air.

Reporting Around the Pattern

As you initiate your VFR approach, make sure your landing and other recognition lights are on, check the area for traffic, and descend to pattern altitude. Since you will now be speaking only to other pilots in the pattern, not Unicom, address your communications to them—for example, "Frederick traffic, Navajo 6723R enter left downwind for Runway 19." Notice two vital points: Because other airports in the vicinity may share the same CTAF frequency, each transmission should *begin* with the name of the airport you are talking to—this will immediately sort you out from traffic elsewhere; specify that you are flying a left or right downwind and your target runway—without this information, other pilots can only guess where you are.

On your reports on base and final you can shorten the N-number to the last three characters (73R), but it is helpful to give some indication of your aircraft type. A pilot taking station behind you can thus know that he should be seeing a twin (Navajo 73R) or a high-wing aircraft (Cessna or Skylane 82G) ahead of him. If he sees something different, he can check if he is mistaken about his place in the pattern sequence or if he is following a non-announcing plane. This method isn't flawless, but it can help. It is also a public service to declare early if your landing will be a full-stop or a touch-and-go; this will help others in the pattern to plan their arrival at the threshold and prepare to go around if traffic is too closely spaced. If you are practicing touch-and-goes, announce that you are flying "closed traffic," as you enter the pattern.

When there are a number of airplanes in the pattern, it is radio-effective to announce your position in the landing sequence by saying, for example, "Frederick traffic, Navajo 73R on extended left downwind for Runway 19, number three to land." Or you can identify the airplane you are following (Navajo 73R, following the Grumman" or ". . . following Grumman 99Q"), which will notify the traffic ahead that you are aware of their positions and notify planes behind you that you are indeed in the pattern on an extended downwind and not merely passing though the area at pattern altitude—as some pilots are unwisely wont to do. Be reasonably descriptive. A pilot flying a large twin on a wide pattern at 1,500 feet would report a "high, wide" downwind or base.

It is crucial to report final, including short final, to discourage the Ace of the Base who may otherwise ignore you as he takes the active for a quick-and-sneaky takeoff, or that obtuse captain who moseys leisurely onto or across the runway, blissfully unaware of or unconcerned about your imminent arrival on his tail or skull. He, of course, should have announced his intentions before making his move, but for such pilots that may be too much to ask. Always report "taking the active," "crossing the active," or "back-taxiing on the active." Similarly, when you turn off the active, report doing so.

A Flexible Instrument

Noncontrolled airports present the great advantage of flexibility. The procedures are simpler and the requirements fewer there than at tower-dominated fields. For their pilots, with freedom comes a need for self-discipline in flying and in talking. Self-service traffic management calls for avoiding extraneous and nonstandard phraseology, as well as overlong reports and chit-chat. For a pilot trying to call his pattern entry or to get traffic information, it is not only frustrating but dangerous to have to wait for a couple of good ol' boys to finish their har-de-hars. Yet there is room on the frequency for such legitimate uses as making stopover arrangements or having a Unicom operator notify a local contact of a late or early arrival or, late in the day, asking a mechanic to stick around to check a faulty gizmo. It is up to the pilot's judgment and good sense to determine if what he wants to say can wait until he is on the ground or if the traffic is light enough to allow him mike time to make arrangements without hogging the air waves. The instrument is flexible, and so must be its users.

Whenever possible, CTAF is used to control airport lighting systems at uncontrolled airports. Operators of ground vehicles frequently monitor CTAF, Unicom or multicom when they drive on airport premises. Furthermore, although it is not the emergency frequency of preference (121.5 MHz is always monitored by specialists), the frequency serving any uncontrolled field may be used for making emergency broadcasts and warnings concerning hazards on the airport or in the pattern. Remember that you will be broadcasting in the blind and that no one may be monitoring the frequency.

Finally, the CTAF frequencies can function in conjunction with ATC. They can be used to give IFR pilots altimeter settings—on many IFR approaches, an altimeter setting from the relevant Unicom allows descent to the lowest published minimums. IFR pilots approaching uncontrolled airports usually are authorized by ATC to switch to the CTAF. Unicom and multi-com can also be used for the verbatim relaying of such information as revision of departure time; takeoff, arrival or flight plan cancellation times; and ATC clearances, provided that arrangements are made between the ATC facility and the Unicom/multicom licensee to handle such messages.

Grass Roots Avoidance

Our friendly little airports in their great numbers remain the foundation of American general aviation and thus of all our aviation. It is here that most of our new pilots join our ranks. At these sometimes scruffy, sometimes splendid noncontrolled fields, flying for business blends with flying for fun. That they can be dangerous is our fault, but we can avoid that detriment by avoiding each other's planes when we are aloft. Some simple rules can help us do the job:

• Avoid ignorance of your own and others' pattern position. Avoid taking other planes for granted, and pinpoint all traffic in the pattern or near it as best you can.

• Accommodate your pattern to the traffic flow. Avoid cut offs.

• Avoid hogging the runway. If on an IFR departure you must pause to set a DG or perform another necessary chore, check and wait for the final approach path to be clear of inbound airplanes.

• Avoid dramatic departures. Announce your intentions and fly the standard takeoff and departure path for your field.

• Avoid dawdling on roll-out. Make *reasonable* speed to the turn-off.

• If while on base or final you foresee a conflict near the runway, prepare to go around early and high.

• For practice crosswind landings or uses of runways other than the active, announce your intentions and check to avoid conflicting with the general pattern flow aloft and on the runway.

• Avoid allowing your ego to dominate good practices and good sense. Don't contest for airspace or pattern priority or step on others' transmissions. If a pilot cuts you off or otherwise bugs you, save your vituperation for the ground, or just save it and cool it.

Cooperating with standard procedures and maintaining good radio vigilance help greatly to prevent aerial conflicts, but even more crucial to safety than observing the rules is observing and evading other aircraft. At the root of collision prevention is a militant looking to avoid. That is not always easy, and it, too, calls for a well-honed, practiced technique, which we shall examine in the following chapter.

2
Seeing to Avoid

Just as constant vigilance is the safeguard of liberty, for pilots it is a vital protector of life, limb, and aircraft. Relaxation and distraction can wreck us:

• The pilot of a Grob Speed Astir II sailplane was climbing within a thermal with three other sailplanes. A Schleicher ASW-20 was 500 feet above him; other sailplanes were 1,000 feet below. The Grob was at 4,000 feet and nearing a cloud base when the pilot lost sight of the Schleicher. As he prepared to leave the thermal, he again spotted the Schleicher. They were on a collision course. He maneuvered to evade, but the Schleicher took about ten feet off the Grob's right wing as it lost about nine feet from its left wing. The Grob's pilot was seriously injured but managed to bail out successfully. The pilot of the Schleicher was killed after his parachute failed to open.

• A student pilot and his flight instructor were practicing touch-and-goes in a Cessna 152 at an uncontrolled airport. After four landings on the active, Runway 18, they switched to Runway 7 for a crosswind practice. The airport advisory service was being provided by a FSS on the field, and the instructor advised the station of his intention to switch runways. Meanwhile the pilot of a Cessna Skylane reported on the advisory frequency that he was taxiing for takeoff on Runway 18. The FSS specialist advised the Skylane that the 152 was on downwind for Runway 7, but its pilot apparently did not hear him. Shortly after beginning his takeoff roll, the Skylane pilot spotted the 152 touching down. He aborted his takeoff, and the Skylane came to a stop at the runway intersection. The instructor initiated an evasive maneuver, but the 152's left wing still struck the Skylane's windshield.

Other pilots report similar incidents:

• "While preparing for departure, I taxied into position for runup so that I could see any downwind or base traffic. During the runup, incoming traffic called Unicom to ask the time, stating as an aside that he would be landing 'shortly.' By now, I was ready for takeoff, and, after scanning the pattern, I announced my intentions and started my takeoff roll. As I proceeded down the runway, I glanced up—just in time to notice another Cessna, not more than 50 feet agl, directly over me. The other traffic had done a straight-in without ever announcing his position or intention. . . . . A lesson I have been taught but failed to remember this time was to turn the airplane on runup so that I could see any downwind, base or *final* traffic before taxiing onto the active. Also, straight-in approaches at uncontrolled airports are dangerous and arrogant—but to fail to announce you're coming in is plain stupid and deadly."

• "I was cleared for takeoff on Runway 10, with no reported traffic in the area. About halfway into my takeoff run, I noticed an airplane about three miles dead ahead, at about 500 feet, coming straight in, head-on and downwind on Runway 28. I asked the tower, 'What's that airplane doing down at the other end of the runway?'

" 'Sir, we don't know. He hasn't contacted the tower, and we don't have him on radar,' was the response.

"I flipped on my landing lights, rotating beacon, and nav lights but received no response from the incoming airplane. Not being in a mood to play 'chicken,' I chopped the throttle, dumped full flaps and rode the brakes to a grinding halt off the runway and into gravel and brush as the other airplane went boldly on its way. The pilot's unannounced, straight-in, downwind approach threatened the lives of six innocent people."

Only one of these cases involved a fatality and injuries—those that did not were still very near misses—but they all reveal how crucial it is to see other aircraft in order to avoid them. Losing a bogey in marginal visibility, relying on the good sense of others to report their positions, taking for granted that no one is on final as you enter the active, and believing that the presence of a traffic cop—a tower—can enforce responsible flying, these and other factors can relax and distract us from manning our ultimate line of defense, visual vigilance.

Accepted Custom and False Impressions

The compounding of such hazardous factors can be insidious, as was dramatized by a recent midair that cost 15 lives. It took a while for all but one of the factors behind the accident to converge. The final element—failure of vigilance—lasted only seconds but was fatally decisive.

On April 17, 1981, Sky's West Parachute Center had been in operation as a sport parachuting firm for two years at the Fort Collins/Loveland Municipal Airport, in Loveland, Colorado. On a year-round basis, it had conducted more than 10,000 jumps annually, which qualified its jump site—two nautical miles east-southeast of the Fort Collins Airport—for charting on the Cheyenne sectional. However, the site was not depicted on the chart. Neither was it mentioned in the *Airport/Facility Directory* for the region. The National Oceanic and Atmospheric Administration, the publisher of these documents, had not been notified of the site's existence by Sky's West or the FAA.

At about 1:58 p.m. that day, a Sky's West official phoned to inform the Denver FSS about proposed jump activities for the afternoon and evening. A Cessna 205 and a Cessna 206 would drop parachutists 1.5 nm southeast of the Fort Collins airport from altitudes up to 18,000 feet msl. The jumps were to begin immediately. The FARs stipulate that notifications of intended parachute drops must be made to an ATC facility or a FSS at least one hour before the first flight, to allow specialists time to prepare a Notam, which, if requested, can be passed on to pilots planning to fly near the jump area.

The fact that the call came late mattered little in this case, because, while the FSS supervisor prepared the Notam and posted it on his own weather board, he did not tell any other FAA facility. He later testified that he "was under the impression" that Fort Collins/Loveland was an approved jump area listed in the *AFD* and that there was therefore no requirement "to do anything about it." The regulations say he was required to pass the information on.

At 2:10 p.m., on his first flight of the day, the pilot of Sky's West's 206, an ATP and CFI with 4,600 hours, contacted the Denver ARTCC: "Six-Two-Fox will be skydiving a mile-and-a-half southeast Fort Collins/Loveland Airport at 8500 feet approximately one minute, then will be climbing to 15,500."

Denver Center simply replied, "Roger."

At 2:21 p.m., the Cessna pilot again called Denver Center to say, ". . . Cessna Six-Two-Fox skydiving 15,500 feet one minute . . ." Seven seconds later, a controller again replied with a "Roger." The pilot had no further radio contact with ATC during the flight. This was a typical exchange and skydiving flight for Sky's West.

The firm's airplanes were not equipped with Mode C transponders capable of reporting altitude, yet FAR 91.24 prohibits any flights above 12,500 feet msl without an operating Mode C transponder. An exception to the rule that is pertinent here calls for at least a four-hour notice to ATC prior to flights where such equipment is required. Denver Center personnel were aware of Sky's West's operations, but ATC had not authorized their deviation from the rule and had not taken any actions concerning the ongoing violation.

The Cessna pilot later stated that he believed that the "Roger" responses from Center on his first flight of the day constituted an "authorization" to climb to higher altitudes without Mode

C. He had another misconception, for he believed that Center always had radar contact with him whenever he selected 1234 on his transponder, a code that Center had sometimes assigned Sky's West skydiving flights. That practice was not always followed, but the pilot stated that he believed he was permanently assigned that code and that squawking 1234 guaranteed positive radar identification.

Of course, a controller can see the radar return and code of an aircraft without Mode C—unless he erases all returns without altitude information. That is just what happened: To reduce the clutter on his scope, the controller working Sky's West's sector "deselected" all non-Mode C targets. His only targets were Mode C and primary target returns, which appear only if the radar energy bouncing off an aircraft and returning to the screen is strong enough. Sky's West's primary return was weak and appeared only 75 percent of the time. The 1234 squawk code never appeared, for it was not on the controller's code select list. Having no knowledge of the flight's altitude, the controller did not track the movements of the 206.

The Encounter

The second skydiving flight of the day took off at 3:30 p.m. Using the customary procedure, the pilot climbed in a left racetrack pattern over the airport on his way to the first jump altitude of 15,500 feet. Never during this flight did he communicate with Denver Center. As usual, his transponder was set at 1234. Five skydivers were on board.

At 3:46 p.m., Air U.S. Flight 716, a Handley Page H.P.137 Jetstream, took off on a scheduled commuter passenger flight from Denver's Stapleton International Airport, destination Gillette, Wyoming. Its captain held ATP and flight engineer-turbojet certificates and 4,784 total flight hours, with 1,784 in H.P.137s. Following regulations, Flight 716 was operating IFR, even though the weather at the time was 7,000 feet scattered and 20,000 thin broken with 60 miles visibility. Three crewmembers and ten passengers were on board.

At 3:59 p.m., as the Jetstream was approaching the jump site, its pilot acknowledged a clearance from Denver Center to maintain 13,000 feet. The flight was being routed direct from the Denver VOR to the Douglas (Wyoming) VOR.

At about 4:01 p.m., the Cessna and the Handley Page collided over the drop zone. The Cessna was in a climbing left turn. The nose and left wingtip of the Jetstream struck the Cessna's left side, and its left propeller slashed through the Cessna's aft fuselage, killing two parachutists.

Both airplanes went out of control. In a near vertical attitude, Flight 716 crashed in an open field, killing all on board. The Cessna pilot and the three remaining skydivers were able to bail out safely. The pilot and the skydiver seated next to him received minor injuries. The skydiver seated behind the pilot's seat suffered an ankle fracture, and the one next to him had his right foot nearly severed by the Jetstream's propeller. The 206 crashed in the same field as the Jetstream; the remains of the two airplanes were approximately 4,000 feet from each other.

The Decisive Failure to See

According to one popular theory, an accident is the culmination of a chain of events. Remove any of the links, the theory goes, and the accident would not have happened. In this instance, we have: an uncharted jump zone; an FSS supervisor who failed to distribute the Notam (which might have helped, had the Flight 716 flight crew asked for Notams during their preflight briefing); Denver ATC's allowing flights above 12,500 feet without Mode C equipment; a controller who deselected all non-Mode C returns and knew nothing of the 1234 code; and the pilots' contributions to the accident.

The Cessna pilot was at fault because he failed to communicate with Denver Center on the second flight. He mistakenly believed he was in radar contact. Had the controller known of Sky's West's presence in the jump zone and had he known that the Cessna was climbing to 15,500 feet, he might have made an effort to identify the Cessna and warn the Jetstream.

Yet there is another, simpler explanation of the cause of this accident: The pilots failed to see and avoid each other. In 60-mile visibility, the Jetstream, with two pilots up front, ran over the Cessna. This was an accident that could have happened had all the other preconditions not existed and in any radar environment. That is the chief lesson of this sad event.

The NTSB performed a computer simulation of the pilots' visual fields. Using radar plots and binocular photography from the cockpits of the types of airplane involved, the board learned that the Jetstream would have been in the binocular vision envelope of the Cessna pilot's windshield for at least 45 seconds, beginning two minutes before the collision. But for the minute just prior to the collision, the Jetstream was out of the Cessna pilot's field of vision.

The turn that helped blind the Cessna pilot was contributory enough, but the pilot also testified that he was not looking for traffic before the collision. He was looking at the airport and at the drop zone.

The NTSB determined that the Cessna was visible in both Jetstream pilots' windshields for about a 45-second interval 60 to 75 seconds before the collision. The Air U.S. pilots were not advised of any traffic and apparently were not scanning in the moments before the clash. Though the white Cessna would have created a visible contrast against the blue sky or the dark terrain, this advantage may have been diminished because the Cessna was in a turn. From the Jetstream pilots' viewing angle, the Cessna presented no wing surface area.

Had he looked, the Cessna pilot would have had a harder time seeing the Jetstream. The H.P.137 was coming straight at the 206 and showed a very small frontal profile.

The NTSB ruled that the probable causes of the accident were the failure of the Cessna pilot to establish communication with Denver Center, his climbing into controlled airspace above 12,500 feet without an authorization to deviate from the Mode C requirement, Denver Center's practice of routinely condoning Sky's West's jump operations above 12,500 feet without a Mode C transponder, and the failure of both pilots to see and avoid each other. The board also named as a contributing element the fact that existing regulations do not prohibit parachute jumping in or immediately adjacent to federal airways.

When the "All-Seeing" Eye Blinks

It bears repeating that whether you are IFR under positive control or VFR on your own but expecting ATC traffic advisories, you can't afford to take an absence of advisories as gospel that no conflicting traffic may be near. It has often happened that pilots reporting near misses have discovered that the most surprised folks to learn about it were the controllers at their "all-seeing" scopes.

An ex-Navy combat pilot, Richard H. Mansfield, describes how dangerous such circumstances can be, even when the airspace is a supposedly closely monitored terminal radar service area:

The clock-radio woke me at six a.m. with the bad news: "Two lightplanes collided yesterday, killing all occupants." The announcer said that the accident had occurred five miles south of a small airport that I had landed at many times. The report ended with, "The weather at the time was clear."

I immediately remembered a close call that I had been involved in just a few weeks before: a near collision that had been a little too "near" for me. I was climbing out VFR westbound from Albany, New York, in a Skyhawk, with Stage III traffic advisories. The weather was clear, the visibility was excellent, and there was very little traffic.

As I leveled at 4,500 feet, I heard Albany Departure talking to a light twin, clearing it to descend below my altitude. I knew that the Cessna twin was west of Albany (they split their frequencies east and west), but I had no idea that it was nearby, since neither of us has received any traffic advisories.

Just then, I received a frequency change: "Cessna Three-One-Lima, you are leaving the TRSA, squawk 1200, frequency change approved."

As I switched the radio, I spotted the airplane, dead ahead, descending right into me. I broke right, rolled out and watched the twin dive past at high speed. I was scared and mad. I switched back to Albany Departure and informed them, "That twin had me boresighted." All I got back was a laconic "Roger."

Fortunately, I had spotted the traffic with plenty of time to react. But here we were, in CAVU conditions, under radar advisories with transponders on, in a low-traffic-density situation, and we nearly met head-on. It was a classic midair situation.

Those who fly in combat or even in simulated combat know that the phrase "check your six" and the willingness to swivel your head is a survival skill. When I was flying Navy jets, I always liked to see my flight leader's head moving, scanning, because one has to twist the neck to scan properly. . . . It is comfortable to lapse into the womb of the high-glareshield, fully instrumented airplane and be lulled by the soothing voice of Center or Approach. But as I found out at Albany, that may be the time to be most vigilant. Nearly three-quarters of your time should be spent looking out of the cockpit when flying under VFR. Instrument pilots, too, should scan as much as possible— an IFR flight plan doesn't relieve the pilot of the responsibility to see and avoid other aircraft operating in visual meteorological conditions.

Federal Aviation Regulations Part 91 has been amended to require that all aircraft equipped with an operable radar beacon transponder have the transponder turned on, including Mode C equipment, if installed, while airborne in controlled airspace. (The new rule does not require installation of a transponder in any aircraft that currently operates without one.) The purpose of the rule is to provide an increased degree of aircraft target visibility to ATC radar controllers. It is intended to help increase controller awareness and facilitate recognition and resolution of potential traffic conflict situations.

Nevertheless, the FAA admits that "at certain times and in certain places, a concentration of beacon targets could possibly confuse and interfere with the efficiency of ATC rather than assist it."

This panaceatic "solution" may well create a serious problem: Because controllers who reach a level of traffic saturation selectively suppress the transponder emissions of VFR aircraft so as to reduce workloads, the new rule would encourage that practice. The FAA responds to this criticism by saying that it "does not expect that the rule would encourage the suppression of select transponder codes." However, it also allows that "during periods when . . . excessive VFR presentations derogate [from] the separation of IFR traffic, the monitoring of the VFR code may be temporarily discontinued." In other words, if you are VFR, don't count on the help your transponder is there to provide.

Height Failure

This need for concern is heightened by the danger that the altimeter or encoder may register erroneously. Such a menace develops insidiously. An unsuspected leak in a static line or gradually worsening and excessive friction in some part of an altimeter can lead to an error of several hundred feet as the pilot or the controller reads the data on his instrument or scope. This affects not only IFR but VFR pilots.

A recent incident illustrating the problem involved one aircraft flying VFR and another on an IFR flight plan. On the controller's radar display, the VFR traffic was shown at 7,500 feet and the IFR airplane at 8,000. When he was advised of the approaching traffic, the IFR pilot spotted and reported the VFR airplane as passing *overhead* at about 8,200 feet. A subsequent check of the VFR aircraft's static system revealed a leak in the static line.

In consequence of the FAA's having found many instances of static system failures, the FARs require the altimeter systems and altitude encoders of aircraft flown IFR to be tested every 24 months. Strictly VFR aircraft are not so required, but periodic checks should be made for all aircraft. During the altimeter and encoder check, and at any time a part of the static system is removed for maintenance, a correspondence check must be performed to ensure that the altimeter and encoder are reading within 125 feet of each other.

Unless your transponder is checked every 24 months, it may not be activated for IFR or VFR flying. The test is meant primarily to determine if the unit is operating on the proper reply frequency with the appropriate pulse codes.

Blanking and other Delinquencies

Controllers have complained of numerous instances in which light aircraft targets temporarily or permanently vanished from their radar displays. The FAA has been investigating this unsettling phenomenon. One suspected culprit is "blanking," which can occur when an aircraft is placed in certain pitch and bank angles that cause the airframe structure to block signals from the transponder antenna.

Between periodic equipment checks, monitor the performance of your altimeter and encoder. It is important to know whether your aircraft is equipped with an encoding altimeter or a "blind" encoder. In an aircraft with an encoding altimeter, the encoder gets its altitude information from the panel-mounted altimeter. The main advantage of this arrangement is that the pilot is assured that his altimeter agrees with the altitude on the controller's display—if the electronic encoder is working properly. The main shortcoming of the encoding altimeter is that an altimeter error will cause an altitude reporting error; the pilot and ATC will see the same—but potentially wrong—altitude.

Blind encoders are remotely located and are not connected to the panel-mounted altimeter—they have their own altimeter. Their major advantage is redundancy. If either the pilot's altimeter or the encoder is in error, a controller may notice the discrepancy, because the altitude he sees on the display will differ from the assigned or selected altitude. For this reason, it is a good practice to ask a controller's assistance in checking your altimeter from time to time. All center and many terminal area controllers have displays that show the altitudes of encoder-equipped aircraft. If you have a blind encoder and the controller's displayed altitude matches your indicated altitude, your altimeter and encoder are working properly. A discrepancy of 300 or 400 feet is probably due to a static line or excessive friction in the altimeter mechanism. Errors of several thousand feet often are caused by an electronic malfunction in an encoder.

An electronic problem may also cause the encoder to transmit an intermittent signal. An intermittent reading is more dangerous than no reading at all, because a controller may assume that an aircraft is at its last observed altitude, when, in fact, the aircraft may have climbed or descended since its last altitude report.

If you become aware of an intermittent or erroneous signal, operate the transponder in Mode A (non-altitude reporting). When you file an IFR flight plan, indicate that your aircraft has no altitude encoding capability through the appropriate equipment-code letter (for example, "/T," for a transponder with no encoding capability) in the aircraft designation.

Some new transponders can display reported altitude, but keep in mind that they always report the encoded altitude based on a barometric-pressure setting of 29.92. Ground radar equipment factors in the local altimeter setting to arrive at an aircraft's altitude. Therefore, to check the correspondence between altimeter and encoder, the pilot momentarily would have to adjust his panel-mounted altimeter to 29.92 inches.

Some of the conflict alerts issued by ATC computers, particularly at high altitudes, may be explained through inaccurate altimeters and altitude encoders. Altimeters are inherently more accurate at lower altitudes. At sea level, they must be calibrated within ±20 feet; at 30,000 feet, the allowable error increases to ±180 feet.

Problems such as these have led some avionics engineers to express concern about the workability of proposed traffic alert and collision avoidance systems (TCAS). A few airlines have been testing TCAS II, which not only reports the traffic's range and azimuth but suggests evasive action such as "fly up" or "fly down." The equipment determines the conflicting traffic's position by interpreting transponder returns. Critics argue that if altimeters or encoders are in error, it is *possible* that TCAS could command a pilot to fly into the path of another aircraft. For example, the TCAS could sense traffic at, or slightly above, an airliner's altitude, when the other aircraft was slightly below. Given the increased changes of altimeter error at high altitudes—say, 45,000 feet—even well calibrated altimeter-encoder combinations could inspire wrong commands.

In view of the flaws within the system and the equipment on which controllers and pilots rely for groundborne traffic control, there is still no all-encompassing substitute for see-and-avoid if you are flying either VFR or IFR in visual conditions.

Perennial Blind Spots

Scanning for traffic is like accurately painting the sky: It is an art, it is a compounding of details, and it is subject to physiological, psychological, and mechanical problems—the construction of our eyes, our fallible human nature, and the design compromises that are inherent in the aircraft we fly.

Good vision is obviously the key to successful traffic scanning, and there are physiological factors that can affect how we see. Light coming through the lens of the eye is focused on the retina, which is made up of cones and rods, the light-sensing cells. The cones are sensitive to color; the rods are sensitive to black-and-white images. When we look directly at an object, the light is focused on the fovea, a section of the retina directly opposite the lens where visual acuity is greatest. This region is composed entirely of cones.

Visual acuity, the relative ability of our eyes to resolve detail, is of primary concern. A person with 20/20 vision can detect an aircraft with the fuselage diameter of a Cessna 210 at approximately 4½ miles. A nearsighted person would not be able to detect the aircraft until it was closer. Visual acuity decreases rapidly with myopia (nearsightedness). It also rapidly decreases toward the periphery of vision. During the daylight hours, we cannot depend on peripheral vision to detect approaching aircraft. At night, when only black-and-white images are seen in the darkness, looking directly at an object can cause it to seem to vanish—the effect known as night blindness. The apparent disappearance stems from the black-and-white image's falling on the cones, which are sensitive to colored light. Therefore, at night we should use our peripheral vision, using the sides of our eyes so that the light is focused on the rods. (It usually takes at least 30 minutes for the eye to adapt completely to darkness.)

These factors, as well as a tendency of visual acuity to change as we grow older, are why frequent, periodic eye examinations—at the minimum, those given with regular FAA-required medicals—are important. It is critical to a pilot's defenses to make sure that his vision is fully capable of seeing to avoid and, if he needs to wear eyeglasses while flying, that his prescription currently meets his visual needs. Those needs also include the ability of his eyes to move efficiently and effectively for good scanning.

Another nighttime phenomenon is the *autokinetic effect,* or stare vision. When we stare at an object in the dark, it may seem to move erratically, an effect caused by an involuntary, continuous horizontal movement of the eyes. This movement is so rapid that we are unaware of it.

Relative motion—or rather a lack of it—can create a form of blind spot. Our eyes can much more readily detect a moving object, yet dangerously conflicting aircraft will appear to each other to be relatively motionless. A cardinal rule of bogey spotting is that if your traffic remains essentially stationary in the windshield but is growing larger, you and he are on a collision course.

Distractions can be psychological—concerns over decisions regarding the flight and personal worries are but two of them— or mechanical, but they affect our ability to see and avoid. When our eyes are turned "inward," that is, when we are not concentrating on the airplane and its protection, we scan less fully and efficiently, and our minds are less likely to register bogeys our eyes may pick up. Social or business conversations in the cockpit and simple daydreaming can have the same effect. As we shall see later in this book, even more dangerous distractions are the effects of hypoxia, fatigue, illness, alcohol, and drugs.

Glare is always a problem and sometimes can only be reduced with tinted windscreens, sunglasses, or sunshields. However, many pilots fly behind windscreens fogged by dirt, rendered nearly opaque against the sun by scratches, or spotted with insect remains and other tiny objects that obstruct or distract vision. It is not uncommon for an in-cockpit aircraft spotter to fixate on a fly speck as traffic to be viewed with suspicion. It is essential to keep the windscreen as clear and scratch-free as possible by cleaning it before every flight and making sure that no residue from the procedure remains to cause glare. Be sure what cleansing materials are right for your screen, determine the best method for using them and then, though it may be a bother when you are raring to go, do the job yourself, unless you can fully trust your line personnel to do it.

Unfortunately, conscientiously scanning our instruments and charts can also diminish our outward-scanning acuity due to accommodation time. That is the period required for our eyes to change focus from an object at one distance to an object at another distance. It is estimated that it takes about three to five seconds to shift our eyes from outside the aircraft to the instrument panel and back outside again. That is a good reason for enlisting your co-pilot and passengers to watch for traffic, even to the point of making bogey spotting a contest. Believe it or not, kids can be very good at the game. Teach your spotters the 12-hour clock method, indicate what you mean by traffic that is worrisomely near or is too far distant to be a factor, and have them point at the targets they call out. If you are flying an IFR clearance but are not wrapped in cloud, don't bury your eyes in the panel but *watch out* to pick up intruders into your supposedly sacred, ATC-reserved airspace. Only you and the other pilot may know he's there—and he may not be talking.

Just as important, don't follow ATC instructions blindly. As pilot-in-command, you have the authority and responsibility to refuse a controller's instruction if it promises to endanger your flight.

Structural Blinders

Every aircraft design involves compromises that reflect a balancing of performance, economies, safety, and market preferences. The results can limit our see-and-avoid capabilities. Every model has its own advantages and liabilities in that respect. The question for the pilot is not whether a high wing or low wing is superior, but what visual limitations and opportunities does it offer.

In straight-and-level flight, our field of vision is blocked downward and in front of the nose. This is true for high- and low-wing airplanes. How much our vision may be blocked depends on the design and how high we sit in the seat. For this reason many student pilots cannot find landmarks that are literally right under their noses. The wing of a high-wing plane will block vision above and behind the aircraft in an area that is somewhat in the shape of a cone. The wing of a low-wing craft, on the other hand, will block an area somewhat in the shape of an inverted cone behind and below the plane.

In a turn, a low-wing aircraft will have a good field of vision in the direction of the turn. However, the wing will block the area opposite the turn. With a high-wing airplane, the reverse is true; the field of vision is blocked in the direction of the turn and is unobstructed in the area opposite the turn. During climbs and descents, the actual flight path of both high- and low-wing aircraft may be blocked, depending on such factors as the design, speed, and flap setting of the aircraft and even how tall is the pilot.

Aircraft manufacturers place obstacles in our field of vision, some of which, such as braces, struts, and compasses, are due to unavoidable structural considerations. A primary way of compensating for such limitations is making clearing turns. Depending on the aircraft's attitude and airspeed, the visibility in its flight path may be blocked. Shallow turns should be employed at regular intervals to "clear" the flight path. Similarly, to compensate for visibility limitations in turns, clear the area as well as you can before initiating the turn and then complete the turn as rapidly as practicable—with due consideration for safety and your passengers' ease of mind. Clearing before climbing and descending is always advisable.

Due to manufacturing considerations, windshields are often obstructed by braces and assorted instruments. Be sure to move your head and check for bogeys that may be hidden behind these obstructions. Pilots add to the problem by putting charts, computers, and other paraphernalia on top of glareshields, where they can reduce visibility as they are reflected in the windshield.

Scan Plans

The most effective see-to-avoid method is scanning, which is not an instinctive way of looking at things. It must be learned and then practiced until it is instinctive. You may be annoyed at first because it takes the casualness out of gazing about the sky—at first, scanning gets to be a lot like work—but you will discover how much more you can see and how much more justifiably confident you will be about your safety.

Because of the limitations brought about by the nature of visual acuity and accommodation time, we cannot scan in one continuous sweep. We must divide the area we are surveying into sectors. After this is done, a proper scan is accomplished by stopping and looking, then moving to the next sector for another stop-and-look, all the while checking behind braces, struts and other obstructions. If necessary, ask your right-seat passenger to lean forward or back or to shift his or her seat so you can check the airspace on that side of the plane. If the passenger offers to help, say yes.

Concentrate your search on the areas most critical to you at any given time. In the traffic pattern especially, clear yourself before every turn and always watch against someone improperly entering the pattern. On descent and climbout, make gentle S-turns or adjust your pitch to provide a better view ahead. When turning final, look both ways along the extended runway line and check below your glideslope, just in case. On final, don't stare at your aiming point, but also scan for aircraft that may blindly cut you off or knock you off.

In cruise flight, you generally can see to avoid any collision threat by scanning an area 60 degrees to the left and right of your center visual area. This includes checking out the side windows every few scans. You may not be able to check your six in your cocoon-like cabin, but you can stretch your scan around to past four o'clock on your right side and, with a little effort, to seven o'clock on your left. Statistical theory holds that your chances of detecting aircraft increase when you scan ten degrees up and down. This will allow you to spot any aircraft threatening your flight path, be it level with you, below and climbing, or above and descending.

Knowing what you are looking for during your various flight regimes and how much airspace around your plane you can expect to survey, you can apply the "stop-look" method. This system is based on the theory that traffic detection can by made only through a series of eye fixations at different points in space. Each of these fixes becomes the focal point of your field of vision (a sector or block 10 to 15 degrees wide). By stopping and looking every 10 to 15 degrees, you should be able to detect any contrasting, moving, or enlargening object in each block of airspace. This will give you 9 to 12 blocks in your scan area, each of which will require a minimum of one to two seconds for accommodation and detection.

One method in the system relies on a side-to-side scan movement. Start at the far left of the visual area and make a sweep to the right, pausing in each block to focus. At the end of the scan, return to the panel. Another method is from front to side. Start with a fixation in the center block of your visual field (approximately the center of the windshield in front of the pilot). Move your eyes to the left, focusing on each block, and swing quickly back to the center block. Repeat the action to the right.

There are other methods of scanning, some of which may be as effective for you as the ones just described. The key point is that unless some series of fixations is made, there is little likelihood that you will detect all the targets in your scanning area. When your head is in motion, your vision will be blurred to some extent, and your mind will not register targets as such. Yet you may *feel* secure.

Also remember that your eyes are subject to illusions. For example, at one mile, an aircraft flying below your altitude will appear to be above you. As it nears, it will appear to descend and go through your level, yet all the while, it will be straight and level below you. At least one midair collision has occurred because the pilot of a higher-flying airplane experienced this illusion and dove right into the path of the aircraft flying below him.

The Cost of Dropping One's Guard

The flying weather was good when a Cessna 182Q Skylane and a North American Rockwell 560E Aero Commander collided at 2,000 feet over Livingston, New Jersey, on November 20, 1982. The midair occurred about one mile within a lateral boundary of the New York Terminal Control Area. Not only was the weather good but the crowded sky still seemed friendly with helpful traffic call-outs from ATC. That, so it proved, was the danger.

The Skylane was flying VFR from picturesque Kupper Airport, in Manville, New Jersey, to Ramapo Valley Airport, near Spring Valley New York. The pilot—private certificate, 250 total hours—had often flown a direct course between those airports. The pilot's course line, as drawn by him across a New York TCA chart, touched the perimeter of the TCA boundary extending from 1,800 to 7,000 feet msl.

The Aero Commander was en route VFR from Blairstown Airport, New Jersey, under vectors by a New York terminal radar approach controller for a practice ILS to Teterboro Airport. The pilot held a commercial certificate and had about 730 hours of flight experience. He was instructed to turn from a heading of 120 to 170 degrees and to maintain 2,000 feet. The approach controller also told him that there were "numerous targets in your 12 o'clock position—one showing 1,000 feet, altitude unverified, the others altitude unknown." The pilot responded, "Okay, roger, sir. That's Caldwell Airport."

At the time, the Skylane was between the Aero Commander's one and two o'clock positions and about seven miles away. According to the NTSB, the closure rate of the two airplanes was 236 knots—400 feet per second.

Several people on the ground witnessed the crash and said that both airplanes were in level flight; the Skylane was slightly higher than the Aero Commander. Just before the collision, the Skylane banked steeply. The NTSB determined that the Skylane hit the right side of the Aero Commander's rear fuselage and sheared off its empennage. The aircraft hit the ground about 1,500 feet from each other. The impact occurred in a residential area, but no one on the ground was hurt. Both pilots and a passenger in the Aero Commander were killed.

The NTSB said that "the probable cause of this accident was the failure of the pilots to exercise adequate vigilance to detect and avoid each other. Contributing to the accident was the failure of the pilot of [the Skylane] either to keep clear of the New York TCA or to avail himself of the traffic advisory capability of the New York terminal radar approach control. Also contributing to the accident was the failure of the controller to observe the potential conflict and to adequately convey traffic information to [the Aero Commander]."

Since completing his training at the FAA Academy in January 1982, the controller had been checked out on three radar positions in the New York terminal radar approach control facility as a full-performance controller. His workload was light at the time of the collision, said the NTSB, which added that he "could have and should have observed the potential conflict and issued an appropriate advisory."

In addition, the Aero Commander pilot may have relegated his responsibility for collision avoidance to the controller. "The pilot may have been overconfident that the controller was protecting his airspace because his airplane had been radar identified, his altitude had been acknowledged, and he was flying in positive control airspace," the board said.

According to the FAA's *Air Traffic Control Handbook*, ATC's primary purpose is the prevention of collisions between IFR aircraft. Controllers must provide radar traffic advisories to VFR aircraft only when their workload permits. The FARs state that when weather conditions permit, regardless of whether an operation is conducted IFR or VFR, each pilot must maintain see-and-avoid vigilance. ''When weather conditions permit'' is ambiguous, but a liberal translation is that when a pilot can see past the nose and wingtips of his aircraft, he had better be looking out for traffic.

The NTSB said that the two pilots could have spotted each other, had they been looking, with enough time for avoidance. The board's summary also stressed that ''the system of providing separation is not error-proof, nor in all probability will it ever be. Conflicting traffic, particularly near the boundaries of a TCA, may be a threat detectable only by pilots, and then only if they are looking for it. There may be one common denominator to all midair collisions, and that fact might be described as pilot complacency particularly when an airplane is under positive control.

''Separation can be maintained most effectively by pilots who recognize that outside scanning must be an aggressive procedure . . . in order to take timely evasion action.''

Thus, VFR pilots must not assume that ''traffic advisories'' are an umbrella, a blanket, or insurance against conflicts with other aircraft. Regard such service as a luxury that may complement see-and-avoid, a luxury that can be withdrawn or simply can fail to do what we may expect of it. Furthermore, pilots flying under IFR clearances also cannot assume protection when VFR aircraft are in the same airspace, though the IFR planes are under positive control and the VFR airmen may be monitored. Nor is the proximity of positive control airspace necessarily going to help, as we shall see in greater detail in a subsequent chapter. Flying defensively by seeing to avoid remains the responsibility and life-preserving necessity of the pilot-in-command.

Pilots must beware another traffic threat, one that also consistently takes lives and that demands more than one kind of defensive vigilance, even though those aircraft fly under strict procedures and their pilots are highly disciplined professionals.

We shall now enter the realm of the "green demon."

3

Living with the Green Demon

This time the bogeys are really warbirds. They are flown by military airmen in United States airspace on various missions, including training flights meant to bring out the combat capabilities of planes and pilots. With depressing regularity, general aviation aircraft turn up where the military planes are doing their work. In the unintended conflicts, the civilians always lose. For instance:

• In December 1981, an LTV A7E, pulling from a practice bomb run, struck a Cessna 180F in a restricted area near Fallon Naval Air Station, in Nevada. Both pilots were killed. According to the NTSB, the probable causes of the accident were the Cessna pilot's failure to follow directives (he had entered the restricted area without a clearance) and his failure to see and avoid the A7E.

• In February 1980, a Cessna TU-206G and a General Dynamics F-111D collided at 5,800 feet (about 1,500 feet agl), 11 miles northeast of Cannon Air Force Base near Clovis, New Mexico. The Cessna was descending to land at Clovis Municipal Airport, and the F-111D was conducting a simulated instrument approach to Cannon when the collision occurred, killing both occupants aboard each of the aircraft. The safety board said that the probable causes of the collision were: the failure of the F-111D pilots to see and avoid the Cessna (the board determined that the F-111D, flying at nearly 400 knots, was not within the Cessna pilot's field of view prior to the accident); the failure of the pilots of both aircraft to follow approved procedures (that is, to request radar advisories); and the failure of Cannon Approach to "observe the Cessna radar target and to issue traffic advisories to the F-111D."

• In September 1977, a Cessna 414, cruising near but outside the boundaries of a restricted area, was struck from above and behind by a McDonnell Douglas F-4E that was descending to enter the area for gunnery practice. All four people aboard the Cessna were killed, as was the Air Force pilot-trainee in the front seat of the F-4E. The instructor-pilot, who was copying weather information when the collision occurred, managed to eject safely from the rear seat. The NTSB determined that the probable cause of the crash was "the failure of the pilots of Reed 11 flight [the F-4E] to maintain adequate vigilance in order to see and avoid the light aircraft."

In these midairs we have the old nemeses: neglect of regulations intended to prevent collisions, inadequacy of ground-based traffic surveillance and warning, and failure of the airmen involved to look out for the bogeys that struck them down. Defensive-flying procedures could have averted what happened.

About one in every three near-midair collisions reported to the FAA involves a military and a civilian aircraft. In 1979, 35 percent of the 540 reported near misses involved military and civilian aircraft; in 1980, the percentage of near misses was 37; in 1981, 36 percent; and in 1982, out of 311 reported near misses, 43 percent involved military and civilian aircraft.

For many years, actual military-general aviation collisions have averaged about one per year. This figure might indicate that one's chances of being downed by the military are slight; however, given the speeds at which many military aircraft fly, the number of close encounters each year is much more sobering. The risk increases when civilian pilots unwittingly or negligently fly into areas with substantial high-speed military traffic, or when pilots run afoul of our national air defense system, as in the following case, in which the mission flown by two Air Force fighters was in deadly earnest.

Fatal Intercept

A few minutes after four o'clock on the afternoon of January 9, 1983, North American Air Defense (Norad) radar picked up a slow-moving airborne target in the air defense identification zone off the cost of South Carolina. The target could not be correlated with any known or proposed aircraft movements in the area and was declared an "unknown." Two McDonnell Douglas F-4C Phantom IIs were scrambled from Seymour Johnson Air Force Base, in North Carolina, to intercept and identify the intruder.

The Air Force contacted the FAA and learned that neither Washington Center nor Jacksonville Center were in contact with any traffic in the vicinity of the unknown target. Seven minutes after the detection of the intruder, the Phantoms were climbing to Flight Level 250 on vectors toward the target. Their pilots, who were Michigan Air National Guard officers on active duty at Seymour Johnson, were told to make a stern intercept (to approach the target from the rear) and to stay at least 500 feet away from the unknown aircraft. The target was reported at 9,500 feet, tracking 010 degrees at 200 knots groundspeed. The objective of the intercept was to find out what type of aircraft the target was.

The Phantoms—Juliet Lima 25 (JL25) and Juliet Lima 26 (JL26)—entered a dense undercast as they descended through 13,000 feet to begin the intercept. Neither of the weapons systems officers (the "backseaters") was able to pick up the target on his airborne radar, and the Phantoms were ordered to turn away from the target and reposition for another attempt.

Meanwhile, Washington Center had informed the Air Force that it had just received a transmission from a pilot who reported flying a Beech Baron VFR at 9,500 feet, 56 miles southeast of Wilmington. Center gave the Baron's N-number and suggested that the airplane could be the intercept target. The senior director of the Norad facility considered this information. During the

preceding year, fighter interceptors had been scrambled to identify about 160 unknown targets off the coast between the Virginia Capes and Florida. Ten of the unknowns had turned out
to be Soviet bloc aircraft. The director decided that Washington
Center's possible identification of the target (not yet identified
on Center's radar) was not good enough. He told his subordinates,
"We have to get an ID." The intercept would continue.

At this time, the Phantoms were level at 14,000 feet and in
instrument weather conditions. After acquiring the unknown target on its airborne radar, JL26 began to descend for intercep-
tion. The pilot again was instructed to approach no closer than
500 feet. JL25 remained at 13,000 feet and about two miles in
trail. As JL26 set up its intercept, the following conversation
took place between the pilot of the D-55 Baron and a Washington Center controller:

"Say, you have us in radar contact?"

"Yes, sir. I want to advise you of something, sir. You are
in a warning area, and they did send out military aircraft to
scramble on your flight. Are you proceeding from your present
position direct Norfolk?"

"We were coming up [Atlantic Route 3], and we hit pretty
good cells. We just deviated around them."

"Okay, sir. Well, you have some F-4s right on your tail,
sir. I just want you to be aware of that. Is there any way at all
you can proceed direct New Bern, direct Norfolk?"

The request confused the pilot somewhat, as a turn toward
New Bern would take the Baron only about five degrees to the
left of its current heading, direct to Norfolk. The controller's
intention, however, was to get the aircraft out of Warning Area
W-122 as quickly as possible.

As this conversation was taking place, the Norad senior director learned that Washington Center had identified the Baron
on radar and had confirmed that it was the unknown target for
which the Phantoms were searching. Having a positive target
identification, he ordered the intercept discontinued.

As the order was being relayed to the Phantoms, JL26 collided with the target.

Although the Phantom pilot repeatedly had been reminded not to get closer than 500 feet to the target, this limit applied only to an intercept in VMC. The clearance limit for an intercept in IMC was 1,500 feet, and the radar system aboard the F-4C was programmed to provide a "break" command at a target slant range of 1,500 feet. The pilot of JL26 had not acquired visual contact with the Baron. He had been adjusting his Phantom's airspeed so as to close on the target at 50 knots and had been receiving heading corrections from his backseater to keep the target 15 degrees to the right of the Phantom. When the break command had appeared on his radar screen, the backseater had called for the pilot to make a hard left turn.

The pilot had applied military power (maximum power without afterburner) and had begun a climbing left turn. He did not know that the Baron pilot also had begun a left turn to comply with the controller's request to fly direct to New Bern. The Phantom pilot later said that he was looking out of the right side of the cockpit when he felt "a thump."

The F-4C was flying 127 knots faster than the Baron when the two aircraft collided at 9,300 feet, about 30 miles south of Cherry Point, North Carolina. The bank angles of the planes were nearly the same at the time of impact. The Phantom was climbing, and the Baron was in level flight. The left wing of the 56,000-pound F-4C struck the Baron's vertical empennage and continued down and through the fuselage and cabin. Although the Phantom was damaged, it was flown back to Seymour Johnson AFB and landed safely. Neither the pilot nor the backseater was injured.

Search and rescue efforts turned up only some debris from the Baron. The airplane's seven occupants are presumed dead.

In its report on the collision, the NTSB cited mistakes by both pilots. The pilot of the Phantom failed to maintain a safe closing speed and separation distance while intercepting the Baron.

The pilot of the Baron failed to follow regulations in FAR Part 99, regarding penetration of an Air Defense Identification Zone (ADIZ).

The flight had originated in Nassau. Before takeoff, the pilot—a 47-year-old private pilot with multi-engine and instrument ratings and about 4,455 hours—filed two VFR flight plans with the local FSS. On the first flight plan, he indicated that he would fly Atlantic Route 3 to Wilmington, North Carolina, and then direct to Norfolk. He was informed that this flight plan was unacceptable because of regulations that require flights entering the United States from the Bahamas to clear Customs at one of five designated airports in Florida. The pilot then refiled. His new flight plan indicated that he would enter at Fort Pierce, Florida, and then fly direct to Norfolk.

The pilot never activated the plan. Instead, he flew the route he originally had intended to fly. He entered the Atlantic Coast ADIZ without letting anyone know who he was or where he was going. When he finally contacted Washington Center, the pilot was more concerned with obtaining vectors around thunderstorms than with the importance of identifying himself.

We will never know if that pilot recognized the extremely hazardous situation in which he had placed himself and his passengers. As an official from the FAA's Southern Region put it, "The Baron pilot's big mistake was that he didn't activate his flight plan with Nassau Radio. If he had, ATC would have known he was coming and there would have been no intercept." Instead, through his disregard of regulations intended, in part, to prevent just that kind of confusion and response, he precipitated an intercept by a much larger and faster aircraft in instrument weather conditions. He placed himself in harm's way.

Lacking positive identification of him, the Air Force had no choice but to go through with the intercept mission. A year earlier, ten Soviet aircraft had been intercepted in the area and escorted away from the United States. For all Norad knew at the time, the unknown target that appeared on its radar that January 9 could have been a Beech Baron or it could have been a

Tupolev Badger Bomber. The situations for which military planes and procedures are designed are not games. Like it or not, civilian pilots who treat them as such run the worst kinds of risk.

Where Are They?

To ensure that our military airmen stay proficient, the aerial services have their pilots and crews constantly practice missions such as aircraft intercepts, air-to-air combat, low-level bombing, and photo reconnaissance, in conditions as close to the real wartime environment as they can devise for friendly airspace. The warplanes fly fast and close to the ground to simulate penetration of enemy radar. They maneuver swiftly, with close timing, guided by sophisticated equipment and the "Mark-I eyeball." The airspace in which they conduct these exercises is set aside for them, and in a surprisingly large number of places throughout the United States, there will be a good chance that military aircraft will be out there preparing for the worst. The camouflage many of the birds wear does its job well, and the speed at which they travel further complicates the job of spotting them. Few general aviation pilots have the experience and training to look expertly for needle-like attackers that purposefully barrel low over the terrain.

The defensive pilot's first recourse, therefore, is to know where the "combat zones" are. This demands attention, for avoiding those areas can be tricky.

About two percent of our airspace is designated for "special use"—again, because of the areas' locations, the smallness of that percentage is not really a cause for nonconcern—though not all special-use airspace has been assigned to the military. ("Special-use" is regarded by the FAA as areas to which certain activities must be confined or wherein nonparticipating aircraft are subject to restrictions.) In addition, much of the airspace over our coastal waters is devoted to military training. However, military traffic does not confine itself entirely to these areas. Aircraft ranging from T-37 jet trainers to B-52 bombers practice navigation and low-level flying along military training routes (MTRs), which crisscross the country. In some of these areas and along the MTRs—the realm of the green demon—military aircraft are permitted to exceed the 250-knot speed restriction they otherwise must obey below 10,000 feet. The speed restriction is also waived for certain aircraft, such as an F-106 heavily laden with fuel and ordnance, because such planes do not handle well at airspeeds below 250 knots. More about MTRs later.

Special-use airspace can bedevil the general aviation pilot, particularly if he is not flying with an IFR clearance, when a big chunk of it lies across his route of flight. Yet not all such areas should be considered impenetrable barriers to navigation. Here are the types of special-use airspace and the rules to follow when you are considering a flight through such zones:

Restricted Areas

These zones are scenes of hazardous activity, such as artillery firing, aerial gunnery, and guided missile launches. Flight in a restricted area is not allowed without the permission of the using or controlling agency. A VFR pilot must obtain a clearance from the controlling ATC facility *before* entering a restricted area. Many restricted areas are joint-use airspace, meaning that civil aircraft are permitted into an area when it is not "hot" (in use by the military). To find out the status of a restricted area, call or radio a flight service station within 100 miles of the area. ATC will also know its status.

If an IFR flight plan sends you on a dogleg around a restricted area, you may be able to cut the corner if the area is cold. ATC can clear you through areas it has confirmed will be cold when you get there.

Temporary restricted areas established for large-scale military exercises lasting no longer than two weeks may not be shown on a chart but will be published in Notams. Hours of use for restricted areas are listed in a table on sectional charts.

Military Operations Areas

MOAs are used by the military for training activities that include primary jet training, aerial combat maneuvering (old-fashioned dogfighting), and airdrops. The military long has used certain sections of the country's airspace for training purposes, but it was not until 1974 that the FAA started to depict MOAs on aeronautical charts in an effort to apprise pilots of the potential danger of flying in these areas.

These areas used by the Air Force's Air Training Command are mainly found in Texas and the Southwest and may be divided into 20 different practice areas. At certain times, each of these divisions may be in use by an aircraft. For example, Desert MOA, north of Ellis AFB, in Nevada, is used for large-scale air-combat exercises that resemble a busy day during World War III.

Some southwestern cities, such as Phoenix, appear on sectionals to be almost entirely surrounded by MOAs. However, many airways are outside the MOAs' boundaries. Airways that run through MOAs must be available for IFR traffic more than half the time. Also, most MOAs do not extend all the way to the ground and are not in use all of the time. In the Phoenix area, for instance, the Williams 4 MOA extends from 14,000 feet up to but not including 18,000 feet, and the Sells 1 MOA extends from 10,000 feet up to but not including 18,000 feet. This information does not always appear inside the MOA on the sectional but can be found in a table along the top of the chart.

The military provides nearby flight service stations with information on any planned activity in a MOA 24 hours in advance. ATC also can provide information to VFR traffic on the status of a MOA and will authorize an IFR flight to pass through it if aircraft separation can be guaranteed. An aircraft flying on an IFR flight plan to an airport with an instrument approach inside a MOA will be permitted into the area. However, there may be a delay while ATC clears the airspace of conflicting traffic.

Prohibited Areas

These locations are not necessarily designated for military use. According to the *Airman's Information Manual,* they are established for "security" or other reasons "associated with the national welfare." Among our several prohibited areas are the airspace over the White House, Camp David, the Reagan ranch in California, Jimmy Carter's home in Plains, Georgia, and a nuclear warhead assembly plant located in Amarillo, Texas. Aircraft are not permitted in prohibited areas at any time.

Alert Areas

Some alert areas are used by the military for pilot training conducted at speeds less than 250 knots. Other alert areas, particularly in Florida, are used by various aeronautical institutes for training. Still others are used by aircraft manufacturers for test flying. Alert area 381, which stretches along the Gulf of Mexico from Houston to New Orleans, was established to alert pilots to the large amount of helicopter traffic flying between offshore rigs and the coast.

Flight service stations do not receive reports about activities in alert areas, and since all pilot training there is conducted VFR, neither does ATC. There are no restrictions to flight in alert areas.

Warning Areas

The same sorts of activities that occur in restricted areas take place in warning areas, which lie exclusively over water beyond the three-mile international limit. There are no restrictions to flight in warning areas, because the FAA has no authority in airspace over international waters. However, ATC will not allow an IFR flight to fly an airway through a warning area unless the controller can provide separation. Flight service stations are not aware of the activity in warning areas. VFR aircraft should exercise extreme caution when flying into them.

Air Defense Identification Zone

As we have seen, pilots can make trouble for themselves and others by ignoring the stern rules regarding such a zone. ADIZs are not special-use airspace but boundary areas along our borders that are under constant radar surveillance. Orginally established for scanning the skies for enemy attack, coastal and border radars these days are more concerned with identifying and tracking dope smugglers, which means that the people at the scopes are more sensitive to the movements of "unknown" general aviation airplanes.

The distance at which a target will be picked up depends upon how far the coastal and border radars can "see" and the altitude of the incoming aircraft. The first radar contact usually is made within the outer ADIZ line, which extends up to 200 miles off the coast.

Norad computers store flight plans for aircraft expected to cross into the ADIZ. If an aircraft enters the ADIZ and is within its 'correlation circle,'' it will be identified as friendly. To be within the correlation circle, the aircraft must be within 20 nautical miles of its expected flight path and five minutes of its expected time en route. If an aircraft is not in correlation, it is put into a "pending status." Norad will then take two minutes to identify the pending aircraft as friendly, hostile, or unknown. Military controllers use a hot line to FAA centers to identify pending targets. If the aircraft cannot be identified within two minutes, the order to scramble is given. It takes two to three minutes for fighter pilots to climb into their aircraft, complete their preflight, and take off. They can be on top of the unknown target within minutes after that.

The best way to avoid becoming an unknown target if you will be flying into an ADIZ is to file a flight plan, open it after takeoff, and stay in contact with ATC. Be as predictable as possible—Norad does not relish surprises—and don't presume that you may fall unnoticed through a crack in the busy system. Remember, "they" are always faster than you.

Military Training Routes

Like the ADIZ, MTRs are not considered by the FAA to be special-use airspace, although some specialized activities take place along them. MTRs are represented on sectional charts by faint gray lines and on NOAA IFR charts by light brown lines. Jeppesen does not publish these routes on its commercial en route IFR charts; the firm has stated that its subscribers are primarily interested in the national air route system, which is designed to provide aircraft separation, military craft included, for pilots flying on IFR flight plans.

In recent years, the military has placed increasing importance on low-level flying proficiency. MTRs are flown mostly below 10,000 feet, with much of the flying being done at about 400 knots, as close to the surface as possible—often at just a few hundred feet. There are some 500 MTRs in the continental United States. Some of them are instrument routes (IRs) flown on IFR flight plans, and others are visual routes (VRs).

Help from the Green Demon

MTRs are located over sparsely populated areas all around the country, but they often run through airspace that can have substantial general aviation traffic, such as desert areas just a few miles north of Phoenix. Their greatest concentration is in the Southwest, between Tucson, Arizona, and Las Vegas, Nevada—the area is referred to by military pilots as the "spaghetti bowl," because of the great tangle of routes on the training charts. Many simulated bombing runs by B-52s take place at the Strategic Training Range Complex, which encompasses most of Wyoming and great chunks of Idaho and Montana.

To fly at your defensive best in the crackling areas where MTRs may stretch and bend, you may want the help of the "green demon," as the military call it. This is a set of three charts covering the entire United States and issued by the Department of Defense every 56 days to indicate all the IR and VR routes in service. The charts accompany a flight information publication (FLIP) AP/1B, which contains further MTR information. FSSs and some FOBs have the green demon. It is more current than the MTR information on sectionals, which are issued every six months. The routes are shown on the green demon in red (IRs) and blue (VRs), with the altitude range at which each segment may be flown also given. Pilots may subscribe to or purchase single copies of this publication by writing the National Ocean Survey, Distribution Division C-44, Riverdale, MD 20840, asking for "DOD Flight Information Publication—Area Planning, Military Training Routes U.S., AP/1B." If you do your preflight weather briefing by phone, you can ask the FSS briefer—if you are fortunate enough to contact a living-breathing one—what routes are in your flight path and which of them are likely to be hot when you will be in the vicinity. It can be time-consuming and perhaps a bit aggravating, but you can make it easier for the briefer if you can pre-identify likely MTRs on your green demon and ask about their status. Don't rely merely on a sectional. If you have no green demon, the FSS specialist should be using his along with a teletype message FSSs and ATC Centers receive daily confirming in-use times for routes lying within a 200-mile radius of the FSS. This information is also broadcast at 15 minutes past the hour over VOR TWEBs and on PATWAS, where available. If your flight will carry you more than 200 miles beyond your local FSS, you can radio ahead to FSSs while en route for MTR in-use times in their areas.

Self-Defense from the DOD

In addition to knowing where you are likely to encounter military traffic, some common-sense rules should help you to avoid military conflicts.

First, always refer to a chart before a flight. As an example, a sightseeing flight around Martha's Vineyard that begins and ends at the island's main airport may not require a chart for navigation, but in neglecting the chart, a pilot would not be aware of the restricted area just off the western tip of the island. Similarly, one must scrutinize the Phoenix sectional carefully to realize that flight is prohibited between 2,000 and 5,500 feet msl east of the Buckeye VOR on Victor 16. Those altitudes are used by military jets on approach to Luke Air Force Base. Familiarize yourself with established arrival and departure corridors and published instrument approaches for military air installations where you fly. Information on these corridors and the types of aircraft that use them generally is available from local airport managers and fixed-base operators.

That brings us to another rule: Stay alert for military traffic in terminal airspace. In many parts of the country, military and civil airports are located near each other, and in some cases, military and civil aircraft share airports. A high-speed jet fighter can pose more of a danger to slower moving general aviation aircraft in a busy terminal area than it would during a low-level run out over the desert. Of 13 collisions of military with general aviation aircraft between 1970 and 1983, five occurred just after one of the aircraft involved had taken off or was preparing to land. Four others occurred while one aircraft was climbing to cruise or descending.

First Duty: Guard Duty

The risks of conflicts with military aircraft are not limited to charted areas and routes. Extra caution must be exercised *near* charted military activity areas. That means flying heads-up for all on board, to avoid 600-knot surprises. Many warplanes zip around like bullets—some fighters capable of 900-feet-per-second speeds fly as fast as a .45 caliber slug the moment it leaves the gun barrel.

Apply everything you know about seeing to avoid, with two main additions. First, if you spot one aircraft, look for his buddy—or buddies. He may well be flying with a wingman, and oftentimes, multiple aircraft missions are flown with as many as four planes involved. Second, keep your scan extended not only wide but as high and low as you can. Depending again on the maneuvers they are flying, the bogeys' flight paths can vary from straight-and-level to dazzlingly acrobatic. If you are flying low, remember that low is where many military training flights are supposed to be.

A word of consolation: As you see to avoid, know that the military pilots are looking out for you, too. The pilot is instructed to spend about 95 percent of this time watching out for checkpoints and other visual references. His GIB (guy in back) has responsibility for running groundspeed checks, timing, determining headings, and handling other in-cockpit chores. Military pilots are drilled on keeping their heads and eyes moving. In fact, not looking outside the aircraft on a MTR checkride results in automatic failure. The F-111 aircrew operational procedure manual stipulates see-and-avoid as a mandatory practice with the aircraft's flight path being visually cleared by at least one crewmember at all times.

Nevertheless, the fact that they are looking does not guarantee that they will always see or avoid. We have seen cases where such failure has tragically occurred. Collision avoidance is a *cooperative* effort by us potential victims to prevent lethal encounters. We do it by heeding a lesson drummed into all fighter pilots:

"Keep your head on swivel!"

4
Under Control

On charts and in diagrams, they look like castles in the air. Their neatly arcing sector boundaries strongly suggest walls built to counter intruders and to contain chaos. Their stark acronymic designators—TCA, TRSA, and now ARSA—and their operational rules create a powerful impression of maintained order: If you are not licensed or equipped to enter here, or if for another reason you are not admitted, stay out; if you legally enter this domain, you will be embraced with protection; confusion and conflict will be purged to assure you safe passage.

These castles have been created to prevent violence in the traffic maelstrom near busy airports, and perceptions of their airspace can resemble those of storms with vicious cores. Progressing inward, there is increasingly heightened activity until, at the churning terminal vortex of the system, the area of greatest danger descends to the surface, like a funnel cloud when meteorological hell breaks loose.

So, in our terminal areas, while we know there is hazard, we find depicted planned protection tidily laid out and graphically schematized for us to convey benevolent, effective, and efficient *control*.

In the real atmosphere, the picture may well be otherwise.

Although most midairs and near misses occur near uncontrolled airports, a disturbingly sizable number still turn up where ranks of aerial traffic cops man their scopes and binoculars to keep things orderly. We have already seen one instance where assumed TCA protection in the New York Terminal Control Area failed to prevent a collision, and very recently, a midair near

Teterboro Airport, coincidentally at the heart of the New York TCA, not only destroyed two airplanes and all their occupants but took lives and razed property on the ground. The fact is that while the mandated castles may have improved safety around busy terminals, problems that led to their creation and widespread deployment remain. It isn't as easy to legislate, mandate, or dictate against fallibility as we would like.

It is clear, also, that the *positive* in positive control must be augmented by the pilot-in-command's flying defensively. In tightly controlled airspace, groundborne men and machines can let us down, and when they do, our skilled self-reliance must take up the slack.

A Seminal Disaster

In examining how this can be done, we would do well to start by reviewing the failures that led to an event which spurred the ongoing regulatory rage for low-level airspace policing. The accident, which killed 144 people in the air and on the ground, was the worst in U.S. aviation history at the time.

On September 25, 1978, at 8:34 a.m., Pacific Southwest Airlines Flight 182, a Boeing 727, departed Los Angeles with 96 passengers, seven crew, and 32 PSA employees. It was en route to San Diego's Lindbergh Field on the second leg of a flight that had originated in Sacramento. The 727's arrival at Lindbergh was scheduled for 9:05 a.m.

At about 8:15 a.m., a Cessna 172, N7711G, departed Montgomery Field, near San Diego, on a round-robin instrument training flight to conduct approaches at Lindbergh, the only field in the vicinity with an ILS. On board were an instrument flight instructor and a commercial pilot pursuing an instrument rating course through an FAA-approved school. The Skyhawk was fully equipped for the operation.

The weather was cool, with good visibility.

To understand the traffic control situation that developed before the crash, it is helpful to know that while Lindbergh Tower (local control and ground control) was on the airport, San Diego Approach and Departure Control was located at the Miramar Naval Air Station several miles to the northeast of Lindbergh. Miramar had ARTS III radar, which displayed altitude, speed, and other data for transponder/encoder-equipped targets, and provided Stage III radar service within the designated terminal radar service area airspace. The TRSA airspace overlay Lindbergh with a floor 4,000 feet above the airport. Stage III service provides separation between all participating VFR aircraft that do not decline it, and all IFR aircraft.

Miramar provided Stage II service to Lindbergh below 4,000 feet. Stage II service did *not* offer separation service to VFR aircraft but did provide radar sequencing of arriving participating aircraft as well as radar traffic information to departing aircraft.

Lindbergh Tower did not have its own radar but did have a repeater radar scope from Miramar. The repeater scope did not repeat the ARTS III data.

Cessna N7711G was operating VFR and made a couple of practice ILS approaches to Runway 9 at Lindbergh. On the last, a low approach, the Cessna advised Lindbergh Tower that he wanted a practice NDB approach to Runway 27 and was cleared over to San Diego Approach Control. The Cessna reported in to San Diego Approach at 1,500 feet, northeastbound, and remained with that facility to the time of the collision, one minute and 45 seconds later.

PSA also was under control of San Diego Approach, nearing Lindbergh from the northwest. The 727 had the airport in sight and was cleared for a visual approach to Runway 27.

What the Participants Said

The following is a transcript of the transmissions of the various participants (APP = San Diego Approach Control at Miramar; CAM-1 = cockpit voice of the PSA captain; CAM-2 = cockpit voice of the PSA first officer; CAM-3 = cockpit voice of the PSA second officer; CAM-4 = cockpit voice of an off-duty PSA captain; RDO-1 = radio voice of the PSA captain; TWR = Lindbergh Tower):

0859:30   APP:PSA One-Eighty-Two, traffic twelve o'clock, one mile northbound.
0859:35   RDO-1:We're looking.
0859:39   APP:PSA One-Eighty-Two, additional traffic's, ah, twelve o'clock, three miles just north of the field northeastbound, a Cessna one-seventy-two climbing VFR out of one thousand four hundred.
0859:50   RDO-1:Okay we've got that other twelve.
0859:51   N7711G:[*Unintelligible*] Seven-Seven-One-One Golf [*unintelligible*] one thousand five hundred, ah, northeastbound.
0859:56   APP:Cessna Seven-Seven-One-One-Golf, San Diego Departure, radar contact, maintain VFR conditions at or below three thousand five hundred, fly heading zero seven zero vector final approach course.
0900:08   N7711G:Zero seven zero on the heading, VF'nR below three thousand five hundred [*unintelligible*]
0900:15   APP:PSA One-Eighty-Two, traffic's at twelve o'clock, three miles, out of one thousand seven hundred.
0900:21   CAM-2:Got 'em.
0900:22   RDO-1:Traffic in sight.
0900:23   APO:Okay, sir, maintain visual separation, contact Lindbergh Tower one three three point three, have a nice day now.
0900:28   RDO-1:Okay.
0900:31   APP:Cessna One-One-Golf, and traffic's at six o'clock,

two miles, eastbound, a PSA jet inbound to Lindbergh
out of three thousand two hundred has you in sight.

0900:34 RDO:Lindbergh, PSA One-Eighty-Two downwind.

0900:38 TWR:PSA One-Eighty-Two, Lindbergh Tower, ah, traffic
twelve o'clock, one mile, a Cessna.

0900:41 CAM-2—Flaps five.

0900:43 N7711G—One-One-Golf, roger.
CAM-1:Is that the one we're looking at?
CAM-2:Yeah, but I don't see him now.

0900:44 RDO-1:Okay, we had it there a minute ago.

0900:47 TWR:One-Eighty-Two, roger.
APP:Cessna One-One-Golf, a traffic, ah, in your vicinity,
a PSA jet has you in sight, he's descending for Lindbergh.

0900:50 RDO-1:I think he's pass[ed] off to our right.

0900:51 TWR:Yeah.

0900:53 CAM-22:Yeah.
TWR:How far are you going to take your downwind, One-
Eighty-Two, company traffic is waiting for departure.

0900:57 RDO-1:Ah, probably about three to four miles.

0900:59 TWR:Okay.

0901:07 TWR:PSA One-Eighty-Two, cleared to land.

0901:08 RDO-1:One-Eighty-Two's cleared to land.

0901:11 CAM-2:Are we clear of that Cessna?

0901:13 CAM-3:Suppose to be.

0901:14 CAM-1:I guess.

0901:20 CAM-4:I hope.

0901:21 CAM-1:Oh yeah, before we turned downwind, I saw him
about one o'clock, probably behind us now.

0901:38 CAM-2:There's one underneath.

0901:39 CAM-2:I was looking at that inbound here.

0901:45 CAM-1:Whoop!

0901:46 CAM-2:Aghhh!

0901:47 CAM:[*Sound of impact*]

0901:49 CAM-1:Easy baby, easy baby.

0901:51 CAM:[*Sound of electrical system reactivation tone on voice
recorder, system off less than one second.*]
CAM-1:What have we got here?

0901:52   CAM-2:We're hit man, we are hit.
0901:55   RDO-1:Tower, we're going down, this is PSA.
0901:57   TWR:Okay, we'll call the equipment for you.
0901:58   CAM:[*Sound of stall warning.*]
0902:04.5   CAM:[*Sound on cockpit voice recorder ceases, electrical power to recorder stops.*]

Steps in a System Breakdown

With the pilots and controllers apparently on top of the situation, how could the collision occur, especially in a relatively light-traffic and high-visibility environment?

Shortly after Cessna N7711G reported in to Approach, PSA was advised by Approach of the Cessna traffic at 12 o'clock, three miles. PSA reported the traffic in sight, was advised by Approach to maintain visual separation, and was then turned over to Lindbergh Tower. Approach advised the Cessna that PSA was two miles behind him and "has you in sight." The tower (with information from the repeater scope) also gave PSA a traffic call—"traffic 12 o'clock, one mile, a Cessna." PSA replied, "Okay, we had him there a minute ago," and a few seconds later, "think he's passed off to our right."

What is more illuminating is the conversation in the PSA cockpit, which indicates more uncertainty than was confessed to the controller. The captain: "Is that the one [we're] looking at?" The first officer: "Yeah, but I don't see him now." The captain: "He was right here a minute ago." First officer: "Yeah. . . . Are we clear of that Cessna?" The second officer: "Suppose to be." The captain: "I guess." (*Sound of laughter.*) The off-duty PSA captain: "I hope." Again the captain: "Oh yeah, before we turned downwind, I saw him about one o'clock, probably behind us now." The first officer: "There's one underneath. . . . I was looking at that inbound there."

Then suddenly, from the captain, "Whoop!" and from the first officer, "Aghhh!"—Impact.

At the NTSB hearing, a great deal of attention was given to the conflict alert system of the ARTS III radar at Miramar, the location of the TRSA at Miramar and not at Lindbergh, the ATC procedures in the overlapping airport traffic areas, the state-of-the-art of the collision avoidance systems, and other marginally relevant matters. These seemed to obscure the crux of the accident—the illusion of positive separation in the radar environment and the conflict it represents with what pilots expect of controllers and other pilots in such a "control situation."

Both aircraft were under air traffic control. PSA was IFR and was being provided separation service. The Cessna was VFR and was being provided radar traffic advisory service. PSA was cleared for a visual approach to Runway 27, was given traffic advisories about the Cessna, reported the Cessna in sight, and was instructed to maintain visual separation from it. The Cessna was advised of PSA's presence behind him. With all this working, what weakness can point to ways of preventing similar accidents when potential conflicts develop?

The Meanings of "Visual Separation"

ATC effects aircraft separation in various ways. It can assign different altitudes or flight paths, and it can provide spacing in terms of time or distance. In radar coverage, a minimum of three miles separation is provided between aircraft operating within 40 miles of the antenna site and five miles between aircraft flying beyond 40 miles from the site.

However, in terminal areas in good visibility, visual separation is frequently used. In fact, it is *the* method by which controllers expedite traffic at our busiest airports, because the weather is good most of the time. Visual separation is, of course, basic to the visual approach, without which we would have intolerable delays in our major terminal areas.

Visual separation can be accomplished by a tower controller who sees the aircraft involved and issues the necessary instructions to ensure that they avoid one another. But the type of visual separation that concerns us here is accomplished from the cockpit, upon instructions from the controller, by the crews' seeing the other aircraft and maneuvering as necessary to avoid conflict. This may involve following in-trail behind another aircraft or keeping it in sight until it is no longer a factor.

The PSA crew was providing its own visual separation from the Cessna, upon instructions from the controller.

The *Airman's Information Manual* specifies the roles and responsibilities of the pilot and the controller in visual separation: "Acceptance of both traffic information and instructions to follow another aircraft is pilot acknowledgement that he sees the other aircraft and will maneuver his aircraft as necessary to avoid it or maintain in-trail separation." The *AIM* goes on to make very clear that the pilot has the responsibility to notify the controller if he is unable to see his traffic, unable to maintain visual contact with it, or for any other reason cannot accept responsibility for providing his own separation.

The conversation in the PSA cockpit suggests that there was uncertainty about the traffic from which the visual separation was being maintained. The PSA crew had the obligation to report this uncertainty to the controller. If they had done so, this would have shifted responsibility to the controller to try to effect a different kind of separation.

Many of us can confirm from our own experience that we too seldom hear transmissions from other aircraft to ATC that indicate uncertainty or lost targets. This accident is a tragic reminder of the gravity of that responsibility.

Another valuable lesson, which conspicuously has appeared in various guises as we have analyzed midairs in different environments, is that it can be dangerous to rely blindly on someone else to maintain visual separation from your aircraft. The situation must be evaluated each time. If ATC tells you that your traffic is overtaking or converging with you and you neither can see nor find it, immediately ask for vectors out of its way. That may be the only way to protect your vulnerable six. Pilots and controllers with their equipment are all part of the same collision-avoidance system. That a pilot needed help should not become clear to ATC only upon the merging of two blips on a scope.

TRSA Service and Disservice

PSA Flight 182 and Cessna N7711G were working in a terminal radar service area. TRSAs have long been a subject of controversy because they have been areas of dangerous confusion. The search for collision protection led to TRSAs, full-blown TCAs, and to the more recently conceived airport radar service area (ARSA). Controversy has centered around whether the voluntary pilot participation regulated for TRSAs is actually uncompelled and whether the collision avoidance guidance intended for these areas is provided well enough for pilots to trust it.

TRSAs were originally designed to provide three stages, or levels, of separation service. Stage I has been eliminated.

Stage II facilities provide traffic information as the controllers' workload permits. The primary, and at times all-consuming, work is the separation of IFR traffic. When possible, controllers will sequence IFR and participating VFR into the airport traffic pattern. Once radar contact with him has been established, a pilot may navigate on his own into the pattern, or, again depending on traffic conditions, he may be directed to specific headings into a properly separated position behind a preceding aircraft in the approach sequence. When the pilot reports that aircraft in sight, he is instructed to follow it. For an IFR aircraft, standard separation is provided until it is sequenced and the pilot reports having the correct preceding airplane in sight. He then assumes responsibility for maintaining separation. Standard radar separation between IFR and VFR aircraft—or between VFR aircraft—is not provided. (Departing VFR aircraft may request radar traffic information on initial contact with Ground.)

Stage III provides sequencing and separation between all participating VFR aircraft and all IFR aircraft operating within the TRSA, the boundaries of which are depicted on sectionals and in the *AIM*.

It is important to know that pilots are assumed to be participating in the radar service program, that is, accepting instructions to that effect, unless they specify "negative Stage II" or "negative Stage III" when they initially contact Approach or, for departures, Ground. In other words, by "voluntary," the rules mean that the pilot must *volunteer negatively*.

For Stage III, this means that a pilot who does not *initiate* his exemption from the service is assumed to accept all Stage III operations. He will be expected to maintain the altitudes assigned him by ATC until he is instructed to "resume appropriate altitudes." If he is not assigned an altitude, he must inform the controller, with whom he must coordinate before climbing or descending. Again, within the TRSA, ATC will inform pilots about observed but unidentified aircraft *to the extent possible*. If a pilot is within the controller's airspace jurisdiction and requests vectors to avoid observed traffic, he will receive the service—on a workload-permitting basis." But the pilot must request it. If you are a participating VFR pilot, ATC will tell you if you are leaving the TRSA, but this does not mean that radar service will be terminated, unless the controller specifically tells you so.

At all times you are in the TRSA, you remain responsible for seeing and avoiding other aircraft and maintaining appropriate clearance from terrain, obstructions, and below-minimums weather. If the controller's instructions threaten to compromise your safety, tell him and request other instructions. If collision or weather avoidance is immediately necessary, do it and then tell him.

Needing Protection from "Protection"

There have been many accounts of pilots running afoul of the services offered within TRSAs. In this case, Larry F. Ferguson found that instincts developed as a fighter pilot were needed in such "guarded" airspace:

On a number of occasions when departing Tallahasee, Florida (TLH), I received commands first from Ground Control and then from the tower after becoming airborne to contact Departure Control on 120.8. Looking in Jeppesen, sure enough, I found that Approach was 120.8. I assumed that I was required to contact 120.8 when arriving or departing, never realizing that it was Stage III—a false assumption.

Coming in one day, I dutifully contacted TLH Approach: "Twin Cessna 69730, 20 miles west, descending through 7,000 with Echo." My groundspeed was 180 knots, and I assumed that control knew of my rapid approach. Another false assumption. Five miles west, the sequence went:

"Cessna 69730, TLH, five miles, 12 o'clock, do you have field in sight?"

"Seven-Three-Zero, roger, field in sight."

"Seven-Three-Zero, contact Tower on 118.7."

"Seven-Three-Zero, roger."

"TLH Tower, Twin Cessna 69730, five miles west on close-in base leg."

The tower acknowledged and indicated 730 to land on Runway 36, wind calm. My speed was 150 knots indicated.

I prefer to make a high, close-in, power-off approach, traffic permitting. Not only do I find this an easier approach to make, it also gives the airspace more quickly to the next aircraft and appears to have many built-in safety factors that are missing in a long, low, power approach.

I continued on a close-in base, 1,000 feet agl. There had been no radio transmissions. I came within five to ten seconds of turning final—wheels lowered into place, flaps extended to 15 degrees, and throttle about to be retarded to idle with full flaps then to drop. Then came the transmission from the tower that gave me one of the greatest chills I have had in 35 years of flying: It told an aircraft—not mine—"you are cleared for a touch-and-go landing."

Furiously, my co-pilot and I searched for the aircraft. It certainly was not on final. I was so unglued that I temporarily forgot to drop full flaps. I later learned that it was a Cessna single, with an instructor and student, under my nose, and that the instructor "saw me."

Meanwhile, back in the tower, excitement had suddenly developed. I received an excited, garbled transmission about being on too high a base "anyway" and something about going around. The tower was talking as if a crash was impending, and apparently the single and I were somewhat close. The next tower transmission gave me clearance to land. My second? I don't know, but I thought so.

I landed slightly long because of the flap delay. The single did a 360 somewhere and landed. Apparently, everyone else had as rapid a pulse rate as mine. The tower never did send out an apology to the instructor.

Had I not thought that contacting Approach was mandatory, I would have been talking and listening to TLH Tower, rather than Stage III. I would have known that there was a plane shooting landings. In this case, there were two aircraft in the pattern shooting landings. In World War II as a fighter pilot, I learned radio silence, and rarely do I talk to anyone unless it is mandatory or absolutely necessary. I prefer always to deal directly with and monitor the tower to know about traffic in the pattern. Stage III or mandatory Approach contact prevents this and had a direct bearing on this incident at TLH.

If that instructor saw me, as he later told me, I have a strong opinion that he contributed to what happened. At TLH most of the base legs of training flights are at least a mile out. I was well inside a mile. How could he see me if he was on base, as he vaguely indicated? Did he not see me as he was flying downwind and deciding to make a close base to cut the big twin out? Of course, I will never know; however, his manner left me with the impression that he might be capable of such an action.

A week later, my feelings cooled, I went up to the tower. The same controller was on duty. He wanted to apologize, saying that he didn't realize I was so fast and close and that he had not seen me. I said that no apology was necessary; we were all at fault in various ways. By being on Stage III, I did not know of the two aircraft shooting landings. During the last four miles, there were no radio transmissions, for the training flights were in the crosswind or downwind legs. Had I known about these flights, I additionally would have alerted the tower of my rapid approach and restructured the approach. Not seeing other traffic at four miles out, I felt that the close-in base was sufficient.

Stage III opened a near-fatal gap in this landing sequence. The controllers were not very busy at the time, yet they failed to recognize or alert the tower to my rapid approach to TLH. The tower had a lapse, and of course it was my responsibility to see other traffic.

Protection we need from the hazards within ATC's guardian system includes our own accurate awareness of what procedures are in effect and our responsibilities under them, and our alertness to the traffic situation based on what we can spot from our cockpits. If you are uncertain about what you, your traffic, or the controller are doing or are supposed to be doing, ask the controller for clarification.

Fortress TCA

Consider that in 1981, Chicago's O'Hare International averaged a takeoff or landing every 47 seconds around the clock. O'Hare's daytime controllers that year would have considered 47-second intervals a picnic, for their traffic loads normally demanded intervals of 20 to 30 seconds. While O'Hare admittedly was the nation's busiest terminal that year, the others among the nation's 50 most hectic airports weren't that much more serene, especially during peak hours. Especially with carrier proliferation brought on by deregulation, their skies are crowded to the point where many must use special local control frequencies for different active runways, often to accommodate simultaneous instrument and visual approaches and departures from parallel and intersecting runways. In several terminal control areas, such as New York, which has three of the busiest 50 airports, heavy traffic of all types shares the airspace.

The complexity of communication and operating procedures at high-density terminals presents a challenge to pilots who mix aircraft of widely varying performance.

Experience is, as usual, the best teacher, and a newcomer to high-traffic areas can do everyone a service by conducting his first flights there with another pilot who knows the ropes. Preparation is the fundamental key. There is a wealth of information on the applicable rules, procedures, and services in such publications as the *AIM, Jeppesen's J-Aid,* the *Airport/Facility Directory,* and AOPA's *Handbook for Pilots* and *Airports USA.* Studying the instrument approach procedures can also provide a good idea of what to expect.

Many terminals are dominated by TRSAs, which we have examined, but the highest-density airports are ensconced in TCAs, which to some pilots seem to be governed by a siege mentality. Certainly, whether you are operating IFR or VFR, you must receive clearance from ATC to operate within a TCA. For that, certain equipment is generally required: a two-way radio capable of receiving and transmitting on the appropriate frequencies; a VOR or tacan receiver; and a 4,096-code transponder; for operation in a Group I TCA—the busiest—a Mode-C transponder. For operating in a Group I TCA, you must hold at least a private pilot certificate.

The guardians of the fortress do allow exceptions. For example, ATC can waive the transponder requirement, but the pilot must request the waiver from the appropriate ATC facility at least one hour before his proposed entry into or exit from the TCA. Also, helicopters operating below 1,000 feet and in accordance with written agreement with the FAA need not have a VOR or tacan receiver or transponder.

Within the TCA you will be provided with Stage III radar

service, meaning vectors and associated instructions for sequencing and separation from other airplanes. The separation criteria vary among different facilities, but generally they involve minima of three miles horizontally and 1,000 feet vertically between IFR aircraft and 1.5 miles horizontally and 500 feet vertically between VFR aircraft and between VFR and IFR aircraft.

Gaining Access

TCAs can block a lot of airspace horizontally and vertically for aircraft not precleared into them. The granting of VFR access depends on the controller's ability to handle that traffic plus whatever other aircraft he can accommodate without reaching workload saturation. If you are trying to negotiate entry with a controller who is up to his ears in aircraft, expect a detour. The frequent rejection of entry requests has given many TCAs a bad name, but several of them are trying to provide pilots better opportunities to proceed without undue rerouting, vectoring or other ATC restrictions that force extra work on pilots and the controllers alike.

There are ways for pilots to help. First, use good radio technique. When requesting a TCA clearance, attempt to establish radio contact on the *correct* frequency, which is available on IFR and VFR TCA and sectional charts, in the *AFD,* and from ATIS and FSSs. Make your initial call when you are ten miles outside the TCA, even if you are above it. This can make accommodation easier and quicker. Listen to avoid blocking other transmissions, then get the controller's attention by stating the appropriate facility's designation, your number, and "TCA request." Brevity helps. After the controller responds, provide your aircraft's number, type, position, altitude, and squawk code; state your request and your destination—for instance, "Cessna

One-One-Two-Three-Delta, a 172 over the Van Nuys VOR at 7,500 feet, squawking 1200. Request descent through the TCA direct Long Beach, landing Long Beach.''

Operations in peak traffic periods are toughest. Acknowledgment of your transmission or an instruction to stand by is not a clearance into the TCA. A controller may stipulate ''remain clear of TCA,'' but if your controller does not, still you must stay clear until he announces that you are ''cleared to enter the TCA.''

Requesting the line of least resistance or a preferred route through the TCA may help you get through rather than being forced around or over the dedicated airspace. Some TCAs have readily accessible VFR corridors. If you are unfamiliar with a TCA along your planned flight route, check with Flight Service, local FBOs, or a local ATC facility for indigenous procedures and preferred routes, if they exist.

Fort ARSA

Just as forts are small, less formidable, versions of fortresses, the new airport radar service areas that are increasingly dotting the airspace have proved to be lesser specimens of TCAs. They are a source of deep concern and controversy within aviation for political as well as aeronautical reasons. Their rapid implementation by FAA fiat has raised questions about whether they actually enhance collision avoidance and also about the FAA's willingness to obey the spirit of its own rules by making regulatory changes in a democratic manner. By various bureaucratically deceptive and high-handed means, the FAA has forged ahead with its program of turning voluntary-participation TRSAs into obligatory-participation ARSAs without allowing a full review and expression of views by the pilot community.

Particularly as airline pilots and corporate aircraft operators have seen it, the central problem about TRSAs is that many general aviation pilots choose negative participation within them. In ARSAs, traffic separation under positive ATC control is required from the floor of the airspace—which at its core descends to the surface—to the ARSA's 4,000-plus-foot top.

By the rules, a person seeking entry into an ARSA must establish two-way communications with the applicable facility *prior to entry* and must maintain contact while within it. A person departing a satellite airport within an ARSA must establish and maintain two-way communications with ATC as soon as practicable. While within an ARSA, he must operate according to ATC clearances and instructions, except in an emergency. He may not take off or land within an ARSA except in compliance with FAA arrival and departure traffic patterns. Parachute jumps and ultralight flights within an ARSA must have authorization by the governing ATC facility.

Officially, you need not have a transponder for in-ARSA flights, but since control there is by radar, positive radar contact must be established prior to entry or no dice. The "advisability" of carrying a transponder thus becomes evident. This is compounded by the fact that where the workload has mightily increased for controllers in the replacement of TRSAs by ARSAs, pilots have often been denied entry until room could be made for them in the controllers' workload. Many problems are emerging, the key ones being that at peak traffic periods (which are growing longer) the control frequencies are congested and saturated and new radar positions and equipment are needed to handle the load. The result has been increased time and fuel-consuming delays through imposed holds outside the ARSAs and detours around them.

The stated purpose of the ARSAs is to prevent midair collisions; to simplify airspace designations and standardize ATC services; to resolve conflicts between VFR and IFR aircraft; and to provide traffic advisories and arrival sequencing.

However, pilots have complained that ARSA operations have created confusion, hardships, and dangerous conditions. In fact, just as many controllers have handled TRSA traffic as if participation were mandatory, many ARSA controllers have overseen their forts like mini-TCAs. The Aircraft Owners and Pilots Association and other pilots' groups have been campaigning for a hold on new ARSAs and for a termination of most of the existing ones until the workload can be handled. They are also calling for a hard, realistic look by the FAA at whether they are truly needed.

Winged Vectory

In spite of problems that have accompanied efforts at improved ground-based collision protection, ATC incorporates many procedures that can add confusion and reduce position awareness. For the defense-minded airman, that environment can be rendered safer by his knowing what radar vectors can do for— and to him, if he doesn't watch himself.

While you may derive a certain amount of security from the knowledge that vectoring lifts a great deal of the navigational burden from your shoulders in terminal areas, this luxury carries with it a demand for more, not less, vigilance. You can't fully and blindly relinquish responsibility for avoiding collision with other airplanes or terrain to the controller. Great risks can ensue if the controller loses radar contact, there is a communications failure, or he simply forgets about you and you are caught without a clear picture of your orientation with respect to the airport. The last thing you need, especially when on instruments, is to be misplaced, particularly in areas with high terrain or obstacles. Pilot David G. Martin learned what such a thing could mean on what was to be a simple, vectored hop from San Jose to Visalia, California:

The tower controller at San Jose's Reid-Hillview Airport read me the clearance. "ATC clears Bonanza 576Q to the Visalia Airport via radar vectors to Mount Hamilton Intersection, Victor 107 Panoche, Victor 230 Fresno, Victor 23 Laton Intersection, direct; maintain 7,000;

Departure Control frequency 121.3; squawk 4528; departure instructions: left turn after takeoff to 290 degrees for vector.''

I read the clearance back and was soon airborne and climbing through the overcast. At about 2,500 feet, we burst out of the tops into brilliant sunshine. Level at 7,000 feet, my passengers and I settled down to enjoy the serenity of smooth, calm-air flight above the clouds.

Everything went smoothly until Oakland Center handed me off to Fresno Approach: ''Fresno Approach, Bonanza 576Q; 7,000.''

''Seven-Six-Quebec, Fresno Approach; squawk 0415; altimeter 29.98.''

''Fresno, 76Q; roger.''

A short delay and then, ''Seven-Six-Quebec, descend and maintain 4,000; fly heading 095, vector for the ILS.''

''Seven-Six Quebec is out of seven for four; right to 095.'' I then began setting up the radios for the approach. I set the Visalia ILS on the Number 1 radio (it is hard-wired to the HSI) and the Visalia VOR/DME on the Number 2. The DME is tuned separately, so I set it up to the Visalia VOR/DME, and then verified the idents. No ident on the ILS yet; still too far away.

I had not even reached 4,000 when Fresno came back to me: ''Bonanza 576Q, turn right, heading 120; descend and maintain 2,000.''

''Seven-Six-Quebec is out of 4.8 for 2,000.''

About a minute later, Fresno came back with ''Bonanza 576Q, contact Fresno Approach on 118.5.''

''One-one-eight-point-five; 76Q, good day.'' After I had changed to the appropriate frequency, I called Fresno: ''Fresno Approach, Bonanza 576Q is with you, out of 3.2 for 2,000.''

''Bonanza 576Q, Fresno Approach; report level at 2,000.''

''Seven-Six-Quebec.'' At about 2,500 feet, I entered the soup; a total grayout—no breaks. I leveled at 2,000 and called, ''Fresno, 76Q is level at two.''

''Seven-Six-Quebec, turn left, heading 070.''

''Left to 070 for 76Q.'' I do not know exactly when that gnawing sense that something was wrong began to grip me, but it was somewhere on this base leg. Something just did not seem right. I glanced at the instruments. Everything looked normal, with the exception of the Off flags on the HSI. I thought they would have been showing by then—maybe when we got in closer.

''Bonanza 576Q, turn left, heading 330.''

"Fresno, 76Q is coming left to 330." Still those Off flags for both the localizer and the glideslope. I wondered if maybe the Number 1 radio or the HSI had gone haywire. There was something there, though, because there was an occasional flicker of the localizer flag.

"Bonanza 576Q, Fresno; turn left, heading 290; intercept the localizer; maintain 2,000 feet until established on the localizer; contact the tower, 118.2."

It took about one second before I knew what had happened: Visalia does not have a tower—so he must have been vectoring me to Fresno! I stayed at 2,000 feet and verified that theory by centering on the OBS on the Number 2 VOR. Sure enough, I was on the 350-degree radial of Visalia at 24 nm. "Fresno Approach, Bonanza 576Q; I was cleared to Visalia, not Fresno; over."

"Seven-Six-Quebec, Fresno; say again the nature of your, ahhh, request; ahhhhh, stand by one."

There was a long pause; and then, "Bonanza 576Q, climb and maintain 3,000; turn left, heading 180; vectors for Visalia; we're sorry about that."

After a normal landing, I talked by phone to the Fresno Approach watch supervisor, who apologized profusely and said there was some sort of mix-up with the computer.

When we are on radar vectors, there is a tendency to assume that ATC has us thoroughly in sight and in hand, but they and we can be wrong. In Martin's case, the problem was not severe; in fact, the ILSs for Visalia and Fresno were oriented within ten degrees of each other—which deceived the pilot for a while. However, what if high terrain had been a factor, as it has been in wrong-routing cases? Similarly, pilots vectored to the right airport have also been accidentally vectored, through error or controller forgetfulness, far from the approach. It is critical to keep abreast of where you are, even if in cloud, and if, upon examination, something seems wrong, tell ATC. It is a good habit to keep one of your navigation receivers tuned to a navaid other than the one used for final approach. On approaches with a LOM, some pilots forget to monitor the ADF, which provides an excellent indication of the aircraft's position. Remember that if a controller has forgotten you as you fly his vectors *in the blind,* your separation from other airplanes may be in jeopardy. Should you suffer a communications loss while being vectored, having a good idea of where you are positioned with respect to the airport and the approach fixes can enable you remain within protected airspace and quickly adjust to flying the approach procedure on your own. If you receive a vector that seems cockeyed—such as one that sends you toward outer space rather than angling you to intercept the localizer, begin the turn but also briefly request a clarification. Again, the controller may be in error, or you may have responded to instructions given to a similarly numbered airplane.

Keeping track of your position may not be easy, especially if you have little or no ground contact or you are unfamiliar with the area. Being familiar with the published approach procedure helps, as does following your progress with respect to the approach plate as you are vectored. Just noting the directions in which you have been steered—north or southeast, whatever—and reading what your navigation instruments tell you about your position with respect to fixes and courses, you can see how the controller is setting you up for the approach.

Vectoring offers the time- and effort-saving advantage of not having to fly full approach procedures. This has become a basic and welcome practice but one that tends to make pilots complacent.

Another time-saving option is the contact approach, which is assigned only upon the pilot's request and only if weather reports made at the airport indicate at least one mile horizontal visibility. You must be able to remain clear of clouds. Once you are granted a contact approach, you are responsible for navigating to the airport by reference to the surface, as well as maintaining proper separation from other aircraft. If you are approaching over unfamiliar territory in marginal visibility, it is wise to consider how well you will be able to navigate—for instance, can you see the airport and your traffic?—before requesting a contact approach. The visual approach, which we have discussed, can be requested by the pilot but is usually assigned by ATC when the airport is at or above VFR minimums and you have the airport and your traffic in sight. Again, navigation and separation become your responsibilities. You can follow the traffic as closely or as far away as you deem necessary or safe, but you must also be on the alert for any VFR traffic that may be in the vicinity. The radar controller is not obligated to provide advisories or separation once you accept a visual approach or visual separation; he will do so only on a workload-permitting basis. Such an approach increases your workload. You will be looking for arriving and departing traffic and may even be getting radar advisories. Your attention may be diverted to spotting called-out traffic while you lose sight of a plane you have been watching. There are dangers of confusion and misidentification.

One day, over Denver, a Bonanza pilot inbound on a visual approach reported "the Otter" in sight and was told to "follow the Otter." Two Otters were on final; he had sighted the first. Turning to follow it, he collided with the second.

Clearing out Clutter

Urban ground clutter can make things worse. By day, a low-flying plane can be lost in a mosaic of colors and shapes; at night, street lights, neon signs, and other distractions can combine to obscure even dramatically illuminated targets.

In any conditions on a visual approach, if you don't have the traffic in sight, if you aren't sure which plane the controller is talking about, if you think he has forgotten about you, or feel that you can't comply with an ATC instruction or aren't sure of the exact procedure you are to fly, then ask for clarification or refuse the clearance. It's always better to confess ignorance than to blunder into disaster.

Separation during landings under visual conditions rests upon the pilot's discretion as to how much distance he needs between himself and his preceding traffic. However, this pertains only if the tower reports the braking action as "good." That is important, for at larger airports landing at the highest rate possible is often the custom. You can keep things smooth by keeping up your speed on final. A full-flaps, 65-knot approach, with airliners pursuing you at 150 knots to a runway two miles long, is neither good airmanship nor professional nor safe for all concerned. Add IFR conditions and a stack of holding, waiting aircraft to the situation, and your slowness can cause bad vibes all the way down the line.

Mixing with the big guys in the air around high-density airports is challenging and demanding, but it is really no more or less skill-stretching than flying into a swarming noncontrolled airport on a Saturday. The keys to successful operation in either environment are preparation, knowledge, experience, and courtesy. Know the procedures, keep alert, and look to avoid, and you can elude conflicts with other aircraft and ATC. Failing to be sharp, aware, and bright-eyed in any airspace, controlled or noncontrolled, can lead to tragedy.

We have seen examples of how the System and its controllers can fail pilots. Yet it remains a fact that pilot error is an essential ingredient in a majority of accidents. At such times, what pilots do on their way to a collision may be a mystery, as it happens, to the controllers handling or observing them.

If there is a midair or other kind of crash, an investigation may reveal what circumstances the pilot or pilots faced and what they may have attempted or failed to do to prevent or survive the situation. But all too often, as incidents unfold, the controller may only be able to watch and listen at his scope as the pilot-in-command meets the burden of his responsibility head-on and alone.

Sometimes, the crunch comes with a bewildering suddenness, sometimes the agony is long and drawn out. Be the incident a midair or another emergency, even one that ends without injury, its impact upon the controllers can be brutal. The radar eye may then remain hard and cold, but as we shall see in the following chapter, the people watching what it reports are anything but that.

5
"6241 Yankee . . ."

Every airman owes it to himself to visit a major ATC control facility at least once, to watch the System at work and to witness the interaction between pilots and controllers at the "other" end of the frequency. (Controllers can gain the same benefits of realization and understanding by riding in cockpits.) On one such visit in 1978, *AOPA Pilot* not only observed controllers at work but sat with a particular controller as he handled a sudden, unexpected situation such as controllers dread. Although parts of the ATC System are different today, the elements of this crisis are perennial.

The room underneath the glassed tower at Dulles International Airport was dark. Six gigantic radar scopes lined the wall, casting an eerie green glow. This was the center of operations for Dulles Approach/Departure Control. Outside, thick fog and light rain engulfed the airport.

Frank Stile, a 40-year-old former New Yorker, was between duty assignments and was free for a time to explain what the puzzle of lines, circles, and dashes on the scope mean. For him they are part of a common language that he can manipulate for better comprehension. Various overlays on the scope could be illuminated, independent of the ever-present sweep that continuously traveled around the 22-inch tube, marking various reporting points and approach courses to the runways at Dulles.

Stile explained the alphanumeric tag of computer-generated information. Aircraft identification, altitude, and groundspeed appeared alongside the target display of an airplane. A keyboard allows a controller to change and update the information as well as to coordinate the assignment of transponder codes, which are essential to the system's operation. "Transponders are a help," Stile said. "Targets are often unrecognizable without transponder information. Watch what happens when I depend on just raw data for a return on this airplane coming from the Front Royal VOR."

He pointed to a display that showed an airplane "tagged" 6241Y approaching the western limits of the radar's coverage. A few adjustments to the radar display, and the tiny blip that represented the aircraft disappeared. There was no transponder information on the scope, and the targets displayed were from actual returns from the aircraft skins. Several sweeps showed no target from the plane that had been at the outer limits of the radar's 55-mile coverage, although there were other small blips illuminating the scope, representing other aircraft.

"See, there it is," Stile said as he pointed to a tiny speck that was barely discernible when the sweep line crossed it. It wasn't visible with every sweep. "Now we put the transponder display back on, and it is clearly visible, no mistake," the controller declared as the target became larger and brighter alongside the data-tag information. "A lot of times people may not believe me when I tell them 'no radar contact,' but I'm telling the truth. And when things get really busy and there are a lot of transponder-equipped aircraft on the scope, it can get real tough trying to find an airplane without a transponder return. Transponders make my life easier."

Moments later, Manuel Vaamonde, assistant chief of the Dulles operation, assigned Stile to relieve the controller handling the approach position.

"Look, Frank," said the man vacating the chair in front of the scope, "I gave this guy in an Aztec a heading of 130 degrees, but he doesn't seem to be holding it. Tell him again. I've got him level at 6,000."

Stile seated himself in the empty swivel chair, pulled himself up to the console and spoke in a clear and authoritative voice: "6241 Yankee, say your heading, please."

A clock on the console indicated 1827 GMT—1:27 p.m., local time.

"One-thirty—uh, 110, sir," came the reply from the pilot flying in the overcast nearly 50 miles away.

"Four-One Yankee, roger, turn right heading 130," advised Stile, who watched the scope to verify the pilot's compliance. Then he turned to the controller he was relieving and exchanged additional information regarding two airliners—a United Airlines 727 and an Ozark DC-9—he would also be responsible for directing to Dulles. The light from the scope cast a silhouette of the controller as he guided the three airplanes toward the airport. His feet worked floor pedals which controlled the radios and left his hands free to push buttons and turn switches that illuminated all quadrants of the console in front of him. As he kept watch on the tiny targets on the radar screen, he said he believed that many pilots did not have an accurate idea of the problems a controller faces in getting his job done.

"General aviation pilots do not seem to fully understand how many rules we have to follow just to get them safely to the airport. The day of 'kick the tires and light the fires' is gone— except maybe in Australia," he said.

Moving Mountains

Stile added that instrument traffic was his biggest concern. On a day such as this, there as no VFR traffic to conflict with it. He usually attempts to provide advisories to VFR traffic but cannot always comply with such requests.

"If I'm busy on approach and have several guys lined up for the ILS, well, I can get pretty tied up. Providing traffic advisories is my last option, if it won't interfere with my ability to take care of IFR aircraft needing my service. It's a judgment call, my choice.''

A particularly bright elongated mass of light illuminated a section of the scope that represented an area northwest of Dulles. The controller attributed the image to a line of mountains in the area and said that he could eliminate the display from the scope. "I can program the system to remove any target from the scope that isn't moving.''

He made adjustments to the equipment, and the reflected radar image of the mountains disappeared. This influenced none of the other targets. Stile made another change, and an even greater display of the terrain than had shown up before appeared. The controller settled on a point somewhere in between. (A day short of three years before, Trans World Flight 514 had flown into that same stretch of ground, killing all 92 occupants. At the time of the crash it was being worked by Dulles Approach.)

Stile said that the constant sweep of the scope and the contrast of the faded display that trailed the bright, moving line was something he had grown accustomed to. "The light doesn't bother me a bit,'' he said as he penciled information on paper strips for tabulation of the flight, "I'm used to it. What's worse for me is when I'm not busy. When I'm busy, I'm reacting a lot, and time passes quickly. But on a day like this, with nothing going on, well, it's tough, just waiting for something to happen.''

Handling several planes at a time was not unusual, by his account. The time he spent behind the scope varied, and he also spent time in the tower cab. He is a 14-year ATC veteran.

"I may have to handle as many as 15 airplanes at one time,'' said this short, stocky man with a day's growth of beard on his face and his shirt cuffs folded back above his wrists, as he pondered the screen, "and sometimes I might spend as little as 15 minutes or maybe as much as two hours behind the scope. The rest of the time I usually spend in the tower. Today, for exam-

ple, I'm working my sixth day. I'm on overtime. We're a little
short of people, and I'm fully qualified to work any position, so
here I am. I'll be glad when tomorrow comes and I can take the
day off."

A Braniff Airlines pilot advised the approach controller that
if the RVR (runway visual range) went below 1,800 feet, he
would have to divert his jet to Washington National Airport,
located nearly 25 miles to the southeast. Stile acknowledged the
pilot while looking up at a display of three revolving drum
counters that were receiving input from electronic equipment
near the runway in use, and he relayed the information to the
pilot: "RVR, touchdown 1,800, midpoint 2,000, rollout 2,000,
altimeter 30.20. And how about giving me a report on the cloud
tops?" The pilot, cleared earlier for a descent to 7,000 feet,
reported that he was descending into the overcast at 8,000 feet.

The airline target was some distance behind the Aztec, but
its data tag indicated a groundspeed of 250 knots, while the
Aztec was indicating 140. The smaller, twin-engine airplane was
going to be overtaken by the jet. The controller said that he
would make allowances for that. "Even though the Aztec was
here first," Stile said, "I'm going to send in the jet first. I can
zip him in and still get the Aztec on the ground in about the
same amount of time. Besides, the jet uses a lot more fuel, so
why keep him waiting?"

Stile cleared the Braniff for the approach and gave the crew
the current RVR: "touchdown 2,400, midpoint, 1,800, rollout
1,800." A diversion to National would not be necessary for the
big jet.

The Aztec was next.

"Six-Two-Four-One-Yankee is seven from the marker, cleared
ILS One Right approach, RVR 2,000, midpoint 2,000, rollout
2,000" was spoken into the tubelike microphone that jutted out
from the left side of Stile's face.

"Forty-One-Yankee, roger." The time was 1:45 p.m.

The information tag moved with the bright blip that represented the Aztec, following the illuminated line that marked the way to the runway, and one minute later, Stile's commitment to its pilot was over.

"Six-Two-Four-One-Yankee, contact the tower, 120.1."

"One-twenty point one. Good day, sir."

"Good day."

First Miss

Stile's attention turned to a United jet he was vectoring to the airport. He was momentarily interrupted by another pilot's readback of the altimeter setting as "20.19." Stile shook his head and corrected the pilot. "Negative, 30.19."

The Aztec information tag continued to move down the line representing the runway and off the other end in a right turn. The altitude readout began to increase from 600 feet msl. The Aztec was executing a missed approach. The published approach allowed a descent to 200 feet above the runway.

"He wants to try it again," said the intercom voice from the tower cab.

"Yeah, I see," Stile replied.

The departure controller questioned the pilot about his reason for making the missed approach. The reply was garbled and mixed in a hash-like interference.

"He says the glideslope is out!" a voice shouted in the dimly lit control room, an offered interpretation of the unintelligible communication from the pilot.

The room suddenly filled with voices and movement. Moments later, another person yelled that the ILS equipment was okay. The electronic monitors indicated no problems, and no malfunction alarms had sounded.

The departure controller had continued to issue instructions to the Aztec pilot, who appeared to be calm and expressed no concern about making a second approach. The controller did not ask him again why he had just missed. He advised the Aztec to contact Approach Control.

"Approach, Aztec 6241 Yankee is level 2,000."

"Six-Two-Four-One Yankee, roger, fly heading 190, vectors back to the final, ILS One Right, RVR now 2,200, midpoint 2,000, rollout 1,800."

From somewhere in the room came questions—people wondering aloud—why the pilot had elected to make a missed approach and agreement that the visibility was so low that he probably didn't see the runway. The airlines preceding him were able to descend lower because they were certified for Category II and Category III approaches.

The pilot may have been calm, but tension had risen in the control room. Several more persons were hovering behind the controllers. Stile continued to vector the Aztec down the east side of the runway, careful to keep it from Washington National's airspace farther east. Five minutes later, the plane was lined up on the final approach course, and Stile advised, "Four-One Yankee, RVR 2,000, midpoint 2,000, rollout 2,000."

"Roger."

"Six-Two-Four-One Yankee, contact the tower 120.1."

"One two zero point one, roger."

The target descended steadily to 600 feet along the approach course and leveled off along the runway. It began to climb. The Aztec was making a second missed approach. The two approaches had been executed smoothly on the radar display, with proper descents and headings maintained by the pilot.

Rising Apprehensions

The room was restless again. There was talk among the men at the other positions. The low murmur of their voices filled the room.

"How come he missed this time?"

"I dunno."

The tower intercom buzzed back and forth with voices as Stile compiled the Washington weather reports that had been requested by the Aztec pilot, who had decisions to make and who shortly would again become the approach controller's responsibility. Stile was now busy, and his voice off-mike was no longer casual and relaxed. He spoke quickly, and his concern was evident. Yet in his radio communications, he gave no hint of his otherwise apparent uneasiness.

"Dulles Approach, Aztec 6241 Yankee is with you, level 2,000."

"Aztec 6241 Yankee, fly heading 180. One eight zero on the heading. We're getting the latest weather on Washington."

"Okay."

Someone in the room said loudly, "Hell, Washington is not any better. Nothing is any better around here."

Although the pilot hadn't requested it, Stile decided to include the Baltimore weather as well. His voice was composed, with no sign of apprehension, as he transmitted the data to the Aztec: "Washington's reporting sky partially obscured, measured 200 overcast, visibility one-half mile, light drizzle and fog, and the ceiling is variable 200 to 400. And at Baltimore, it's indefinite 200, sky obscured, visibility one-quarter mile, light drizzle and fog."

"Okay. Well, I'll tell you what, we'll go back towards Columbus and we'll go to Martinsburg." The Aztec pilot wasn't going to try another approach in the immediate area.

"You want to go to Martinsburg now, sir?" Stile's voice rose in pitch as he verified the pilot's statement.

"Affirmative." The pilot's voice was firm.

"All right, turn left 360. Left turn heading 360, maintain 2,000," Stile advised while he began to gather weather data for Martinsburg.

"Roger."

The target on the scope was now about five miles east of the airport. The time was 2:10 p.m.

"Six-Two-Four-One Yankee, squawk code 4276, please," Stile requested as he reprogrammed the computer for the new code. The alphanumeric display momentarily dropped from the screen until the pilot reset his transponder. Moments later, the controller was providing the Martinsburg weather: "Six-Two-Four-One Yankee, Martinsburg is reported indefinite 300, sky obscured, visibility one-quarter mile, light rain and fog."

The pilot did not respond, and Stile stared at the scope as he began to push the computer keyboard.

"Six-Two-Four-One Yankee, Dulles." Stile was staring at the scope, moving his face closer to the giant tube. "He disappeared! He just dropped off the scope!" he exclaimed, his voice strained.

"Yeah, he's gone," echoed another voice in the room.

Vaamonde, who was standing close by, moving quickly to the supervisor's position, picked up a phone and began dialing a number. His deep frown was made sharply visible by the desk lights.

An air of anxiousness spread through the entire room. Attention turned to Stile's position, but no one spoke to him. He continued to give instructions to the United jet, interspersing them with calls to the Aztec.

"Six-Two-Four-One Yankee, Dulles." There was no answer, and his voice wavered as he haltingly explained to the airline crew that they had to enter a holding position because another aircraft had disappeared from the scope.

Another man settled into the unmanned position next to Stile and offered, "Hey, Frank, I'll take over your traffic while you try to raise him."

"No, I only have this United guy, and I have him holding on the west side of the airport," Stile said. His voice was high-pitched, and his head was shaking from side to side, as if he were saying no through its movement. His eyes remained aimed at the glass scope. "I just don't understand. He just dropped off."

Stile's distress was obvious, but he continued to call to the missing airplane. No one interfered with him. As the Aztec pilot had been doing only minutes before, Stile was making his own decisions.

Several persons stood quietly nearby and looked toward the scopes. They waited for the Aztec's display to reappear, for the pilot to respond to the controller's calls.

"Wait, I think I have him!" shouted Stile as he peered into the scope.

"Where?" came a voice, equally excited, from the darkness.

"No, I guess it isn't him," said Stiles, his voice slowing and dropping off to a whisper before he finished the sentence. "Six-Two-Four-One Yankee, Dulles," he said into the mike, his voice reflecting hardly a trace of the concern he was showing among his colleagues.

"He crashed!" A man standing next to the assistant chief had said this and then leaned over and exchanged more words with Vaamonde, who was holding a telephone handset to his ear. The time was 2:14 p.m.

The Ordeal of Confirmation

The waiting was over. A strange wave of relief spread among the people crowded into the room. No words were spoken. Most eyes were trained on the supervisor's position.

"He crashed into a townhouse," said the man who had been talking with Vaamonde. "It's confirmed." Almost simultaneously, a voice spoke over the tower intercom: "Frank, someone just called the tower and said there was a crash about five miles east of the airport. You heard yet?"

"Yeah, I know. He just dropped off," Stile mumbled as he began to shake to his head back and forth.

"You have to get somebody to relieve you," said the intercom voice, "that's the procedure."

Someone slipped into Stile's position as the controller was ushered from the room, which was now crowded with at least 12 people. Some of them followed Stile out of the room.

"Preserve the tapes!" someone called out.

"That's being taken care of," came a reply from the gloom. "Better be sure to get the radar records. We need a special weather observation, too."

A low, steady drum of voices filled the room. There was no confusion, only a sense of urgency. Telephones were ringing at the supervisor's position. No sooner would a line be cleared than the phone would ring again.

"I'll never understand how those news people find out what's going on so fast, even before we do," blurted Lyle Hartman, the operations chief, as he hung up one telephone. Between answering those calls, he was placing others to area police and fire departments to verify the conflicting information being reported about the crisis. No one seemed absolutely sure what had happened, except that the plane had crashed.

A review of the aircraft's flight plan and the ensuing telephone checks revealed that the Aztec had departed Columbus, Ohio, at noon. Only the pilot was on board. He was ATP-rated and the chief flight instructor for Ohio State University.

The equipment monitors were checked again, and two technicians appeared. They talked of shutting down the entire ILS system in order to do a thorough check. The assistant chief didn't agree that such an action was warranted. "Hell, that would shut down the airport," Vaamonde insisted. "I don't think we have a problem with the ILS. The system checks okay on the monitors, and nobody has reported any difficulties with it."

The discussion ended with the technicians claiming that they could check "just about everything" without interfering with landing traffic.

"Someone says he landed on a golf course at Reston," said Hartman as he hung up one of the telephones in front of him. "I'd sure like to go with that." His comment went ignored.

Vaamonde was making a series of telephone calls. A notebook on his desk lay opened to a page marked "SAMPLE" in bold, red letters. "Facility Accident Identification Record" was printed on the top of the page. Another page, which he held in his hand, had "Priority Notification" printed at the top.

Hartman and Vaamonde were clearly in control of the operation as they directed various people to double-check information. They appeared unruffled, and their actions were deliberate as they exchanged information, making sure that all the proper procedures were followed.

"I've called everybody I can think of," sighed Vaamonde. "Now I guess we better get some statements."

"Yes, we should do that now," said Hartman. "We need to know who was working him. I guess we should get one from everybody."

Nearly 40 minutes after the Aztec disappeared from the scope, Stile returned to the control room. He stopped a few feet from the entrance and told everyone that he was physically in good shape. At 3:45 p.m., he and a fellow controller were sitting on metal chairs in front of a gigantic tape machine. Bob Logan, the Dulles tower chief, claimed that the complex-looking machine made situations such as this much easier.

"That is the most modern unit of its kind," explained Logan, who had quietly begun overseeing things when the crisis began. "It cost several thousand dollars, but it does in a matter of minutes what used to take hours. That machine can locate specific time periods by computer, so in this case, we can go right to the spot where we began working him."

Logan left the immediate area, and a technician began to run the tape through the machine, but nothing came over the speakers. He spent several minutes trying to discover why nothing could be heard. Suddenly he realized what he had done wrong. Seconds later, the whole scenario of 6241 Yankee's last flight was relived, including the pilot's conversation with Stile, the tower operator, and the departure controller. The tape yielded no new information, no hint of difficulty from the pilot.

At 5:00 p.m., the men were left alone to discuss the statement that Stile would have to make, now that his memory was refreshed by the tape.

The control room was no longer crowded with people. The shift had changed, and more aircraft were being vectored to landings on Runway One Right.

The six-o-clock radio news that evening was reporting correctly that the Aztec had struck a townhouse in Reston, Virginia, killing the pilot and two occupants of the house, a man and his wife. Their 12-year-old daughter was not at home when the fire engulfed the building. The broadcast reported that Federal Aviation Administration officials on the scene had no explanation for the fatal crash.

What lay behind the crash of Aztec 6241 Yankee would have to be resolved, if possible, by the investigation that was already beginning at the disaster site and among the Dulles controllers. One thing is clear—in fact, it is the point of this chapter: The fear and anxiety the doomed pilot may well have been hiding behind his professional, calm demeanor, was shared—though similarly masked—by the controllers working him.

The story of 6241 Yankee's last flight makes clear both the benefits and limitations of the pilot-controller relationship. Under certain, not uncommon, circumstances, there are limits to what each party to the partnership can do, and especially when collision and terrain avoidance are involved, if circumstances take the situation out of the controller's power to help, the loss may be painful for all concerned.

As we have seen, we must be vigilant as we work with ATC, just as we must fly defensively in sharing the sky with our fellow pilots. Still, it is good to know that in getting through many of flight's tough moments, we who are airborne are linked to those who guide us from the ground by bonds more compelling than regulations on a page or the progress of blips on a scope.

Part Two
SURFACE CONFLICTS

6
How Clear to Land?

It would be nice to believe that once you are clear of the danger of a midair collision, you can let your defenses down a bit and just land and taxi home free. Don't believe it.

Much can happen near to the touchdown zone and beyond it. For instance, a lot of traffic above the airport means a lot of traffic on it. At large terminals, taxiing among multi-holers and multitudes of mingling smaller craft under the rapid instructions of low-patience ground controllers can be a lesson in humility, especially if the taxiway labyrinth is large and one's knowledge of it is small. Finding oneself stopped and staring head-on at a behemoth whose cockpit is too lofty to see certainly can press home the *light* in lightplane. And having to ask, "Ground, I'm cleared to Taxiway UU, where is it?" is bad enough; being answered, *"Sir,* you've already passed it, hold and stand by one" can be devastating as you watch other airplanes stop while Ground gets you sorted out. On one airport milling with taxiing and waiting planes, Ground's feverish calls to locate a misplaced bird were rewarded with a last-gasp reply from the pilot: "I'm rocking my wings!"

Not only the air contains damaging objects; contact with the ground can also be shocking. Especially at friendly little airports, semi-controlled conflicts with the surface are legion and call for defensive flying all the way to the chocks. Then, though your aircraft may be motionless and tied down, other conflicts *on* the surface can well up to haunt you there or later.

This section is about airports—arrivals thereat, departures therefrom, and vigilance you will need within their boundaries.

Arriving at a large airport not only involves seeing to avoid other aircraft but listening and working to avoid breaking the smooth flow of operations. Preparation before arrival is a good defense against the embarrassment and inconvenience this causes.

Clear of Turbulence

First, however, one last point to remember about aerial conflicts with other aircraft: When you are mixing with aircraft larger and heavier than your own, avoid their wake turbulence. According to the FAA, wake turbulence encounters are factors in about 11 accidents and hundreds of incidents each year. This subject is discussed in greater detail in the companion volume to this book, *Crises in the Cockpit* (Macmillan/Eleanor Friede, 1986), but here are some things to keep in mind.

A wake consists of counterrotating vortices that emanate from near an airplane's wingtips. These vortices—mini-storms that can suddenly and swiftly roll a light aircraft onto its back—are created by the pressure differential of the airflow over the top and bottom of the wing. The most powerful vortices are generated by heavy airplanes flying slowly in a clean configuration. They can hurt even when not at their strongest.

ATC often will provide warnings of possible wake turbulence. Nevertheless, avoidance is the pilot's responsibility. Generally, the best tactics are to keep above and upwind of a heavy airplane's flight path; when following a heavy airplane to a runway, land beyond the point where it touches down. Keep in mind that an airplane need not be a widebody to generate turbulence too strong to handle. Aircraft have been upset by the wakes of airplanes nearly their same size.

Just Getting In

Those pilots who are most leery of large-airport landings tend to be VFR airmen who are inexperienced in such operations. The prepared IFR pilot is virtually led into the airport by procedures he knows, instruments he follows, and controllers who hand him from post to post each step of the way. The one thing ATC won't tell him to do that he must remember—like his VFR brother—is to check the airport's automatic terminal information service (ATIS), for weather, approach, and runway information. Not having "the numbers" can create both a handicap for yourself and an irritant for the tower. Yet even a seasoned IFR pilot, with all his numbers straight, must be careful about a form of technological betrayal on his instrumented approach, as pilot Edward G. Gauss learned early in his IFR career.

Gauss was preparing to make an ILS approach to Fairbanks, Alaska. It was his first such effort after getting his instrument ticket:

I was not quite expecting it. One instant, I was out and the next, there I was, in my first nice wet cloud. Everything stabilized, and it seemed it was taking a long time to get to the beacon. I considered making a crosscheck off the VOR but hesitated. I had set up all of my radios for the approach and was afraid that I would do something wrong if I changed them. The vector still seemed to be taking a very long time. So I relented and tuned my backup radio to the Fairbanks VOR and made a rough triangulation. I was on course.

I began to worry that I might lose my courage and want out, so I tuned my backup radio to a nice safe radial that would get me back to blue sky. The needle went way off to one side and started flagging. I found that distracting, so I turned it off. I told myself that there was a great big pie of blue sky to aim for, and I would have no trouble finding it if I needed to. The backup radio was still set on the VOR, and it looked untidy. So I returned it to the localizer. As I turned the knob, Approach called and gave me a heading toward the beacon. I turned onto the base leg.

Soon I was given a 45-degree turn to intercept the localizer and was cleared for the approach. It was a bit bumpy from the wind bounding off the hills, but there was no problem picking up the ILS. There was a good, strong signal. And on my primary radio, the localizer was functioning normally.

Passing Fox, I started down. Here I go, I said to myself. All I have to do is to keep the needle centered and slide down. The easy part is when you're out; it gets harder as you get closer, I reminded myself. Approach handed me to the tower, and I was told to report at the outer marker. Everything stabilized and was normal. On this approach, at the outer marker you could start using the glideslope, so I began to pay attention to it. The localizer seemed nailed dead center. I passed the outer marker and picked up the glideslope. There was a little bounce, and I began working to get the glideslope on center. The localizer needle remained right on. It had not budged at all.

An alarm went off in my brain. I am not that good! Both localizers were dead center. I had spent too much time worrying about the glideslope. With my skill level, the localizer should have moved off! Something was wrong.

I remembered that I had turned the backup radio off. Quickly I turned it on. The localizer came on, flagged a bit and then settled about a third of the way from the center. I pressed the test button on the primary receiver. There was a good flag, but the needle stayed dead center. The radio had failed.

I got the localizer centered using the backup, and the glideslope stayed within an acceptable error. I found I could ignore the localizer on the primary display and use the indicator on the backup receiver. And then I was in sunshine. The runway was right there for me to land.

Later, at the radio shop, we discovered that a wire in the meter of the indicator had separated. The only warning I could have had was simply that I was not that good. Had both receivers been on, I would have caught the problem earlier.

Near the ground, a pilot's sixth sense about the health of his airplane or the guidance he is receiving is critical, for there may be all too little time to rectify what is going wrong. This applies not only to brand-new instrument pilots but to ATPs with thousands of hours as they monitor the progress of their airliners toward the surface. Kevin Garrison was such a pilot; a McDonnell Douglas DC-9 was his airplane as he and his captain relearned some lessons about defensive thinking during instrument approaches:

"Only another minute or so, and we should hear the marker."

With these words, I pressed on with my approach into Knoxville. Something was definitely wrong. Cleared for a visual, we should have seen the approach lights long ago.

"Let's see now. We're dead center on the localizer. The glideslope is out of service, but we're at minimum descent altitude. How far out were we when Center turned us onto final?"

I was descending from the clouds with a 30-knot tailwind. Although directly over the airport, I was looking straight ahead into the gloom and snow. As I was waiting for the marker, I got the strangest feeling at the back of my neck. Over the years, I have learned to pay attention to that feeling.

It was snowing harder. I had little experience as the first officer in the DC-9, and though I was flying the airplane, it ws really the captain's call. But something didn't feel right about the approach.

"The heck with it; missed approach." As I grabbed the throttles, the captain's hand was there as a backup to mine. I had decided only a second before he did. "Positive rate, gear up, flaps at 15 degrees, fly the published missed approach, talk."

Back with Center, we got a right turn back to the airport, which was *ten miles* behind us. The approach lights were turned up, and the snow was lighter. We made a smooth landing, and afterward we both shared that inward shudder. Something went very wrong on that approach, and we tried to figure out what it was.

The approach was made late at night. We had been on a quick flight from Cincinnati to Knoxville. Clouds were numerous and broken, but adequate visibility for a visual approach was reported at Knoxville by Flight Service. We couldn't see the airport, but we told Center it would be all right if they vectored us to the final. Notams had indicated that the glideslope and middle marker were out of service, so we set up for localizer-only minimums. We even had a time limit set up for the outer marker to the missed approach point. Sounds nice and tight and professional? No. Actually, Center, thinking "visual," vectored us to the localizer *inside* the marker without telling us, then handed us off to Flight Service for advisories.

We had forgotten some basics of instrument flight; we had become too used to things going smoothly and gotten casual about flying.

Don't rush. That is one rule that is firmly planted in my mind now. I should have demanded the proper information and taken my time setting things up. A procedure turn and tuning the automatic direction finder to the locator outer marker would have taken a few extra minutes in the bumpy, dark air; but it also would have oriented me and gotten us down in time—slow enough to shoot the approach professionally and smoothly.

Details that seem unimportant and that little voice telling me something is wrong are two things I have included in my scan and plan to pay close attention to in the future.

Facing the *Music?*

Preparation for what is not supposed to happen must be part of every pilot's defensive arsenal, especially when he is at that stage of a flight when he must rely on such factors as controller communications and navigational radio accuracy. Not only can radios fail within the airplane, but working flawlessly, they can pick up and relay to the crew bizarre sights and sounds. Maverick signals, in fact, are becoming a serious problem that particularly affects instrument approaches.

For instance, 16 nautical miles west of Runway 8R at Stapleton International Airport, at Denver, a thicket of radio and television antennas sprouts from Lookout Mountain. Pilots familiar with Stapleton have another name for the mountain: They call it Sing-Along Hill, because broadcasts from the antennas can be heard on the localizer frequency for the ILS/DME approach to Runway 8R.

Lookout Mountain may have acquired a whimsical nickname because of the presence of the antennas, but FM signal interference in aircraft navigation receivers is potentially life threatening to pilots. A few seconds of Frank Sinatra over the audio channel of a localizer frequency can provide comic relief during an instrument approach, but when localizer and glideslope needles begin to respond to a wandering FM broadcast frequency, the problem becomes far more serious.

The FAA has been aware of the phenomenon for about a decade and has been working with the FCC to ensure that frequencies for new instrument approach aids do not conflict with existing FM broadcast frequencies and that new FM stations are located not to become part of the frequency interference problem. However, as the FM broadcast industry grows in size, power, and influence, broadcasters' patience for the necessarily restrictive dictates of aerial navigation wanes. For example, the FCC has suggested that the entire service volume, or area of coverage, of a localizer approach (a maximum of 35 degrees each side of the runway centerline, out to 12 miles) may be too much airspace to reasonably protect from frequency interference.

Television antennas with 5,000,000-watt transmitters also are a significant threat. Aviation also has to contend with an increasingly crowded frequency spectrum. Even local, low-power transmitters can interfere with frequencies that control such things as runway approach lights and low-level wind-shear systems.

The problem of FM interference arises from the close proximity of the FM spectrum (88 to 108 MHz) to the aviation VHF navigation and communications frequency range (108 to 137 MHz). A powerful FM transmitter can overpower and spill into transmissions by a nearby 10- to 50-watt localizer or terminal VOR transmitter. Also, because FM broadcast antennas are designed to direct the signal horizontally, toward the audience, an aircraft flying at low altitude on an instrument approach would be in the area of greatest FM signal strength. Furthermore, energy from an FM signal broadcast at the top of the FM frequency range can bleed into the bottom of the VHF range and affect localizers and terminal VORs. Anomalous FM signals accidentally can coincide with an active ILS or VOR frequency.

This last-named phenomenon, along with the existence of inter-fering pirate stations, occurs mainly in Europe.

FM interference may also result from a strong FM signal's overwhelming a VHF receiver to the point where the receiver is unable to pick up any other frequencies. A VHF receiver's abil-ity to keep frequencies separated can be weakened in the pres-ence of more than one strong FM broadcast signal. When that occurs, the receiver is vulnerable to a mixing of the FM signals, which can produce a third signal with a frequency that may be identical to a local ILS or VOR frequency. ELTs also can pick up, mix and retransmit FM signals.

Various proposals are now being considered as potential remedies. These range from protective modifications to navaid transmitters to improving FM transmitters and VOR, ILS, and communications receivers to the required installation of a heavy (15 pounds) in-line filter to provide aircraft receivers with a pro-tection of ten decibels of frequency attenuation.

In areas, such as Detroit and Denver, where interference has created erroneous localizer and glideslope flag indications and needle deflections, controllers normally keep aircraft away from the affected areas, but they aren't always successful. Mean-while, while the possible remedies are being debated, pilots should check to see if their destinations, particularly heavily populated areas, have been cited by pilots experiencing interference. If you experience such a problem, immediately notify ATC or Flight Service, indicating (1) which avionics receivers were affected by the interference and what effects you saw or heard; (2) the frequency affected; (3) the date, time, and location and the air-craft altitude; (4) the source of the interference, such as an FM radio station or TV signal. (The AOPA is also conducting a study of the problem and should be contacted with this infor-mation at its Airspace Technology Department, 421 Aviation Way, Frederick, MD 21701; telephone 301/695-2209.)

Fitting In

For VFR pilots, the potential glitches to arriving smoothly at large, busy airports (outside of harsh wind conditions or lapses in airmanship) tend to involve pilot-controller communications and traffic adjustment. Again, be prepared: Prestudy the airport layout and the surrounding area, including recommended reporting points and prominent landmarks. From approach plates, the appropriate sectional or TCA chart, or the *Airport/Facility Directory* make a preflight list of the ATIS, approach, departure, tower, ground, and Unicom frequencies you can expect to be using. The advantage here is to have something to refer to readily should you have difficulties in receiving frequency assignments when you arrive. You won't necessarily be given the particular approach or tower frequency on your list, but it will be usable in a pinch.

Make your initial call after gathering the current ATIS information—do that early, as far out as you can receive it. Not only will this set the weather and runway picture for you, but it will save your having to tune back to it or the controller from having to give the information to you. When you call, just say you have "Information Hotel" or whatever; that is more accurate than "with the numbers," for if the ATIS data has been very recently changed, the controller may not be sure which information, such as an altimeter setting or runway change, you have. Know, also, the indicated airspeed you will use during the initial phases of your approach. That is key to the controller's strategy in fitting you into the traffic flow and is one of the first things he will ask you. Saying your type aircraft can help, but if you are prepared to fly a higher-than-normal approach airspeed, you should let the controller know it. You will not be expected to match the 160-odd knots of the jets, but, as we have said, it will be appreciated if you can come up with 120 knots or more, even if this will require a fair amount of power. Remember, that the approach controller thinks in term of *indi-cated*, not true, airspeed in *knots*.

From your prestudy of the area, select a visual checkpoint to make your first call from as you overfly it. VFR check-points—which can be airports, towers, tank farms, just about anything that can be spotted easily from the air—are identified on sectional and VFR terminal area charts by magenta flags.

One more point to observe before you begin the business of fitting in and getting in: You will be in rapid-fire communication with the ground, listening carefully as headings, altitudes, and airspeeds are given to you and other aircraft, and it is essential that you respond as promptly as possible—remembering to *fly the plane first*—to calls meant for you. Sometimes it can take a lot of concentration to pick your calls out from the multitude of numbers flowing into your ears. Make it a practice to tell your passengers that no further conversation with you is available. Even if the right-seat occupant is a fully qualified pilot, the pos-sibility of help from that quarter can well be outweighed by the effects of mixups and distractions stemming from his trying to contribute. Unless you and your co-pilot have already worked well together as a crew, concentrate on doing the arrival job by yourself.

Always on Call

Now is your time to sound like an ATP pro, which means being clear and brief on the mike. Give your aircraft identifica-tion, location, and intentions and that you have the ATIS. Ap-proach may then respond with a heading to vector you into the flow, an altitude assignment, and a transponder squawk code.

As you get closer to the airport, you will hear airplanes ahead of you being turned over to the tower. Sometimes it will be the standard "Contact Tower now on 118.6," but frequently the words will be something like, "Monitor (or switch to) Tower on 118.6 and report reaching Romeo (or the twin stacks or the river, or other reporting point)." *Monitor* is different from *contact* in that it means switch to the new frequency and be silent until you are called or until you reach the reporting fix or point. This reduces the amount of talk on the tower frequency. (If you are IFR and are told to report a fix, report the name of the fix rather than just "the marker," for there may be two or three approaches in use simultaneously, and this confirms to the tower which approach you are flying.)

The tower may ask if you can keep up your speed beyond the final approach fix or on a VFR final. If you can't, you must stick with whatever speed will be safe, but if the runway is a long one, you may find it relatively easy to keep up your speed. Before doing it in heavy traffic, give some practice time to high-speed landings on a long, lightly used runway.

A controller may also ask you to use the maneuverability of your light aircraft to fit into the landing traffic flow, provided the conditions are visual. This can result in some interesting procedures, such as a right descending 270 to a landing from a point 2,000 feet directly over the airport; a delaying 360 on short final; a 6,000-foot ear-popper descent straight in from six miles out; and (an old favorite) a last-minute runway switch. These maneuvers are not particularly difficult, but they do demand some understanding of the performance capabilities of the airplane by pilot and controller alike.

It is worth mentioning here that many pilots have noticed a difference in the way they are handled by controllers who have aviation experience, compared with those who do not. The lack of operational flying experience in the current controller force has been recognized by quite a few people. Some controllers even have difficulty recognizing the differences in performance among aircraft types. This is particularly true of general aviation aircraft. The problem has been compounded with the increasing movement of ATC facilities away from airports.

On final, we normally think of ourselves as being pretty busy. Still, if the conditions are visual and the final approach is long, it is possible to seize a chance to get ahead of things by determining which taxiway you will shoot for to clear the runway both safely and expeditiously and which way you will head to reach general aviation parking. Again, studying the airport diagram beforehand does wonders for one's orientation when the real thing is just ahead of the nose.

Courtesy toward other pilots is important here as elsewhere. Once you are cleared to land, you legally "own" the runway, and if you decide you may need all of the pavement, you should use it. But don't land short and crawlingly roll out long, as if you mean to take permanent possession. For instance, if you are cleared to Dulles' Runway 19L, where the first turnoff is more than half a mile from the threshold, landing on the numbers will not offer proof of your virtuosity, while landing long will indicate your intelligence. At Washington National, however, landing short on Runway 15 will enable you to tell the controller you'll be holding short of intersecting—and jet-busy—Runway 18, so he can release traffic on that runway.

Okay, you're down and still in the good graces of all concerned, including yourself, and you dutifully clear that runway with all safe and deliberate speed. Now you must listen carefully, for the tower controller may want to take you across one or more parallel runways before you go to Ground. This is a critical portion of any flight into a busy airport. Several collisions and near misses have occurred at just this stage. One such incident is reported by Joel Hamm, a pilot and controller who discovered that not all such events stem from "pilot error."

At the FAA Academy, we were taught to do everything by the book. Our instructors were particularly picky about radio technique. The business of separating airplanes leaves no time to wonder if the other guy really meant what you think he said. Controllers, they preached, must be brief and precise and, above all, must speak only the language prescribed in "The Good Book."

On a FAM (familiarization) airline flight to Los Angeles, I was riding jumpseat on a United DC-10, enjoying the view and doing some public relations work for the FAA. My hosts had recounted some horror stories of ATC "system errors," and I had been obliged to counter with a protracted tribute to the devotion and sterling performance of the FAA's ground troops.

I was just running out of wind when Center handed us off to Approach, who lined us up and turned us over to Tower while we were still up high and a long way out. The guy who answered our call-up was one of those super 'trollers I had been bragging about. The Los Angeles skies were dark with exhaust trails, the radio jammed with calls; but the man in the cab had the big picture. My unease at being mixed up in the rush-hour melee calmed under his nonstop monologue of combined ATC, CB-ese, and Buck Rogers jargon—not exactly standard phraseology, but it kept everyone moving.

We touched down on Runway 25L and made a fast right turn for the terminal on the other side of the parallel runway. Local control held on to us.

"Keep 'em spooled up, United. You'll be across in a minute."

What did that mean? Were we cleared to cross? The captain shrugged and pushed the throttles. As we nosed onto the runway, the first officer swung around for a look.

"STOP!"

Someone stood on the brakes, throwing me against the harness, as a blue-and-white blur filled the windshield. A wingtip slashed by, scarcely out of reach of our nose, as the departing jet rotated and disappeared. We had come within yards of hitting a 727 on a takeoff roll. Joe Cool and his snappy lingo had nearly gotten us creamed.

"Hold short of 25 Right." That is what he should have said. Only the crew's vigilance and reflexes saved us from a replay of Tenerife. We sat there for a moment, tight-lipped, staring out the windows. I knew what they were thinking: Good Ol' FAA does it again. As a representative of the agency charged with promoting air safety, I prayed to the god of bureaucrats that I might die there unnoticed.

Tower's clearance to the gate broke the silence. Joe must have gotten the message: There was no more jive talk, just a straight "Cross 25 Right. Contact Ground, 121.9."

"Are you going to write up that incident?" I asked.

"Why bother?" the captain grumbled. "It won't help. Happens all the time."

Well, not to me it won't. I stepped into the sweltering smog, determined to learn from that experience. When I am in the air, I am going to keep my eyes open.

And on the ground, speak only by the book.

On the ground as in the air, wherever other airplanes are in motion around us, procedures and the pilot's etiquette of looking out for oneself and for the other guys must be carefully followed. The rules and our eyes are our protection. We shall examine groundborne operations more fully in a subsequent chapter, but there are other hazards that attend approaches and landings to defend against, where the surface is not always smooth or the runways long.

7
Roughing It

After a tiring flight, there is nothing quite so welcoming as a sharply visible, dry, smooth, and spacious runway swelling gently before us in the windscreen, cleared for us to land. Unfortunately, some runways prove to be dimly seen or suspiciously wet or rough-skinned or small or all of the above. Also unfortunate is the fact that as we approach them, they don't always seem to rise slowly to meet us just right but instead threaten certain conflict when we slam awkwardly onto their surface. Landing accidents account for a very large proportion of airplane mishaps and are largely caused by pilot error. Some landing crashes are caused by the runways themselves, conditions which pilots fail to handle or prepare for. Whatever the conditions, we need to have defenses prepared against them.

Familiarity is not necessarily a defense:

• As the pilot (3,060 total hours, 400 in type) approached his home field in his Piper Apache, he discovered that an aircraft had become mired in mud on one end of the 3,500-foot, turf runway. After a short radio discussion with the pilot of the immobilized aircraft, he decided to land on the other end of the runway, which usually was drier. The pilot configured the Apache for a short-field approach. With a tailwind of about five knots, the plane began to sink on short final. The pilot applied power too late to arrest the sink. The Apache touched down hard, and its left gear sank into mud and collapsed. The three occupants escaped injury, but the Apache was substantially damaged in the accident. Asked by the NTSB for recommendations on how the accident might have been avoided, the pilot replied, "An attitude of caution at one's home airport might be stressed. Familiarity breeds false assurance."

Off the Great Bright Way

That truth applies both day and night. Landing by night at a large, well-equipped airport should pose no major problems for a night-proficient pilot who follows the procedures. Spotting other airplanes against a background of city lights can be difficult, but finding the airport is made relatively easy for us through vectoring and batteries of flashing approach lights and dazzling runway lights that make landing seem like motoring up Broadway. At small airports, however, approaching after sunset can range from the irritating to the hazardous, as pilot Bruce Barton found, even if the field is an old friend:

It had been a typical day of flight instructing, and, as usual, I was running a half-hour behind schedule. As I returned to Seattle's Boeing Field in my Cessna 150 with my last student, I could see that time was going to be tight. I still had to make my weekly flight over the Cascades in order to instruct at a small airport the following morning. The flight would take less than an hour and a half. The summer was waning, and the days were growing shorter, so I would have to hurry to make it over the mountains before sundown. The runway lights at my destination airport would not be on, unless the Forest Service happened to be conducting night operations.

After a quick departure from Boeing Field, I air-filed a flight plan. It looked as if I was just going to make it to my destination. I thought to myself, "One of these days, I have to figure out a way to stay on schedule so that I do not have to go through this last-minute rush."

The sun had set by the time I reached my checkpoint at Lake Wenatchee, but I was counting on enough twilight remaining to make my landing. As I approached the rim of the Methow Valley I closed my flight plan with the Wenatchee FSS, but I could see that I was a few minutes too late—the valley floor already was enshrouded in darkness. "Well, maybe it's not *too* dark to land," I thought. The nearest lighted airport was more than 30 miles away; I would have to stay at a motel and then return in the morning. It would be too much trouble, and, anyway, my cash supply was low. I decided to head for my original destination and try to spot the runway numbers.

Using the single outdoor light of the Forest Service station as a guide, I found Intercity Airport, and, sure enough, there were the white runway numbers beckoning me to give it a try. No problem—my landing light would pick up the reflectors that lined the runway edges. Lining up on downwind, I noticed someone working on an airplane, using the headlights of a truck for illumination, in the tiedown area. I could still see the runway numbers off to my left.

Flipping on the landing light as I turned base, I was surprised to see much of the light reflected back at me; I had not noticed the haze and smoke in the air. I could no longer see the numbers, but if I turned off the landing light, my eyes would not readjust to the darkness soon enough to be able to pick out the runway again. If I abandoned the approach, though, it would be too dark to see anything at all by the time I came around. I decided that my landing light would pick up the reflectors. I went ahead and turned final.

As I descended on final, I strained to see the reflectors through the gloom. Long seconds ticked by. Where were they? Suddenly my wingtip brushed past some trees. My mind reeled, and I slowly saw that I had to get out of there. I began to advance the throttle and pull up and found myself flying right over the Forest Service station. I had completely missed the runway on my turn to final and was about a hundred feet to the right of it.

So much for that! I shakily began a climbing, downwind departure. But the man I had seen and someone else had noticed my plight. They parked their trucks at opposite ends of the runway to mark it with their headlights. At the same time, there was some commotion around the Forest Service station, and the runway lights came on. This time landing was no problem.

When I climbed out of the airplane, I walked unsteadily toward the men who had assisted me and thanked them. I later learned that, in Seattle, my student and his family had been praying for the safety of my flight at about the time I had nearly collided with the trees.

This pilot just brushed past becoming one of the dozens of airmen that year who were involved in go-around accidents. In fact, only the slightest of differences in his course saved him from smashing headlong into a tree long after he should have aborted his darkness-wrapped approach.

Delaying Costs

Every year, the NTSB attributes about 80 general aviation aircraft accidents to the pilots' failures to initiate go-arounds. Furthermore, delaying the go-around (that is, making the choice too late) forms as prominent a cause of landing accidents as failing to perform the maneuver when it was called for. In fact, delay, says the board, is far more likely to result in serious injuries and fatalities. A go-around initiated too late often results in loss of aircraft control and high impact forces. Two cases, involving widely differing land speeds, demonstrated this:

• A pilot who had logged all of his 621 hours in a Beech C23 Sundowner landed long and fast with a quartering tailwind of 15 to 20 knots. The airplane was rolling at 65 knots when the pilot initiated a go-around, but it was unable to clear small trees off the end of the runway. The pilot sustained serious injuries when the airplane crashed and burned.

• After an ILS approach, a Cessna Citation landed with a 10-knot tailwind on a 4,470-foot runway that was covered with wet snow. Braking action was poor, and by the time the pilot decided to go around, the airplane was about 1,200 feet from the end of the runway. The NTSB said the Citation did not gain enough airspeed to become airborne before it slid off the runway and down a wooded embankment. The pilot, a 10,460-hour ATP, his co-pilot, and three passengers were killed.

It is far better to go around while you are still airborne than to have to make what amounts to a frantic takeoff in a desperately short distance. In such a situation, any airplane's climb capabilities are tested to the edge of the envelope, as is its pilot's ability. For most light twins, which perform poorly on one engine, a single-engine go-around should be considered an emergency procedure. The decision must be made *early*, if at all:

- A pilot (flight instructor, 8,000 hours, with 2,000 in type) was practicing single-engine landings in a Piper Apache with a passenger aboard. He simulated an engine-out by throttling the right engine to idle. After overshooting one landing attempt, he tried to go around, but the right engine did not respond to throttle application. The Apache crashed into trees, but the occupants escaped serious injury.
- The pilot of the Mooney M20C in which all of his 1,100 hours had been logged started to go around after landing 400 feet past the threshold of a muddy, 2,200-foot runway. He realized that the aircraft would not have flying speed before reaching the end of the runway, and he aborted the go-around. As a result, the Mooney was substantially damaged when it crashed into several junked automobiles at the end of the runway. The pilot was not injured.

Limited Options

A pilot on final approach has two choices: land or go around. That seems starkly simple enough, but making the choice can be difficult, for it involves judgment, discipline, and good timing, while the circumstances of the approach or imminent touchdown are in doubt. Sometimes the choice is easy: Another aircraft cuts in on short final or rolls onto the runway for takeoff; the tower tells us to go around (here, the pilot still makes the final decision to go or not, although if he doesn't go, he must have a compelling reason).

The circumstances of the approach or landing may be unclear because they are complex. For instance, the crosswind component may exceed the value demonstrated by the manufacturer of the aircraft, or it may border on the limits of the pilot's skill. The pilot may be approaching at too high an airspeed or altitude or simply may be misjudging his distance from the touchdown zone. He may even be unknowingly landing downwind but only vaguely sensing that something is wrong. In such cases, the pilot first has to see and *admit to himself* that he has fouled the approach, something that some pilots find difficult to do. Too often, pride gets in the way as pilots attempt to salvage bad approaches. In such cases, a high-and-hot approach may result in an excursion beyond the departure end of the runway. An overshoot on the turn to final may result in a stall-spin as the pilot banks the aircraft excessively in an unwise attempt to get back to the extended runway centerline.

Several factors can gang up on a pilot to hinder both his landing attempt and his recognition that he is in trouble. Each one by itself—for instance, an unfamiliar field, adverse wind conditions, or pressure from controllers to maintain a higher-than-normal approach speed or fly a tighter-than-familiar pattern—can distract a pilot into fixating on one element of the approach at the expense of his ability to see that the other elements are not properly in place. Such "forced" inattentiveness has led many pilots to forget to lower the flaps (or gear) or to keep the airspeed controlled. If the airplane is erratically gaining and losing speed during the descent, with its nose wavering up and down, a decent judgment of the touchdown point becomes virtually impossible. It is important to be able to gauge the relative motion of the ground (by choosing an aiming point) at the approach end of the runway as you descend toward it: If the imaginary point (perhaps the numbers or a hash mark) appears to be moving away from you, you will land short of the point; if it moves toward you, you will land beyond your point of intended landing; the point should not move at all if you wish to touch down there.

Low-Timer's Disease?

One might expect that such confusion is eliminated by good instincts born of much experience and that we are discussing a low-timer's kind of accident. Indeed, low-time student and private pilots are heavily represented in go-around and overshoot accident statistics, but as many as one-third of such accidents involve pilots with 1,000 hours or more:

• A pilot with 3,700 hours found himself high on final, so he put his Piper Tri-Pacer into a slip to lose altitude. The airplane touched down about 1,000 feet beyond the approach end of the 2,000-foot runway. The brakes were ineffective, according to the pilot, who intentionally ground-looped off the end of the runway into a trailer park. During the maneuver, the airplane flipped over.

• A 1,500-hour pilot, with 250 hours in type, encountered a crosswind of 15 knots gusting to 30 during final approach in his Beech 58P Baron. After landing, the airplane drifted off the side of the runway and crashed into trees.

• A 1,000-hour pilot with only seven hours in type overshot his turn to final. When he attempted to correct, his Cessna Skyhawk stalled and crashed short of the runway.

• On final approach, a commercial pilot, with 4,460 hours logged, flew a Piper Twin Comanche into a fog bank and then into a dirt mound.

According to the findings of psychologists, it is not strange that experienced pilots have such troubles. Overshoots are often a result of the "landing expectancy" syndrome. The experienced pilot will have made so many successful approaches and landings in his flying career that he automatically assumes the next will be successful. When an approach goes awry, he may feel that his store of experience will allow him to correct the problem. He may realize the seriousness of his mistakes too late and, not being current in practicing go-arounds, may find himself in the same situation as—or worse than—that of the erring low-time pilot.

"Worse than," because the further removed we are from our primary training, the less likely are we to meet such crises well, unless we have worked to remain proficient. The statistics disclose that many pilots cannot successfully handle a go-around when the pressure is on. With his license in his wallet and perhaps becoming worn around the edges, the pilot may not have practiced the maneuver for months, even years. When the time comes for a rusty pilot to perform a real-life go-around, his instant recall of the proper procedures may have faded. The go-around is a fast-paced series of actions that must be practiced continually if a pilot is to be adequately prepared to avoid an overshoot accident or any damaging conflict with a surface that proves to be inhospitable.

Grass Thrashing

Such conflicts are not rare. It is sometimes amazing what pilots will choose or allow themselves to be forced to land on when no emergency set-down is involved. Runways that pilots use—if only once—at "unimproved" airports range from soft dirt to gravel to cratered asphalt to washboard concrete. They bring out the bush pilot in all of us, and the nuts and bolts out of our airplanes as well. Sometimes such a runway is fit neither for man nor his flying beast, but, according to Philip Handleman, the man may be too late in finding that out, and the necessary go-around may be . . . interesting:

One spring and summer, I led a charmed life exploring out-of-the-way places in Michigan in a rented Cessna 152. I crisscrossed the state, touching down at dozens of remote airports, wandering about, and getting to know the local folks.

One hot day, while I was traversing over central Michigan's timber country, Houghton Lake appeared lustrous from the air, surrounded by the lush green of dense pine forest. I decided to stick to my original flight schedule, which called for a stop at an obscure airport near Houghton Lake.

Near the banks of the lake is an all-grass landing field, Houghton Lake State Airport. I had never been there, nor did I know anyone who had been there before. I was reluctant to set down on the grass runway, since the *Michigan Airport Directory* indicated that the condition of the field was rough. As a form of insurance, I circled fairly low over the field before starting the landing. It looked like it was in pretty good shape, although a small portion of the runway and the tiedown area had a different color and seemed to be more thoroughly mowed than the rest of the field. Another positive aspect was the presence of a sharp-looking taildragger parked in the neat tiedown area to the side of the runway. The wind, though light, seemed to be coming off the lake, so I set up an approach accordingly.

The approach path to the airstrip was bordered on one side by a tall clump of trees and on the other by a very tall radio antenna. These obstacles were unwelcome at a grass runway that was not very long in the first place. As I gradually descended on final, everything appeared as if the landing would work out.

However, just a few feet from flaring, I was suddenly able to see that the grass was quite high. In fact, the high grass cushioned my touchdown and immediately enveloped the airplane. It took a few seconds for my mind to register that the grass was at least waist-high—it covered the side windows, and, at its highest point, the grass pressed against the windscreen! I had never landed on such an awful strip.

I rammed the throttle full forward, knowing that if I did not get off the strip immediately, I would not get out of that airport until the field was scrupulously shaved by an industrial mower. I tapped the flap switch for ten degrees and pulled back all the way on the wheel— just what the manual advises for takeoffs from short and soft fields.

But the airplane just kept thrashing through the thick brush, with the propeller slicing the grass and heaving long pieces over the windscreen like a mechanized machete. I hoped that the innumerable blades of grass would not entangle the propeller and cause it to stop turning. The corkscrewing motion of the propeller kept us moving through the jungle of high grass, albeit at a snail's pace.

I continued to hope that the airplane would keep moving until I reached that small mowed portion of the runway. At that point, I might have a chance of lifting off with enough distance to clear (barely) the onrushing trees at the end of the runway. As I approached the mowed section, in one of those strange occurrences that turn up in the midst of a crisis, I saw through the left side window someone who had apparently been tinkering with the lone taildragger on the field—a mechanic or the owner, perhaps. In the fraction of a second that our eyes made contact, I could see written on his face, "What are you doing, you fool? Shut it down before you kill yourself!" And in my eyes he could probably see my equally fervent determination to get my airplane off the field.

I pulled and tugged on the wheel, shouting at myself and the airplane. "Come on, come on!" I kept yelling as the little Cessna just meandered like molasses, oblivious to my urgent pleas. "You have to nose up now, or we won't get off at all," I implored.

When I reached the mowed section more than halfway down the short strip, the nose finally bobbed up. I kept it elevated until I felt the main wheels lift off. I continued the steep climb out of necessity—the stall-warning buzzer blowing its highpitched whistle all the time—as the trees ahead came perilously closer. I squeezed the airplane over the treetops with hardly any margin to spare.

About a minute later, I took a deep breath and swore I would never again attempt to land at an airport designated as a rough field in the airport directory. And if through some mistake I ever found myself settling onto such a "rough" field, I would not allow my sense of pride to pour on the power for an immediate takeoff. Who knows? A visit to the Houghton Lake community that day might have been a worthwhile stop.

Sometimes, the "go" in go-around should begin before the approach is begun. Whenever a field looks suspect, even if you can see airplanes parked on it, drag it first and be skeptical until you feel absolutely sure that there is more than enough secure surface for a landing *and for a takeoff from a standing start* (more about that shortly). Grass can look deceptively short, and mud can appear enticingly firm. Those airplanes may be parked there, but their pilots may have no intention or hope of getting airborne in the near future. The presence of puddles, snow, or ice anywhere near a soft runway is cause for doubt. Also take into consideration such factors as a steeply sloping runway and the presence of nearby obstacles, which can affect your chances of touching down and then safely getting off and climbing out on a go-around. If high density altitude is an ambient condition, be wary: Because of the thinner air, your true airspeed—therefore, your groundspeed—will be higher than the indicated airspeed, which will further "shorten" the runway.

As you make your final approach, keep reassessing the surface as it grows nearer, and be prepared instantly to start a go-around if you see something there that could conflict with your requirements for landing safely and your expectations of getting off when you would like to leave.

On the Go

The keys to a successful go-around are early decision-making, good planning, and proper technique. So says the FAA *Flight Training Handbook,* and so says common sense. This implies that the pilot has a thorough knowledge of the aircraft's systems, performance, and recommended procedures.

Generally, upon deciding to go around, immediately apply the maximum recommended takeoff power. This is no time to stint. One pilot, whose final approach in a Boeing Stearman was hot and high, elected not to use full power for the go-around for fear of agitating noise-sensitive airport neighbors. The airplane settled into trees at the end of the runway.

Plenty of power is always the first requirement: Before applying full power on initiating a go-around, a student pilot raised the flaps of his Piper Cherokee; the airplane stalled. Also be sure you make all the possible power available: A commercial pilot applied full power to begin a go-around after overshooting the runway, but he left on the carburetor heat, and his Cessna 150 crashed into trees.

After you apply maximum power (with the mixture, propeller, and carburetor-heat controls set properly), generally your next move will be to adjust the pitch attitude to slow or stop the airplane's descent. As you do this, use outside visual references *and* glance often enough at your attitude indicator to assure that the nose is lifting sufficiently to arrest the descent. There have been several go-around accidents due to pilots losing control when sun glare or fog removed their outside visual references; the attitude indicator is a crucial backup.

Just as you must increase thrust, you will have to reduce drag quickly *but without "dumping" all of the flaps at once* at a low airspeed, which would risk bringing on a stall. Retract the flaps to the manufacturer's recommended setting—usually an intermediate or takeoff setting. Remember that your aircraft may well be unable to climb or even to hold altitude with the flaps fully extended. Recently, a 1,675-hour flight instructor attempted a single-engine go-around in a Piper Aztec after receiving an unsafe gear indication. He failed or was unable to retract either the flaps or the gear, and the Aztec crashed.

As your aircraft accelerates, you can expect heavy control pressures. If the aircraft was trimmed for a low-power or power-off approach, it will pitch nose-up during the go-around. (Some flight instructors recommend neutral trim settings for the approach to preclude the necessity for excessive control pressure, should a go-around be required.) You may also have to apply right rudder to counteract torque and P-factor. As the aircraft accelerates to V_x (best-angle-of-climb speed) or V_y (best-rate-of-climb), whichever is appropriate to the situation, trim the controls to relieve excessive pressures.

After a positive rate of climb is established, retract the landing gear. The sequence is important: In 1981, the flight crew of a Boeing 737 retracted the gear *before* obtaining a positive rate of climb. The aircraft was destroyed when it settled onto the runway, gear-up, and four passengers were injured. However, *this rule of thumb does not apply to all aircraft.* For example, Cessna recommends that the landing gear of the Cutlass RG be left extended during the balked landing. Check your airplane's operating manual for the proper procedure.

Once the aircraft has been cleaned up and is climbing, consider maneuvering to a position where you can check for traffic on or departing from the runway. At this point, retract the rest of the flaps and open the engine cowl flaps. Now you must decide whether to reenter the pattern or another landing attempt or just fly for awhile to settle down, soothe your nerves and collect your wits. Several accidents have occurred after a pilot's concentration was shattered or disrupted. Often in such cases, a wheels-up landing follows the go-around. If the surface or other conditions still seem too threatening, take time to consider an alternate destination.

A go-around is not a difficult maneuver. It does require prompt decisiveness, swift and *correct* manipulation of the various controls in the proper sequence, and a thorough familiarity with the aircraft. These things come with frequent practice. Again, most of all, the critical key to a successful go-around or landing is making the right choice at the right time. Never consider a landing as a foregone conclusion. Never take a go-around for granted as a piece of cake.

The Blessings of Consistency

Consistency, it has been said, is "the hobgoblin of little minds." That may be, but it is decidedly a virtue in flying little or large airplanes. When it comes to landing on difficult runways, consistency is safety insurance. One reason why pilots delay aborting an approach is that they do not recognize that the approach cannot lead to a touchdown at the place and speed they want. Flying a consistent pattern from downwind entry through the flare gives us a norm to judge by. If we know what the outside and instrument indications should be, we can tell what is going wrong and what to do to correct it, including, if necessary, aborting the approach and trying again. Such near-instinctive awareness comes only from habit.

Maintaining the proper descent profile for your airplane under particular conditions is one way to prevent an overshoot. Flying at the correct speed for the approach is another. This speed is found in the pilot's operating handbook; under ideal conditions it is usually 1.3 times the airplane's power-off stall speed in the landing configuration and under most conditions will provide an adequate margin above the stall.

If a strong crosswind is present, the wind is gusting or there is wind shear, you must fly the approach with slightly more airspeed than you normally would. This precaution is designed to prevent a stall from a loss of headwind, to provide greater control response against the effects of a crosswind and to give you an extra margin of lift in case of a downdraft.

Sometimes the use of only partial flap extension is recommended for flying an approach under such conditions. Doing so can prevent the airplane's being lifted again by gusts once it is on the ground and can also keep the aircraft from sinking too much if you encounter wind shear.

The excess airspeed needed to deal with these special situations seldom amounts to more than ten knots above the normal approach airspeed. In gusty conditions, the rule of thumb is to add one half the gust factor to the normal recommended approach airspeed.

Unfortunately, a great many pilots are so afraid of stalling that they become carried away with the notion that "more is better." Instead of flying the final approach at the recommended airspeed for the conditions at hand, they fly all their finals at high airspeeds. They may be reasoning subconsciously that if low airspeeds lead to a stall, which can kill at low altitude, then the more airspeed you can carry during the approach, the better and safer. In other words, "more is stronger." This reasoning falls apart, however, when the pilot finds himself overshooting the touchdown zone, waiting for the airspeed and altitude to bleed off. Suddenly the airplane is "stronger" that he can afford, and as the monster floats, precious runway is left behind while ahead looms the rough. We recommend a high approach speed, when wind is no factor, only for airports whose runways can accommodate floating and long roll-outs.

Puddle Jumping

One wet afternoon, on a training flight in a Cessna 152, a 4,000-hour instructor took the airplane from his student to complete a landing as they encountered heavy precipitation at 500 feet. On the turn from base to final, the pilot experienced a severe downdraft along with very heavy precipitation and severe turbulence.

The 152 landed halfway down the runway, with only 2,500 feet of stopping distance left. The instructor applied the brakes and the Cessna immediately began to hydroplane. The pilot retracted the flaps to put more weight on the landing gear and moved the mixture to cut-off to stop the engine. The airplane did not decelerate but continued off the end of the runway into an irrigation ditch. Both pilots received minor injuries, but damage to the plane was substantial.

In his accident report, the instructor stated that he believed he had encountered a sudden wind reversal after touchdown. The NTSB ruled that the causes of the crash were the pilot's misjudging distance and speed, a wet runway, and hydroplaning.

The multitude of causes is complex, but the effect of hydroplaning must not be underestimated, for on that wet runway, whatever the wind did, the pilot had lost his last defenses against an overshoot. Another hydroplaning accident:

• The Beech Baron 58P was cleared for takeoff at Knoxville Downtown Island Airport. The weather was overcast with light rain. Runway 8, which the Baron would use, was 3,500 feet long and 75 feet wide and had a very slight downhill gradient. During the takeoff roll, the pilot noticed a zero airspeed indication and elected to abort the takeoff, believing there was adequate stopping distance. The pilot's subsequent statement read: "Firm, steady braking was applied initially, with seemingly good results. As it became apparent that stopping would be marginal, braking was increased—with no increased result. I considered looping the aircraft to use power to stop it. I got to one side of the runway but could not get it turned more than 15 to 20 degrees from the runway heading. The airplane continued to hydroplane until it left the end of the runway."

The Baron rolled past a grass overrun, became airborne for ten to 15 feet, then impacted in a level attitude on a small pensinsula. The pilot sustained a compression fracture of the spine; the passenger received a minor cut on the hand; the airplane received substantial damage. The NTSB named three probable causes: delay in aborting the takeoff, a wet runway, and hydroplaning.

It used to be thought that hydroplaning was essentially a plague for large planes; we now know any plane is vulnerable.

There are three types of hydroplaning: viscous, dynamic and reverted-rubber.

Viscous hydroplaning is associated with a thin film of water on the runway or taxiway and lower tire speeds. The water lubricates the surface and lessens traction. Though the film may be only a thousandth of an inch thick, it can reduce the friction between the tire and the runway drastically. Ordinarily, maximum braking traction is obtained just short of the point where skidding occurs. On a dry runway, this generally happens when there is sufficient braking pressure to make the wheels roll at 80 percent of their normal speed. Small amounts of moisture can halve the available traction, calling for twice the normal stopping distance and gentler braking power, or else the wheels will lock.

Dynamic hydroplaning is what we usually think of as hydro-planing—a complete loss of contact with the runway. This form requires a deeper layer of water (at least one tenth of an inch) and higher tire speeds. At first, water accumulates in front of a fast-moving tire's "footprint," then it works rearward. The tire begins to ride on a wedge of water, like a surfboard. Eventually, the tire is lifted by the vertical force of the water, because a speeding airplane tire cannot rid its footprint of water completely. The airplane can behave as though it were riding on wet ice, with friction at zero. The slightest braking can lock the wheels, still lengthening the runway needed for safe stopping. Because the airplane is moving faster than under viscous hydro-planing, the risk of injury in a collision or sudden stop is greater.

Reverted-rubber hydroplaning occurs when a locked tire skids down a wet or ice-covered runway. The friction heating caused by the skid raises the tire temperature to where the tread wears off. Rubber particles shred off the tire and accumulate at the aft limits of the tire footprint. This forms a barrier, preventing the escape of water. As the trapped water is heated, steam is produced, and the tire is lifted from the runway by the steam's vertical force. The steam's scrubbing action characteristically leaves white skid marks on the runway.

An episode of this kind of hydroplaning usually follows an encounter with the dynamic or viscous type. The pilot makes an approach to a rain-covered runway, touches down and senses that he has no braking effectiveness. He applies more and more brake pressure and the wheels lock, which is why reverted-rubber hydroplaning often occurs at the end of a landing roll, though it can begin at any speed and continue until the airplane stops.

A Series of Problems

NASA has determined that dynamic hydroplaning will begin to occur at a speed equal to 7.7 times the square root of the affected tire's inflation pressure. For instance, the recommended tire pressure for a Cessna 182 is 42 pounds per square inch for the main-gear tires and 49 psi for the nose-gear. Thus the main wheels will dynamically hydroplane at 50 knots and the nose wheel at 54. (Fifty knots also happens to be the Skylane's flaps-down, power-off stall speed [V_{SO}].)

These figures are for the initiation of dynamic hydroplaning. Once it has begun, it will continue until the frictional coefficient allows braking to become effective. As the airplane's speed slowly decreases, the depth of the water between the tire and the runway becomes shallower, permitting tread contact, more traction, and, eventually, braking power. At this point, viscous hydroplaning can begin. Conceivably, you could manage to handle a bout of dynamic hydroplaning, only to face the viscous sort if you carelessly taxi to the ramp.

Perhaps the worst thing about hydroplaning is that it often occurs at the end of an instrument approach. For a variety of reasons, a nonprecision approach may leave you so high at the MAP that you must descend steeply and fast to make the touchdown zone. At the flare, your airspeed is then likely to be excessive, and with a wet, slushy, or ice-covered runway, hydroplaning can occur. To make matters worse, throw in a gusty crosswind. Let us say that in our Skylane, we ordinarily fly final approach at 65 knots. The winds are 15 knots gusting to 25, so we add five knots, and 70 becomes our target speed. The airplane's dynamic hydroplaning speed is 50 knots, so it would be in the danger range during the flare.

High and hot out of a nonprecision approach is bad enough, but adverse winds multiply the risks. With no traction and steering ability, a hydroplaning aircraft weather-vanes into the wind. A strong crosswind can blow an airplane—and its helpless pilot— in this crabbed position off the side of a runway.

The Defensive Approach

To minimize the chances of hydroplaning, plan and execute the approach carefully. Too much speed or height at the threshold will not only lengthen the landing distance, but on a wet runway you will need at least 60 to 65 percent more stopping distance if there is viscous hydroplaning. It is difficult to predict how much more distance will be needed for dynamic and reverted-rubber hydroplaning. Experts generally accept that the latter case requires roughly *twice* the normal stopping distance.

So you want to arrive in the touchdown zone on speed, on glidepath, and lined up with the centerline. Add a gust factor if necessary, but keep those approach speeds at the low end of the normal range. Do not prolong the flare—grease jobs can be dangerously messy on wet runways. They only increase the stopping distance. Decelerating on the ground uses up much less runway than decelerating in the flare. Of course you must be ready to go around if you have landed long or are taking too long to stop.

The landing should be firm. Lowering the nose promptly and retracting the flaps helps to put more weight on the tires. With the flaps up and all three wheels rolling on the runway at a reasonably slow speed, you are maximizing the tire's footprint and reducing the chances of a lengthy hydroplaning bout. Brake gently at first, then gradually more heavily. You will know if the wheels have locked, so it is a good idea to pump the brakes, allowing the wheels to spin up, and promote braking. A locked wheel generates much less friction than a wheel moving just below the skid speed.

Avoiding hydroplaning can begin with keeping the tire correctly inflated. Underinflated tires contact the runway at the sides of the footprint, leaving the center area elevated. With less tire surface to contact the pavement, there is less friction. Overinflated tires contact the pavement in the center of the tread; the sides do not contact. Again, less friction. It is not surprising that worn-out tires do not ride well on slippery runways. The tire's concentric grooves are designed to sling water away from footprint. When the water depth meets or exceeds the depth of the grooves, they cannot do their job, and the incidence of dynamic hydroplaning will rise.

To obtain an idea of how much distance your airplane will consume while stopping on a wet runway, compute the normal landing distance and then add 60 to 65 percent more. For a twin, add this factor to the accelerate/stop distance. And remember that aborted takeoffs are also affected by hydroplaning. Check your operator's manual just in case it may provide useful data.

Many of our better-equipped airports have grooved runways, which help to dissipate water from the tire footprint. In wetness, the coarser the runway surface, the better. An ungrooved runway covered with skid marks and unburned turbine fuel deposits is undesirable, as is one with too much a smooth texture.

Each year, there are more instrument operations by lightplanes, meaning that more lightplanes must regularly face wet runways and the threat of hydroplaning. VFR pilots seeking utmost utility from their aircraft also find themselves increasingly dealing with the problem. Yet jumping puddles need not always be tough skating. Proper tire maintenance and defensive landing can help maintain healthy surface friction.

On any runway, the hazards of puddle jumping can at least partially be evaded through puddle avoidance. Again, as you set up your approach and steer down final, read the runway. If you see congregations of avoidable puddles, patches of ice or snow, or messes of slush, try to pass around them, if your directional control and the runway width will make that possible. Some runways drain or are canted so that moisture gathers to one side or in areas that can be skirted. In other words, where the runway is wide enough, using one side of it may be safer than touching down and rolling out on the centerline. The same goes for avoiding pot holes, patches of sand, and other blemishes that can affect your braking and control power or jolt your airplane.

At a nontower field, if you are worried about the surface conditions, check with Unicom.

When we land, we merely fly from one environment, the yielding air, to another, the unyielding, sometimes quarrelsome, ground. The ground environment must be given the same respect as the atmosphere, to the point of our being willing to make hard decisions about whether we really want to touchdown on that particular runway, once we've had a look at it.

One reason to ponder is that some landing spots can embrace us gently when we arrive but threaten to hold us captive when we want to leave. In the following chapter, we will look at such circumstances as well as at the regulations and etiquette of getting around through the constant rush-hour traffic of large-terminal ramps and taxiways, plus other airport conditions that demand our careful attention.

8

Getting Up and Around

The essential function of an airport is to provide the space and a surface for aircraft to take off and land. Where there is a lot of space and an excellent surface, there also tend to be a lot of airplanes, hence traffic problems and controls for getting them to and from the runways without clipping each others' wings. For pilots and controllers, that can be a real challenge, for the problems can overwhelm the controls. Still, there the basic functions of getting in and getting off are generally handled smoothly and predictably.

Where the space is limited or the surface is not velvet-smooth, pilots must, as we have seen, view their landing prospects with some circumspection. Furthermore, before they land, they must give at least a passing prudent thought to whether, once down, they will be able to get off and up again.

The perceptible surface condition may give us pause, but sometimes an obscure sign, a factor we don't understand, may trigger a mental alarm, however quiet, that we should heed. Quiet-alarm heeding is central to defensive flying.

Roger Macomber describes a situation in which getting off safely hinged upon a subtle interpretive nuance:

Macomber, who was newly licensed, had decided to give his father a lightplane ride in a rented Skyhawk from Hawthorne Airport, near Los Angeles, to Taft, California. By the time he took off to display the technological wonders of modern light-plane flying, his passenger list included his sister and her husband along with his dad, an ex-Navy flight instructor, who hadn't flown in a small aircraft for 20 years. The weather was excellent, and the flight under the meticulously careful Macomber's command had been smooth as the Skyhawk descended gently into the San Joaquin Valley for landing.

About ten miles southeast of Taft, I called up on Unicom, but there was no response. I was especially alert for skydivers. Although my briefing had indicated that the winds probably would favor Runway 25, we flew over the airport at pattern altitude to look at the windsock. Sure enough, the winds were out of the west, so I began a southerly turn to prepare for a left downwind entry. I was announcing my entry over Unicom when I noticed a very strange thing. While the approach end of the runway had a large 25 painted on it, the opposite end had only an X painted there. Of course I knew that Xs on runways meant they were closed, but I had never heard of a runway with an X at only one end.

I was still unable to contact anyone on the Unicom, so I read my checklist and continued my approach. When I turned on final, I noticed that the far end of the runway seemed to be somewhat higher than the approach end. I recalled reading somewhere to be alert for upslope runways, because they can make your approach seem too high, even though it is actually perfect. So I carefully monitored my airspeed and descent rate, ready to go around if anything seemed amiss. The landing was exceptionally smooth, and we taxied up to the parking area. As my passengers headed for the restrooms and softdrink machines, I looked for someone to ask about the X. But it was midday, and there was no one to be found.

In preparation for our departure, I recalculated our weight, which was now about 100 pounds under max gross. The winds were light but still favored Runway 25. I thought once again about the X and reasoned that it must mean that Runway 7 was closed. Satisfied that it would not affect a takeoff on 25, we strapped ourselves in and taxied back to the end of 25. I performed my runup, announced my intentions on Unicom and began my takeoff roll.

The runway was clearly uphill. Still, the airplane accelerated reasonably well, and I ascribed any sluggishness to our weight. But the end of the runway was getting closer and closer. At 60 knots, I rotated gently, and the Skyhawk left the ground. Unfortunately, the runway was climbing only slightly slower than the airplane. What was much worse, however, was the forest of obstacles coming into view.

In order to receive the Bakersfield television stations, Taft residents all had 50-foot TV antennas on their roofs. This collection of antennas was dead ahead, above my altitude! It was too late to abort the takeoff, and the hills to the left and right precluded much of a turn. I kept the pitch as close as I could to the best-angle speed of 60 knots. All my training was needed to resist the temptation to raise the nose still further.

We cleared the antennas with maybe ten feet to spare, continuing straight ahead until an approaching hill forced us to turn north. I looked at my passengers. No one seemed particularly concerned, though my heart felt like it was going to explode. Whether my dad realized what I had done or not, I never asked. I suspected he did, but he had the courage to let me be the pilot-in-command and not question my actions.

I finally understood what the X meant. It did not mean that Runway 7 was closed. It meant that all takeoffs were to be made on Runway 7, to take advantage of the downslope, while all landings should be made on Runway 25. Or, put more simply, never fly over an X on the end of a runway.

I have since reviewed all my training but have never seen examples of this situation presented. I have seen, however, that in some printed descriptions of the Taft airport, there is a footnote that says, "Land rwy 25, takeoff rwy 7 due to sloping runway." My potentially fatal error, therefore, had been to miss the footnote. The other lesson I learned was that, no matter how conscientious a pilot is or how complete his training, there are bound to be circumstances that require judgments based on common sense. In this case, good common sense would have dictated postponing the takeoff until someone could be found who knew what the X meant.

Ordinarily, a runway marked with an X prohibits landings and takeoffs in the direction of the runway's orientation. At Taft, officials had marked the approach end of Runway 7 with an X to discourage landing on that runway. Other posted information is intended to inform pilots of the takeoff procedure.

For all pilots, Macomber's experience points up a key issue with respect to approaching unfamiliar airports: Make sure you know and understand the circumstances and procedures that can affect the landing and your subsequent takeoff. The surface may be hospitable, but an X or other curiosity can mark a hazardous spot.

Dangerous conditions on an "unimproved" runway can insidiously attach themselves to you. We saw in the last chapter that a grass runway that looks easy from the air can be a clinging wrestler holding you down if you misread it as you approach. Pilot Charles W. Mellon testifies that even caution on the way in may not be protection enough against a potential mishap:

On a leisurely flight in the Finger Lakes region of New York State, Mellon decided to take up a friend's invitation to drop into his home airstrip for a visit.

I checked the sectional and found that it was only 2,000 feet long, but I had flown into several strips as small and had no concerns about my ability or my Skyhawk's capability to make a safe short-field landing and departure. Circling the strip, I found that the grass had been mowed recently. A gentle breeze from the north barely budged the windsock. I elected to land to the south, because there were no obstacles in the departure area to cause concern during a go-around. The touchdown was smooth, but I noticed that the airplane slued slightly when I touched the brakes.

The grass on the sides of the airstrip was quite high, up to six inches in spots. Although the lawn mower had left globs of wet grass on the strip, the runway was relatively smooth and hard. After taxiing to the apron and shutting down the Skyhawk, I browsed among the hangars awhile, looking at some of the vintage aircraft stored inside.

Apparently, my pilot-friend was not going to show up, so I decided to take a rain check on the coffee and hangar talk. After another walkaround and runup, I began a takeoff roll to the south. The Skyhawk seemed a little sluggish but picked up speed when I pulled its nose up for a short-field takeoff. I climbed to 3,000 feet and headed east.

The Skyhawk and I flew on our merry way, but not for long. A slight drop in engine speed brought to mind what the farmer proverbially said when his plow horse died: "First time he ever did that!"

The engine speed dropped again—this time about 500 rpm. "Stay calm, Charlie,'' I cautioned myself. ''Go through your checklist.'' Carburetor heat—full on. Oil temperature and pressure—normal. Tachometer with full throttle—2,200 rpm.

I tried enriching the mixture, but the tach needle dropped even further. So I leaned the mixture almost to idle/cutoff. The engine speed increased to 2,200 rpm again. I ruled out the possibility of carb ice, because the outside air temperature showed 64 degrees F and there was very little moisture in the air. Pushing the carb heat off, however, I found that the tach dropped to 1,500 rpm, and I pulled it back on.

Greene Airport was only six or seven miles away. I considered declaring an emergency but decided to call Unicom first to check traffic. ''Wind is from the north, three to four knots,'' a lady's pleasant voice answered. ''No traffic reported.''

I elected to hold my altitude—2,000 feet—and avoid making any power changes until I was sure that the Skyhawk was within gliding distance of the runway, just in case the engine quit. The engine ran smoothly at 2,000 rpm on downwind and continued to purr when I reduced the power to 1,600 rpm on final. The landing and rollout were normal, and the engine idled faultlessly as I taxied the Skyhawk back to the hanger.

The reason for the loss of power occurred to me as I stepped out of the airplane. There was grass all over the Skyhawk. The wheelpants, the propeller, the underbelly, and the carburetor breather and air cleaner were completely green. The wet, freshly cut grass thrown up by the prop during takeoff had tried to suffocate the engine. Using carb heat had provided another route for incoming air, but leaning the mixture had held the power down. I had started the day by counting on the sun to burn off the morning fog. I learned now that it is also a good idea to give the sun time to dry up a freshly mowed airstrip.

Because *au naturel* runways can be subtly affected by natural phenomena, such as a gathering of morning dew, the completely defensive flier does well to include such possibilities in his calculations, using the experiences of others to guide him, if necessary.

Hero on a Beach

Then there are those times when a beckoning field and challenge may thoroughly distort one's ability to calculate soberly, when circumstances create problems for which bizarre solutions seem perfectly reasonable. All it takes is a touch of the would-be knight in shining airplane that lies within us to trigger a disaster-prone chain of events. In reporting this adventure in his 65-horsepower, 90-plus-mph Taylorcraft, Eugene Roberts perhaps understandably has used a pseudonym:

. . . Then came the day when a chance to play a real hero presented itself; my steed and I were eager and ready. I heard that a young man and his wife were planning to camp out on one of the deserted, offshore islands of Southern California. The wife was six months pregnant. I volunteered to fly out to the island during their stay to check on their well-being. As their camp was to be on a beach quite a distance from the plateau where the airstrip was located, I planned to land on the beach. The T-craft could take it. I had landed it on many beaches. The airplane could handle any type of sand as long as I landed into the wind. The curved under-surface of the wide wing was so effective in ground effect that the airplane would float over almost anything.

When I arrived at the island, it did not take long to locate Dave, who was waving frantically on the beach below. To a hero-pilot on a mission of mercy, he definitely seemed to be frantic. I knew an emergency was at hand and that I would have to land—at any cost. As I circled, Dave kept waving and pacing up and down the beach. Finally, he pointed; I came around and lined my airplane up to land.

The beach was narrow and sloped steeply toward the water. It had a high cliff just inside the surf line, which followed it all the way around the curved inlet of the little bay. My slow, power-on approach seemed unusually fast, and I began to wonder if my machine and I were taking on more than we could handle. We continued down until I could see that the beach was not flat but made of soft, powdery dunes. It was too late to go around now. The wheels took deeper and deeper bites out of the top of each dune as the airplane quickly lost speed. Just as we slowed almost to a stop, the tail came up almost vertical, despite full-back elevator control. We really plowed in. The propeller stopped, and I found myself staring straight ahead at the nose in the sand.

After scurrying out of the cockpit, I realized that the landing had been made in about a five-knot tailwind that had lifted the tail at the last moment. Only the wheels, deeply mired in the soft sand, had kept the airplane from flipping all the way over.

Why had my friend acted like a weather vane and pointed into the wind? He said he thought the beach was too soft for me to land on safely, and he had been trying to wave me off but finally had pointed to another beach farther down. So much for our well-planned signaling system. And what about their emergency? "What emergency?" They were having a ball on the island; he had only been waving excitedly. In fact, I was the one in bad trouble, because the tide was rapidly coming in, and soon, the whole beach would be under water—right up to the base of those cliffs. I shivered suddenly with the vision of a third party camping with them for the rest of the week.

But this was no way for a hero to act. I had to start thinking about how to get my somewhat humbled steed back into the air, and quickly. First, the three of us, slogging around in the soft sand, hauled down the tail—no easy task, since it was beyond our reach. Finally, it yielded to our tugs. Next, we cleaned the caked sand out of the air intake by splashing it with salt water, which already was lapping at our feet. I checked the track of the prop to see if it was bent by watching it scribe an arc in the sand as we pulled it through. Miraculously, it was straight. After that, I let air out of the tires until we were able to roll them back up onto the surface of the sand and turn the airplane around into the wind.

Hurriedly bidding my wide-eyed friends goodbye, I started a take-off roll with only about a 40-foot-wide area of beach left. It was curved and humpy. The slope caused the wing to lean down over the incoming surf. It took just the right amount of tail-up control to keep the tiny tailwheel from dragging in the sand like an anchor, but not too much to cause the main wheels to dig in again.

We were almost airborne, when an incoming wave washed in front of one wheel and swerved us out toward the sea. I frantically caught the swerve with hard brake and opposite rudder, swinging us back toward the shore. Somewhat shaken but still determined and with no time to contemplate what I had done wrong, I taxied back down the beach and turned around for a second try. My entranced friends still stood by in helpless wonder.

I had the correct elevator angle figured out and was holding the control wheel in a desperate, vise-like grip. But apparently I was not feeding in enough aileron to allow for the slope of the beach; again, just before we were airborne, we eased down the slope until the wheel hit an incoming wave. But this time I was determined to get airborne. Onward we charged, with the propeller catching the spray and churning it into a foaming mist up over the windshield, obscuring all forward visibility.

I decided to look out the side window to check on how close the cliffs were to the wingtip. I barely could believe my eyes. The cliff was not out the side window but was some 50 yards behind the airplane. A baffled glance downward showed the left landing gear skiing on the surface of the water as, undoubtedly, so was the right. Sure enough, I even could feel us rising and falling, up and down, with the gentle swells.

"Oh, no! I have lost my beloved airplane to the sea," I thought. What could I do now? Well, there was nothing left to do but haul back on the controls and try to get into the air, even if it dropped the tailwheel into the water. As I did so, we suddenly leaped into the air, as though released from a terrible burden. We had skied on the surface of the water for at least 100 yards away from the shore.

Forty-five minutes later the *pluff* of the soft, spongy tires on my home runway reminded me of my narrow escape from the island and my unbelievable takeoff. I knew no one would ever believe it; I could hardly believe it. Had I really skied out to sea on the surface of the water with a landplane?

Later, Dave and his wife said that they, too, could hardly believe my takeoff. All they could see was a large ball of foam and spray with two wingtips sticking out of it moving away from shore, until, suddenly, an airplane popped out of it and headed for the sky. I always will wonder what they said to each other as my airplane headed for the horizon. Was it "What a hero"? More likely, it was "What a dummy!"

Runway Incursions

The clean, well-lighted place that is a concrete airport spares us such miscalculations and, by its controls, restrains us from such hazardous heroics. But on these expanses of manicured ramps, taxiways, and runways, other sources of confusion may lurk—especially amid congestion in poor visibility.

Such conditions played a large part in a near-collision at New York's La Guardia International Airport several years ago. Thunderstorms had caused lengthy delays that night, and the ramps and taxiways were clogged with aircraft waiting to depart. Attempting to move a McDonnell Douglas DC-9 to its proper position in the queue, a ground controller cleared the airliner to taxi on the active runway. The turn onto the active was greater than 90 degrees, and the DC-9 captain could not see the other end of the runway, where a Cessna Citation had just been cleared by the local controller to take off.

The airliner's nose was about to cross the runway centerline when the captain spotted the lights of the small jet approaching at a high rate of speed. The captain stopped and turned on the DC-9's landing lights. The Citation was traveling at 100 knots, near rotation speed, when the pilot spotted the DC-9's lights. He aborted the takeoff and steered the Citation off the runway and around the airliner. There were no injuries, and the Citation was damaged only slightly during the excursion.

NTSB investigators determined that the accident was caused by a breakdown in ATC coordination. The ground controller believed he had received the required authorization from the local controller before he cleared the DC-9 onto the active runway. The local controller maintained that he did not hear, let alone approve, the request. Another controller, whose duties include coordinating the actions of the various tower positions, was on the telephone with New York Center personnel at the time.

The board concluded, "The quick and decisive actions of

the pilots, particularly those of the Cessna's pilot, precluded a catastrophic accident.'' Following the incident, the FAA revised its ATC coordination procedures. Ground Control can clear an aircraft to cross an active runway, but clearance to taxi *along* an active runway may be issued only by Local Control.

Incidents such as this, including the disastrous collision of two Boeing 747s at Tenerife, has prompted great concern. In 1978, NASA studied 165 reports of hazards due to runway incursions over a two-year period, through the Aviation Safety Reporting System. Controller error—primarily a failure to ensure adequate aircraft separation—accounted for slightly more than half the incursions studied. Forty percent involved pilot error. The rest was due to poor service-vehicle operations.

Surprising to many pilots may be the fact that controllers are limited in their ability to monitor surface traffic visually, even under the best conditions. Often, they must rely on position reports from pilots and on the assumption that crews will abide by their clearances. NASA found that the majority of pilot-induced runway incursions resulted from operations without clearance. Another significant cause of pilot error was disorientation and confusion.

The need for pilots and controllers to be accurate and cooperative in maintaining safe ground movement is heightened by a lack of airport surface detection equipment (ASDE)—a radar system designed to help controllers keep track of all traffic on ramps, taxiways, and runways—at most airports. The primary tools of all concerned are see-to-avoid and radio alertness.

Good Conduct, or . . .

Just as you would in flight, you should verify any clearance that leaves you in doubt. We have seen in a preceding chapter how nonstandard phraseology—''jive talk''—nearly caused a major accident by sowing confusion. A further example is that of a pilot who was approaching the active after being told to hold short of it and then being told to "go right on out there." Did that mean to taxi into position on the runway? The pilot tried to verify the clearance but was unable to find a break in the frequency congestion. Fortunately, he spotted another plane on short final and held short.

Poor visibility, disorientation, and a breakdown in crew co-ordination and resourcefulness were factors in a collision at Anchorage International in August 1984. The airport was blanketed in a dense fog; visibility was one-eighth of a mile. The taxiways were covered with a thin layer of snow and ice, and 30 inches of snow was piled up on infield areas. A DC-10 was cleared to taxi from the ramp to Runway 32; its pilot was instructed to report reaching the east/west taxiway. There was no ASDE there then, and the controller did not see the DC-10. Indeed, in the fog, the pilot could hardly see the taxiway centerlines. According to the NTSB, the DC-10 missed a turn that would have positioned it on the east/west taxiway. The crew held short, instead, on a stub leading to Runway 6L/24R. They mistakenly reported that they were on the east/west taxiway. In time, they were cleared to position and hold on the runway.

Both pilots had logged dozens of takeoffs from Anchorage. The first officer's experience at the airport, however, was more recent than the captain's. After the DC-10 was positioned on the runway, there was a three-minute "discussion" in the cockpit. The captain was not sure that the aircraft was on the right runway; the first officer was sure that it was. Finally, the captain acquiesced and began the takeoff. If the crew had checked either the magnetic or gyroscopic direction indicators, they would have seen that they were on the wrong runway. If they could have seen through the fog, they would have spotted a Piper Chieftain about 2,400 feet ahead, holding on the runway for takeoff.

The DC-10 was rolling at about 100 knots when the captain spotted the Chieftain. He rotated and applied left rudder. The DC-10's nosewheel hit the top of the Chieftain's windshield and tore off its vertical stabilizer. The main gear struck the smaller aircraft's wings, tearing one off at the root, the other outboard of the nacelle. The Chieftain was pushed back about 125 feet, but its fuselage remained intact. Of the nine people aboard the airplane, three sustained minor injuries. The DC-10, which was carrying only cargo, continued off the runway into a gully; its three crewmembers were badly injured.

Playing the Heavies

Having landed and been told to switch to Ground, on calling tell the controller which runway you've just cleared, what taxiway you are on, and where you are going—and don't hesitate to say that you are unfamiliar with the airport and ask for progressive taxi instructions. Since lightplanes are assumed to be newcomers, controllers tend to provide them careful, trouble-avoiding directions.

It helps to have prestudied and to have on your lap a published airport diagram that indicates taxiways and ramp areas by letter and designation. Be ready to copy down a complicated taxi clearance, and be sure of which way and where you are to turn before trundling off. Always acknowledge *specifically* any clearance or request that involves holding short of a particular runway. Controllers are justifiably sensitive about that. Keep a sharp eye on the big jets and maintain a safe distance from them. This applies even more when you are departing the airport and are behind the business end of a heavy as it stokes its fires to go.

In getting to the active, there are procedures to follow. Even if you are VFR, you will need a clearance out. Before you call Clearance Delivery, check the ATIS and then request a TCA clearance for an altitude low enough to put you below the floor of the TCA just as you depart its innermost ring. Frequently the innermost ring is under Tower control, so the clearance can be given immediately. Higher altitude clearances have to be coordinated with Approach. It helps to monitor the ground-based frequencies beforehand to see how things are being handled. Gate hold procedures are used to keep aircraft at their gates with engines off when there are departure delays. You will receive the necessary clearance to start from Clearance Delivery, Ground, or on a special frequency. It there are delays but no gate hold is in effect, ATC can advise you, on request, when to start.

When you give your VFR clearance request, you will need to indicate your intentions, that is, your cruise altitude and destination or direction of flight. If you are going IFR, you will say your number, the ATIS information you have, that you are IFR and your destination. You may be given a Standard Instrument Departure if you have not indicated "no SIDs" on your flight plan; even then, you may be cleared according to the SID procedure, which you will have to receive and copy. After clearance receipt, contact Ground for taxi instructions, if that applies where you are.

Large airports differ in how they hand off flights. At some, the clearance delivery controller, after furnishing the clearance, may say, "Call me when ready to taxi." After you call, he may say, "Monitor (or switch to) Ground on 121.75." Again, this means switch, listen, and wait. Each controller, meanwhile, is passing a slip containing your number to the next along the line, eliminating your calling on each frequency. However, when you receive an instruction, you must promptly respond. Don't just start moving but acknowledge, using your number. Otherwise, the controller won't be sure you are in touch, and he may not be able to see what you are doing.

Points of Departure

Here are some basic FAR-based taxi rules:

• On arrival, taxi clearance to the ramp is via the shortest route available, unless otherwise specified.

• A taxi clearance is a clearance to cross any and all runways along the assigned route of taxi.

• A taxi clearance is not approval to enter, cross, or taxi along the assigned departure runway.

• An intersection takeoff can be assigned at the discretion of the controller, or one may be requested by the pilot.

• If an intersection is to be used for takeoff, use the proper intersection.

To these doctrines, this should be added: If you are asked to expedite your taxi, especially across a runway, do so, but do not hurtle forward pell-mell. Many crunches and embarrassments have resulted from pilots complying with too much zip.

The same principle applies to intersection takeoffs requested by the tower. It is up to the pilot-in-command to accept or decline such an instruction. Only you, the pilot, will know if your airplane can safely get off a truncated runway on a given takeoff. If the full runway is very long, an intersection start can help speed the flow. Some pilots, however, say that taking the full runway is always wise, in case of an early engine failure or a need to abort. When the density altitude is high, the runway is wet or slippery, your airplane is just below or at gross, or other factors make you cautious, it is your right to request the full stretch, as it is to request an intersection departure. Above all, whatever you do, be explicit with the controller. Acknowledge acceptance of the clearance, request the full runway, or perhaps request a different intersection, but, again, just don't move, *talk*. Make no turns that haven't been cleared first. Prevent grief by springing no surprises.

Separation Trials

The break-away thrust from a healthy Pratt & Whitney can toss a tailgating lightplane onto its back. When holding for takeoff behind an airliner, position your aircraft where it cannot be hit by jet blast. A lifting lightplane caught in wake turbulence likewise can be flipped onto its back and otherwise disposed of. Therefore, lift off before the rotation point of the preceding aircraft and climb upwind of its flight path until turning clear of its wake. These are basic tactics of sharing a domicile with the bellowing heavies. There's more.

Technically speaking, a takeoff is not to be authorized unless the preceding aircraft has crossed the runway end or unless certain separation criteria have been met. Were controllers to follow those criteria "by the book," the delays would be horrendous, as past intentional slowdowns have demonstrated. Giving the pilot visual separation responsibility cuts through that iron curtain. As it does in the air, pilot defensiveness to an extent replaces procedural protectiveness. For instance, if you are waiting to take off from the end of a runway, you can get a waiver of the book separation rule if you ask for it and the controller feels it is safe to approve. This even includes takeoffs behind transport-sized turbojets.

However, yours is the responsibility for defending against wake turbulence. Depending on the aircraft you are following, you may or may not be advised "caution, wake turbulence" before being cleared for takeoff. You must then maintain safe separation. Controllers often will clear an early departure turn, which you can request, to facilitate separation from other departures. Keep in mind that for us, "heavies" are not only widebodies. Other jets and fast piston craft are also included.

The need for controlling ground movements and separations to prevent collisions and conflicts exists as much at noncontrolled airports as at major terminals. But where Authority is not present, we all must do the controlling by following standard procedures, being cooperative, observing basic courtesy, and adhering to common sense. The advent of more and more jets and other high-speed airplanes at friendly little airports calls increasingly upon our alertness. Our defensive reflexes may have to be very quick, as this true account by Carole K. Dundas and Michael L. Spaight make clear:

Greenville, Texas, is a small town, 50 miles northeast of Dallas. Our airport is a little unusual in that we have a part-time, non-federal tower operated by a company located on the field. But by the time we were ready to depart that day, the tower was closed. We have an 8,000-foot runway with all the instrument aids. Because we are a top-notch facility with very little traffic, we attract a lot of training flights from Dallas, mostly bizjets working on type ratings.

This particular day, a Learjet was in the pattern. It landed on Runway 35, as the wind blew in out of the north at about 15 knots. A C-150 made a long approach to final behind the Lear and made a touch-and-go. We had completed our Mooney 201's runup and asked the Lear his intentions. Because we were both on the ground at opposite ends, visual contact was not possible. We received no reply. After repeated tries, we assumed he was waiting for us to depart. There was an area where he could clear the active at the north end of the field.

We announced our intentions and took the active, 35, for departure to Love Field. Mike, the instructor who was checking me out in the Mooney, asked me to make the takeoff so as to get used to the bird.

As I applied full power and reached the desired speed, I lifted the nose off the pavement. A split second later, I could not believe what I was seeing. A lot of exhaust and a small white tail soon turned into a very big and fast airplane. Mike took over the controls, pulling our Mooney off the ground and to the right side of the runway.

Barely airborne, with the stall warning blaring, we began to dodge the windsock and the tetrahedron. When we were firmly in the air at an altitude of approximately three feet with the dust beginning to clear, we resumed a normal climb.

Feeling as if I were in the midst of a disaster movie, I began to try to collect the situation and assist Mike. The Lear made his takeoff, appearing to be totally oblivious to our evasive action.

I guess the moral to the story is that there is no substitute for experience. Mike said later that he was aware of the Learjet at the other end of the runway. Even though it was unlikely that a professional pilot would take off unannounced downwind, Mike had considered the possibility and had watched for him. That split-second advantage may have made the difference between a near miss and a fatal accident. Thanks to defensive flying.

How much experience should one need and wait to amass? We hope that the related experience of these pilots will help to do the trick. Or perhaps holding this thought carefully in mind: Do not assume that the other guy is smart or considerate or careful or scared enough to be safe, however heavy the metal he may be steering. Without hysteria, consider worst-case scenarios as just possible enough to warrant keeping an eye out for them. Don't assume that the other guy will.

Feathers in the Fan

While we're being defensive about heavies, we also have to beware of *ultra*-ultralight traffic. Flight remains for the birds, and they can be lousy at collision avoidance. Much to the chagrin of many ornithologists and bird lovers, the evidence that birds are a significant hazard to aviation safety continues to pile up. About 80 percent of reported bird strikes occur on or near airports—usually below 2000 feet agl. Between 1964 and 1981, there were 20 air carrier accidents and other incidents caused by bird strikes. One FAA study listed 73 civilian and military crashes and 138 fatalities caused by strikes between 1955 and 1977. The Air Force incurs about 1,000 strikes a year. Some recent collision accidents have been:

• On takeoff from Miami International Airport in December 1972, a Northwest Airlines Boeing 747 flew into a flock of birds. Two engines were damaged severly, the takeoff was aborted, and the airplane hydroplaned and slid off the runway. In a similar accident in November 1975, a DC-10 taking off from Kennedy International ingested sea gulls. One of its engines disintegrated and caught fire. When the pilot attempted to stop the plane, he found that he could not obtain reverse thrust, and the

DC-10 hydroplaned off the runway. There were no injuries, but the resulting fire cost $25 million in damage.

• A Learjet departing Atlanta's DeKalb Peachtree Airport in February 1973 suffered a nearly complete power loss when its engines ingested at least 20 cowbirds. The airplane flew into buildings two miles from the airport and burst into flames, killing all seven occupants. The NTSB, noting that a municipal dump was located adjacent to the airport, concluded that "responsible authorities had not taken due cognizance of the bird hazards to aircraft . . ."

Not only are jets affected. The first recorded bird-strike fatality occurred in 1912, when pioneer aviator Cal Rodgers struck a gull while flying a Curtiss Flyer. The gull jammed into the Flyer's control surfaces, and Rodgers lost control of the airplane and crashed. Some recent piston-power victims:

• A twin-engine Rockwell 690A taking off from Chicago's Meigs Airport in April 1977 struck a large flock of sea gulls. During the attempt to return to the airport, the right propeller was windmilling, and the landing gear was left extended. The airplane spun out of control and crashed into Lake Michigan, killing all aboard. After the crash, 180 dead birds were scooped up from the departure end of the runway.

• The pilot of a Cessna 414 at Pal-Waukee Airport, in Wheeling, Illinois, was warned about a flock of sea gulls some 3,000 feet down the active runway. As the pilot took off, the engine noise caused the gulls to take flight. At approximately 50 to 75 feet agl, an unknown number of them struck the airplane. Both wing leading edges were damaged, and several ribs in the left wing were bent; the radome was cracked, and the left main gear door also was damaged. There were no personal injuries.

• A Cessna 182M saw a bird just a fraction of a second before it struck the airplane aloft. The pilot and a passenger stated that they both heard and felt the impact of the collision. The force broke the exhaust pipe the bird struck at its junction with the muffler, inside the cowling. The resultant damage stopped the engine and forced an emergency landing.

Propeller-driven aircraft can be damaged severely by birds. A bird weighing only a pound or two can have an impact force of several tons when it strikes a lightplane flying at cruise speed. A four-pound bird (the average weight of a duck) will have an impact force of 15 tons on an airplane flying at 260 knots. Even at the relatively slow speeds of takeoffs and landings, the damage can be catastrophic.

Turbojets, which derive their power from the free flow of air into their compressor blades, are even more susceptible.

Why the Fowl Play at Airports

Bird habits are well documented, and studies have shown why birds are attracted to airports.

Food is an attraction, and garbage dumps (sanitary landfills) are often located nearby. The FAA requires airports receiving federal funds to be at least 10,000 feet from any landfill if they handle turbojet traffic; for fields primarily handling piston-engine craft, 5,000 feet. Lakes, inlets, ponds or low flooding areas also offer food supplies.

Shelter: Hangars are natural bird havens, and nearby trees and shrubbery can provide roosting sites.

Airports are attractive to birds, as they are to human fliers, because they offer a spacious expanse for operations. According to some experts, birds like to alight on runways and large, closely cropped grassy areas, because they want a clear view of their surroundings in order to avoid predators. Furthermore, runway areas are relatively undisturbed by humans—by airplanes, yes, but birds, like humans, quickly become accustomed to aircraft and scatter only momentarily when they pass by. Some airports are located along bird airways, and birds flying their many established long-distance routes often choose to RON there during the spring and fall migrations. In fact, they find airports to be fine places both for resting and for nesting.

Try as they may, airport operators have not had much success in driving away persistent bird populations. They have tried a multitude of methods, including pyrotechnics, distress calls, displaying dead or models of predatory birds, poisons, noxious chemicals, and even the use of trained falcons and model airplanes. Birds swiftly adjust to dramatic noises, such as explosions, aviary Mayday calls, and similar ploys. Falcons work best, but these days there is not an abundance of falconers and trained falcons, especially to be kept constantly on call.

As yet, no one at the FAA has suggested threatening to license the feathered fliers unless they police themselves, so it is up to us to police them, or at least defend ourselves ourselves as best we can. Unfortunately, there is no foolproof way to do this. Still, the defensive flier does have some resources to call upon to fight the feathered groupies:

• *Lighting.* Turn on your strobes and your landing light(s) when entering the traffic pattern or any area of known bird activity—for the same reason you should do so anyway: to give birds and human pilots time to see and avoid you.

• *Pull up.* This tactic is questioned by some experts and pilots, but others argue that a bird's instinctive reaction to a midair threat is to dive; therefore, if a strike looks imminent, initiate a climb.

• *Radar.* Some pilots believe that directing a radar energy beam at a nearby flock of birds will somehow cause them to take flight. The theory has not been proved and is mentioned here only because some pilots—but few radar experts—swear by it.

• *Radar advisories and ATIS.* Since large flocks of birds can show up on radar, controllers can issue radar advisories as well as convey pilot reports to give you warning. If you are flying in an area with high concentrations of migratory activity, ask ATC or Flight Watch for any signs or reports of bird hazards. Airports with ATIS should also broadcast information about nearby bird activity.

• *Approach charts.* Instrument-approach airports with high levels of bird activity may have warnings noted on their charts.

Thus far, bird strikes have not been a major cause of fatalities, but they have caused crashes, injuries, and some deaths. With an estimated population of one million gulls, a half-billion starlings and blackbirds, five million geese and 100 million ducks in our land, the odds favor that a pilot will suffer a bird strike—or near miss—at some time in his flying career. For the defensive pilot, that should be warning enough to care.

Because most of us fly safely most of the time, we tend to take problems that can trouble the airport environment a bit for granted, until, out of carelessness or "bad breaks," we get tagged; however, bad breaks are often things we fashion ourselves, when we forget or choose not be be wary and professional wherever we may roll.

Lamentably, there is still another way of being victimized at the local airport or at fields far away. This comes under the category of trust unrewarded. Again, this is a hazard we don't often think about until the resultant emergency hits, and it often hits thousands of feet up. We turn next to a subtler surface conflict, one compounded of attitudes, personal reliability, and, too often, plain stupidity.

Part Three
PRECARIOUS PARTNERSHIPS

9
Accidental Sabotage

Airplanes and their pilots fly on lift and reliance. We rely on physical laws to take to the air and stay there. Furthermore, though we pilots like to regard ourselves as individualists who can take of ourselves, we must rely extensively on the kindness—or at least the benevolent dependability—of strangers. These necessary partners in safety include not only other pilots and controllers but the mechanics and line personnel who keep our birds "healthy and nourished." We may know them well or hardly at all, but by circumstance and by law, we need them. Repeatedly, we trust our lives to what they do for us.

At times, they let us down.

For a sample period, 1978 through 1980, the NTSB found that 99 fatal accidents were due to improper maintenance, service, or inspection. That came to about seven percent of all fatal general aviation accidents for each of the years involved. Yet in some of these and many other such accidents from year to year, pilots must share the blame: They dropped their defenses and relied too much on the expertise of others.

When reliability breaks down, the effects can be horrifying:

· The flight departed Gallia-Meigs Airport, in Gallipolis, Ohio, VFR, bound for Lexington, Kentucky. On board the Piper Apache were the pilot and four passengers. While flying over Portsmouth, Ohio, the airplane suffered an emission of dark-colored smoke from the left engine. According to a surviving passenger, the pilot altered his course to return to Gallipolis.

"After he made the turn," another passenger said, "he shut

off the left engine and made some changes with the controls for the right engine. A few minutes before we started down, the pilot told us to look out and see if we knew where we were. Nobody recognized anything on the ground. The pilot tried to start the left engine, but it would only make a half turn when he hit the starter. Shortly after that, the plane turned on its left side, and then went into a spin. That is the last I remember.''

The airplane crashed in a small valley. The pilot and his front-seat passenger were killed on impact, as was the passenger behind the co-pilot's seat. The other two occupants escaped with serious injuries.

Both engines had been overhauled just one year before. Tachometer readings indicated that the left engine had been run for only 49 hours since the overhaul and that the right engine had been run for 38 hours.

Accident investigators found that there was no oil indicated on the left engine's dip stick. An interview with the Gallipolis airport manager disclosed that one quart of oil had been added to the left engine before the Apache took off. The manager also stated that the left engine of the crashed airplane had a history of consuming a quart of oil every four or five hours it flew. A subsequent test of the left engine revealed an oil leak in the area of the forward attach B nut connecting the propeller-governor oil line to the crankcase. The oil line was removed and its fitting capped off. The engine was run again for four minutes at an oil pressure of 60 psi. An oil film was visible on the front of the crankcase below the propeller flange, but there was no noticeable loss of oil on the dip stick. The oil line was reinstalled, and the engine was rotated for one minute using the starter motor. The oil pressure reading for this test was five psi. About three ounces of oil gathered below the B nut where the oil leak previously was observed.

The propeller-governor line was subjected to an electron microcope scan, which revealed that there were numerous fatigue fractures around the circumference of the tube. A metallurgical examination showed that the oil line was made of an aluminum alloy, not from cadmium-plated steel tubing, as specified.

The NTSB determined that the probable cause of this accident was improper maintenance, servicing, or inspection by maintenance personnel—specifically, oil exhaustion caused by the fatigue fracture of a wrong part.

• En route from Dubuque, Iowa, VFR to Chicago's Midway Airport, the pilot of a Cessna 210D Centurion heard what he later described as "a loud bang" and lost power just five miles west of his destination. He declared an emergency, and Midway Tower cleared him to land on any runway. However, the pilot was unable to glide to the field and landed instead on a street one and a half miles west of the airport. Just before touchdown, the airplane's left wing struck two light poles. The pilot suffered a broken ankle, and his only passenger received a fatal head injury.

The operational history of the airplane's engine had been routine until 58 flying hours before the accident. Nine months before the accident, the Cessna's engine underwent a major overhaul. In the intervening time, the engine had had five oil changes and one propeller repair. A record of the oil change performed after the propeller repair contained the notation, "ferrous metal found in screen."

The propeller had been repaired because it had been damaged during a hard night landing. According to a mechanic, "The outer three inches were bent back and had quite a large amount of nicks, file marks, and plier marks on them." The propeller had been removed and repaired and was reinstalled after a mechanic performed a run-out check of the engine's crankshaft. "The crank checked out very good," the mechanic stated.

However, inspection recommendations published by Teledyne Continental were not complied with. Teledyne's bulletin on prop-strike accidents concludes with, "Owners electing any inspection procedure other than complete disassembly must accept the attendant risks.'' The engine was not disassembled as part of the propeller repair sequence. When the slivers of metal were discovered, the owner had a compression check and a bore-scope examination of the cylinders performed. No other follow-up actions were taken. When asked his opinion of the meaning of the metal slivers, the pilot's mechanic stated that he believed the metal had been in the engine since the overhaul. He suggested that the oil screen be checked carefully for metal particles at the next oil change but offered no other advice.

When the NTSB disassembled the engine, it was learned that one of the propeller counterweight retention pins had failed, causing the counterweight to flail around in a large orbit. Investigators then discovered signs that abnormal loads on the engine's crankshaft had caused two connecting rods to fail, damaging several other internal engine components. The loss of the counterweight retention pin was attributed to the breakup of the bushings in the counterweight blade bracket. The bushings failed due to overload fatigue caused by the propeller strike.

The NTSB determined that inadequate maintenance and inspection was the probable cause of the accident.

Reliance and Responsibility

One accepted definition of *sabotage* is ''an act or process tending to hamper or hurt.'' Clearly, a mechanic's intentional deviation from maintenance, repair, or servicing procedures created to enhance safety comes under that definition. Whether he does it to save expense (not necessarily the pilot's) or time or effort, the damaging effect is the same. If he simply forgets or does not know how to do the job right, the sabotage may be accidental, but its effect on pilot and passengers is just as hazardous.

If problems with an airplane's systems crop up, the standard advice is to find a qualified mechanic to fix them. And by and large, the nation's aircraft mechanics are so skillful and well trained that competing industries have used higher pay to lure them from aviation.

Mechanics have to earn FAA certification by one of three means. They must either attend an approved school, obtain 18 months (for an airframe mechanic) or 30 months (airframe and powerplant) experience on the job, or prove to FAA (GADO) examiners that they are competent. If they also pass an FAA written examination, they theoretically are prepared to take on a variety of maintenance tasks. Mechanics must have additional, supervised experience on the type of aircraft they intended to work on. By the time this apprenticeship is finished, they are legally qualified to work without direct supervision.

However, like pilots, mechanics can be fallible. Unintentional errors, inadequate supervision, poor troubleshooting skills, inattention to detail, unfamiliarity with accepted repair techniques and practices, and, last but not least, pressure from employers and customers can lead a mechanic to make accident-causing mistakes. Yet most pilots trust them almost blindly.

In fact, pilots must share the blame for some maintenance-induced accidents. Whether because of a lack of awareness, negligent preflight procedures, a careless attitude toward the airplane's maintenance requirements, or a misdirected desire to save money, owners often allow problems to go uncorrected, even when they know that "something" is wrong with their planes.

Sure, many pilots will say, but what can we do? How many of us are mechanically savvy enough to know right away if even our car or stereo or toaster has been repaired properly? Even those of us who are mechanically inclined may not be scholars enough about our planes' innards to be able to pass judgment, particularly to pass the ultimate judgment of taking "the job" higher off the ground than we are willing to fall.

The extent of such reliance on our mechanics' word has recently been written into law and has the support of the NTSB. According to the AOPA's Secretary and General Counsel, John S. Yodice:

The law, as it now stands, is that a pilot is chargeable under FAR 91.2(a) ["No person may operate a civil aircraft unless it is in an airworthy condition."] if he was aware, or should have been aware, from an appropriate preflight inspection, of any condition that a reasonable and prudent pilot would conclude made the aircraft unairworthy. A pilot is not chargeable merely because the aircraft in fact is unairworthy or because an aviation mechanic would have found that it is unairworthy. *Administrator v. Hanley,* NTSB Order EA-2090, December 10, 1984.

The comfort of not being chargeable is hardly a factor, nevertheless, when a mechanic's failure jeopardizes us in the air. There are times when legal defenses pale before the value of defenses of another kind, say, of healthy skepticism. Pilot Robert T. Warner tells of such a time:

Tachometer cables for 1960 Skylanes are not in every Cessna shop's inventory, but I had planned ahead, and the shop at the major midwestern airport was waiting for me. After the work had been performed, I went out to pick up the airplane and move it to a smaller airport about ten miles away, where it would remain for a few days. Because we were hurried by the presence of thunderstorms in the area, and since replacing the tach cable is such a simple job, I made the stupid mistake of performing the preflight with the amount of attention I would have given it had no work been done. After a short taxi and a normal runup, we climbed to 2,500 feet, receiving radar vectors from Departure Control toward our destination airport.

As we climbed out, the cockpit became progressively warmer. By the time we leveled at 2,500 feet, about three or four miles east of the airport, it was getting *hot.* I stuck my hand under the instrument panel to see if there was an open fire, but there was only hot air. At that point, I advised the controller that we had a problem of significant heat build-up in the cockpit and that we were landing. I informed him that I was uncertain as to whether there actually was a fire or not. Straight ahead, about one and a half miles, was a private-use, paved strip, and I told the controller that was where we were going. I accepted his offer of fire trucks, since the private strip is adjacent to an Air Force base.

Our landing was a bit fast but uneventful. We turned off the taxi-way, advised the controller that we were on the ground safely, shut down the airplane and jumped out. After a few minutes of determining that the airplane was not on fire, we began to investigate the problem.

Our first clue of things to come was a pair of pliers that we found between the rudder pedals on the right. Still, when I looked up under the instrument panel, I saw nothing conspicuously wrong. When we removed the cowling, the problem became obvious. The cabin air duct connected to the baffling on top of the cylinders had been disconnected from the air-vent box attached to the firewall. This was the only item that had had to be removed to allow the mechanic to connect the ta-chometer cable to the engine accessory section. The mechanic had not reconnected the air duct, and that resulted in air flowing over the cyl-inders and the exhaust pipes and then into the cockpit.

My language before my 13-year-old passenger and brother had been pretty clean on our week-long trip, but that changed when I saw the air duct lying there. We connected the hose and put the cowling back on. After a very cautious runup, we were off on our two-mile flight to our destination airport.

The following Sunday morning, while I was preflighting the air-plane for our departure to Washington, the elevator did not give full up-travel. When I pulled on the control wheel, it came out to a posi-tion, then there was a thump, and the wheel extended another inch. It turned out that the newly installed tachometer cable was rubbing against the right control-wheel shaft behind the instrument panel and bumping over the bolts at the universal joint on the shaft. We repositioned the tach cable so that it would not interfere with the control shaft.

There later was an exchange of letters with the FBO discussing the appropriateness of my payment of the bill. He was very understanding and properly apologetic and eventually waived the entire bill. The me-chanic's pliers remain a paperweight on my desk to this day—a con-stant reminder that when it is not possible to oversee the work done on your aircraft (now my preference), your life depends on doing a very complete preflight after *any* maintenance on the airplane you will be flying.

Another maintenance "war story," such as this account by Edward J. Beatty, has many variations in the experiences of pilots:

Our airplane had come due for its annual inspection. After some debate as to who should do the job, my ownership partners and I agreed upon a mechanic we had known for many years. He said he would do the job right away, if we could provide help. Early the next morning, a couple of us reported to the hangar. By evening, the inspection was completed, but since it was dark, there was no opportunity to test-fly the Cessna 172.

The following day, I wanted to fly to Angola, Indiana. I was told by the maintenance officer of the CAP unit with whom we fly the aircraft that it was ready to go; I would be the first pilot to fly it after the inspection. He also mentioned that excessive aileron play had been discovered and that the mechanic had rerigged and adjusted the ailerons. "Let me know how it performs when you get back," he said in parting.

During my walkaround, I noticed that there seemed to be considerably less movement to the ailerons than I had been accustomed to, which made it difficult to check the attaching bolts and hinges. Knowing they had been rerigged, I assumed that this must be normal. Soon I was on my way. At 3,000 feet, I rocked the airplane a few times to check the action of the ailerons. Everything seemed normal.

Arriving at Angola, I prepared to land on Runway 5, the active, with the wind from 130 at 15. I had landed the airplane under similar conditions on several other occasions and was not concerned about the crosswind—Mistake Number One.

A long time ago, my instructor had told me that if you make a bad approach, you probably will make a bad landing. I now disregarded that sage advice—Mistake Number Two. I did not allow enough for the wind and started my turn to final much too soon. Angling into the runway, I was going to have to make a quick left turn to line up and then immediately correct for the crosswind from the right. I made the left turn, but before I could apply the crosswind correction, I was drifting rapidly across the runway while at the same time trying to flare out. A mad ballet of rudder and ailerons ensued, with the airplane finally crunching down with tires squealing, nose bobbing, and wings rocking. Brakes and rudder finally got it under control.

The return flight was uneventful, including a squeaker of a landing right down the centerline.

The maintenance officer called the next day to ask how the airplane had performed. Much better than the pilot, I told him and related the experience to him in detail. I mentioned what I had noticed during my walkaround; he had noticed the same thing after they had worked on the aileron system but really hadn't given it much thought, assuming, as I had, that this was correct and that the excessive play had afforded us too much access previously. "Maybe we should have someone else check the ailerons out, just to be sure," he said.

A couple of days later, he called again: Another mechanic had been hired to double-check the ailerons and had found that they were improperly rigged. Instead of having the required 22 degrees of up-travel, they had only nine—far less effective.

I had made some mistakes I hope I will not make again. I easily could have wrecked the airplane—I was fortunate.

How many pilots know enough about their airplanes to recognize something like this when it exists? How many pilots would question the knowledge and skill of the A&P who works on their airplane? Almost any pilot can tell if the engine isn't performing properly, by the sound or by the gauges. He can tell if the airplane is not flying correctly if it takes excessive trim or of something fails to operate properly. But how many of us can look at our control surfaces and tell whether they are moving the required amount of travel? In my case, those extra 13 degrees could have made a lot of difference.

Looking at the other side of the coin, if I had not had this experience, we might still be flying the airplane, improperly rigged. Or by this time, one of us might have wrecked it.

This incident had a happy outcome. Others, including actual reverse rigging of aircraft, have ended in fatalities.

Measures Pilots Can Take

Aircraft owners and pilots are not without resources in such matters. Those who have airframe and powerplant certificates can perform their own maintenance, of course, but since most of us do not, even staring over a mechanic's shoulder as he works on our airplanes would do us little good.

Certainly, one of the things we can do is to spread the word about poor maintenance work to forewarn others. If such word comes to you, however casually, check out the reputation of the mechanic and the shop. An even better measure is for us to build up our knowledge of airplane service requirements and to learn as much as we can about service intervals and procedures. What we do not know can hurt us.

An excellent source of information is an FAA publication, *Airframe and Powerplant Mechanics General Handbook* (EA-AC 65-9), which deals with basic maintenance procedures and theory. More specific repair information can be found in Advisory Circular (AC) 43.13A, *Acceptable Methods, Techniques, and Practices—Aircraft Inspection and Repair,* which tells how to inspect and repair aircraft systems and includes sections on fabric and wood structures, control cables, and corrosion protection. As good general information, they are invaluable to pilots. They are available from the Superintendent of Documents, U.S. Government Printing Office, Washington, D.C. 20402. They are also stocked by many of the larger fixed-base operators.

Maintenance guidelines for your airplane can be found in the pilot's operating handbook and the airplane service manual. The service manual contains much more detailed information; this book can be ordered from the manufacturer. Your mechanic, of course, should have a current copy. Other sources of service information and recommended maintenance and corrective procedures are FAA-issued airworthiness bulletins and manufacturers' service bulletins or service letters, which we will discuss later in this chapter.

Do-It-Yourself Options

By studying these publications, you will become more aware of your airplane's peculiarities and be better able to take a more active part in its maintenance. Once you gain proficiency, you may want to perform the maintenance that an owner is allowed to do under FAR Part 43, Appendix A. There are 27 preventive maintenance items that a pilot legally may perform without a mechanic's certificate. Briefly, these maintenance categories are:

- Removal, installation, and repair of landing gear tires
- Replacing elastic shock absorber cords on landing gear
- Servicing shock struts by adding oil, air, or both
- Cleaning and greasing wheel bearings
- Replacing defective safety wiring and cotter keys
- Lubrication of non-structural items
- Making simple fabric patches not requiring rib stitching or the removal of structure parts or control surfaces
- Replenishing hydraulic fluid
- Refinishing of decorative coatings when removal or disassembly of any primary structure or system is not required
- Applying preservative or protective material to components where no disassembly of any primary structure or system is involved
- Repairing upholstery
- Making small, simple repairs to fairings and non-structural cover plates
- Replacing side windows where this work does not interfere with the structure of any operating system
- Replacing safety belts
- Replacing seats or seat parts with approved replacement parts
- Troubleshooting and repairing broken circuits in landing-light wiring circuits
- Replacing bulbs, reflectors, and lenses of position and landing lights
- Replacing wheels and skis where no weight-and-balance computation is involved
- Replacing any cowling not requiring removal of the propeller or disconnection of the flight controls
- Replacing, cleaning, and gapping of spark plugs
- Replacing hose connections except hydraulic connections
- Replacing prefabricated fuel lines

- Cleaning fuel and oil strainers
- Replacing batteries and checking fluid level and specific gravity
- Removing and installing glider wings and tail surfaces that are designed for quick removal and installation
- Replacing or adjusting nonstructural standard fasteners incidental to operations
- Installing anti-misfueling devices to reduce the diameter of fuel tank filler openings, provided the specific device has been made a part of the aircraft type certificate data by the aircraft manufacturer, the aircraft manufacturer has provided FAA-approved instructions for installation, and installation does not involve the disassembly of the existing tank filler opening

Performing these maintenance procedures offers you the benefits of saving money and learning more about your airplane.

Any job other than these should be done by a mechanic or a service facility that specializes in your type of airplane. A mechanic who spends most of his time working on Cessnas, for example, may not be able to service a Mooney adequately— even though his certificate may permit him to work on aircraft manufactured by any company.

Perseverance Pays

There will always be a certain feeling of helplessness when we take our airplanes in for periodic maintenance or a special repair, especially if a glitch has frightened us. Psychological studies have shown that pilots are highly motivated people who enjoy being in control of the situation at hand. Like it or not, when the mechanic rolls our airplane into the service hangar, we lose an element of control. All we can do is to learn more about the people who service them. Beyond this—up to a point— we have to put our trust in the skills of others, knowing that there is always a possibility of human error and oversight.

That point comes when we find, perhaps through grim experience, evidence that a promised cure has not been made. As Anton S. Nesse found, protecting ourselves against malpractice or mechanical mysteries can demand perseverance, time, effort, and money—but the payoff is security. It could mean survival.

As we were flying over the mountain pass east of Bozeman, Montana, the tachometer rolled up 2,000 hours. The Lycoming 0-320 in our Grumman Traveler was purring. I smiled at my wife and said, "I hope it doesn't turn into a pumpkin now." With compression readings in the mid-70s, we had decided to run the engine another 100 hours or so before a major overhaul.

The trouble began as we turned left downwind for Runway 12. I pushed the mixture full rich for landing. The engine started surging, almost stopped, then surged again. I turned a tight pattern, in case it quit, and worked the mixture and throttle to keep it running. We touched down normally, but on the rollout, the engine stopped.

This wasn't the first time the engine had stopped after a normal landing. We had tried to find the cause for months. We replaced gaskets, the accelerator pump, even the mixture needle and sleeve. Each time the carburetor came off, the problem would go away, but in a month it would be back. And always in the same way: The engine would start and run well, throttle back normally for landing and quit after the rollout. It restarted easily, idled poorly, and could not be shut down with full lean mixture—it just continued to chug. My mechanic thought the engine was choking on too much gas, but neither of us could figure out how the gas got through.

We turned off the runway at Bozeman and rolled to a stop on the taxiway. I cranked the engine over to restart. No use; it really was flooded this time. Just a cough, even with the throttle wide open. Then my wife shouted, "There are flames coming out of the engine! We're on fire!"

Visions of planes exploding into fireballs flashed through my mind as we tumbled out and ran. But the fire was confined to the engine compartment, and it just burned quietly. I called Flight Service to send a fire truck, and I tiptoed back, shut off the fuel and grabbed our luggage. In a few minutes, a pickup truck arrived, and the driver put out the fire with a portable extinguisher. Five minutes later, the fire department arrived, as well as the airport manager and a group of volunteers. Not much was left to do except give us a ride to the terminal and haul the smoldering Grumman to a hangar.

Three months, one major overhaul, and $8,000 later, I flew the Grumman home.

The fire had started in the air intake. Gasoline had leaked out of the carburetor and was ignited by a backfire during the restart attempt. I requested a new carburetor but was told that the particular model was no longer available. The overhaul shop said it could rebuild my old carburetor so that the problem would not recur. They thought the leak was caused by a misalignment of the carburetor body halves. But why did the carburetor work fine for 1,900 hours, only to cause a fire at 2,000? I accepted the explanation and the rebuilt carburetor reluctantly.

The summer passed with a few mechanical problems—small ones—as usually happens after a major.

Then one day after a landing, the engine began to choke and sputter on the rollout. I managed to keep it running and to taxi with the mixture full lean. I shut the engine down by turning the fuel off to prevent another fire.

The carburetor was removed and sent back to the overhaul shop with an angry letter. Two weeks later, it was returned along with a tag marked "repaired." I called the mechanic who had signed the tag and asked what he had repaired. "I replaced the carburetor float—it weighed 13 grams more than a replacement float," he said.

The original float had not been replaced when the carburetor was rebuilt. It probably weighed in normally, as any fuel inside the float would have evaporated in the heat of the fire and during the long wait afterward. Nine years of floating in fuel—the last five in 100LL—probably had created a pinhole in the solder joint holding the two halves of the float together. When the float warmed during flight, it would expand, inhale fuel through the hole and eventually sink. This would open the needle valve and expose the mixture valve to the full pressure of the fuel pumps, causing a fuel leak that kept the engine running with the mixture full lean. It also caused flooding and choking with the mixture full rich and the throttle closed for landing.

When you have a malfunction, don't give up the search until you find the problem and fix it. A pinhole could teach you an expensive lesson.

Be Hot on the Paper Trail

There have been many cases of crashes due to aircraft defects about which there were fair warnings that were never heeded. Owners and mechanics alike have been guilty of neglecting airworthiness directives and other publications either willfully or through ignorance.

• The passenger in the right front seat of the air taxi Piper Chieftain had a commercial pilot certificate and about 5,000 hours of flight time. He noticed that neither of the two engine oil-pressure indicators had entered its green arc until the airplane was rolling for takeoff. Shortly after the aircraft lifted off, he heard the tower controller report that the Chieftain was trailing smoke from the left engine. According to the passenger, the pilot began to feather the left engine but then advanced the power controls when the right engine began "sputtering." The passenger recalled that the airspeed was between V_{mc} (minimum control speed with critical engine inoperative) and blue line (V_{yse}, best-rate-of-climb speed with one engine inoperative) when the aircraft climbed into the base of a cloud layer about 100 feet above the ground.

The pilot was attempting to return to the airport when the Chieftain struck powerlines, crashed, and burned. Two passengers, including the person in the right front seat, sustained serious injuries. The pilot and four other passengers were killed.

Investigators were unable to determine what caused the Chieftain's engines to malfunction. The National Transportation Safety Board noted that there were no records of compliance with five airworthiness directives pertaining to the aircraft. Three of the directives affected the Chieftain's exhaust system, magnetos, and fuel injector servos.

Not only aircraft owner/pilots can be badly hurt by such maintenance failures; aircraft renters also face hazards when

FBOs, by intent or by error, fail in their duty to maintain training and other hired aircraft by the book.

Although some owners believe so, the FAA issues ADs not to aggravate or impoverish but to prevent accidents. Undoubtedly, keeping up with these and other warnings means work and inconvenience, but a certain amount of paperwork is necessary if you want to run your airplane safely or buy a used one that will not be a menace or a lemon.

Some of this paperwork falls to the mechanic who performs an airplane's annual inspection. As part of that process, he will research all applicable airworthiness directives. However, he may fail to look up *service bulletins* pertaining to the airplane, and service bulletins often are as crucial to flight safety as ADs. In many cases, a service bulletin on a particular problem precedes an AD. The safety-concerned owner should therefore keep track of all ADs and service bulletins.

ADs are amendments to an airplane's type certificate, and compliance with them is mandatory. They are issued by the FAA and are sent to registered owners of affected aircraft. An AD may call for a change in operating procedures, an inspection, or a modification, or any combination of the three.

Service bulletins are issued by manufacturers, and compliance with them is not required by law. However, some service bulletins are considered "mandatory" by manufacturers, and noncompliance may be grounds for voiding a warranty. Service bulletins in this category usually are sent by manufacturers to owners of record. (Cessna uniquely sends "owner advisories," which notify of the issuance of a bulletin and advise owners to contact their Cessna dealer for servicing.) Service bulletins of a less serious nature are called service letters by some manufacturers. These are usually routed only to company service centers and dealers.

It is well worth the expense to be placed on a manufacturer's mailing list for all service information on an aircraft. This is the only sure way of receiving all service notifications.

AD Advantages

There are three types of ADs: emergency, immediate adopted rules, and notices of proposed rule making (NPRMs). Emergency ADs are issued when the FAA believes the danger is clear-cut and the problem must be dealt with immediately. Owners of the affected aircraft are notified by telegram or priority mail, and the AD becomes effective upon receipt. Immediate adopted rules are sent by first-class mail and are less urgent. An NPRM is published in the *Federal Register* when the FAA believes an unsafe condition has been found in a product but does not see the threat as great enough to warrant an immediate rule. Although 60 days are allowed for comments by interested parties, NPRMs almost invariably are adopted as final rules.

Compliance with an AD may require immediate action—such as grounding an aircraft or changing operations—until a fix can be made. Some ADs require a mechanical fix to be made within so many hours of operation or within a certain time period. Others require mandated periodic inspection intervals, such as every 25 hours or every 20,000 hours.

ADs represent a hidden cost in the price of an airplane, a cost the purchaser of a new airplane cannot anticipate. Buyers of used aircraft are somewhat more fortunate in that they can investigate an aircraft's AD history before buying. But even owners of older aircraft are sometimes hit with costly ADs after more than 20 years of trouble-free service from their airplanes. One compelling reason for researching an airplane's AD history is to avoid paying an inflated price for an aircraft that is due for a costly inspection. The cost of an AD compliance—like the cost of overhauling a run-out engine—should be factored into the purchase price of a used airplane.

To some owners, the FAA may seem capricious in its issuance of ADs, but there is always a specific cause—be it an accident or a series of reports on a defective part. Some ADs result from FAA and/or NTSB investigations. Frequently, the FAA may issue an AD after analyzing a series of maintenance or defect reports (MDRs) submitted by mechanics and operators as part of the Service Difficulty Program. Items deemed potentially hazardous to flight are reported in MDRs to GADOs, which telephone them to the FAA Safety Data Branch in Oklahoma City if they require immediate attention. They are immediately referred to the type certificate holding region for prompt attention. Less critical MDRs are mailed to the Safety Data Branch, where they are stored in a computerized data bank. Once the MDRs have been processed by the FAA, they are referred to as service difficulty reports (SDRs). This data is kept in the data banks for five years to determine trends and failure rates.

Selected SDRs are condensed and published monthly in FAA advisory circular 43-16, *General Aviation Airworthiness Alerts*. This monthly bulletin is designed to be used principally by mechanics and authorized inspectors. However, if you are considering purchasing a used aircraft, a list of SDRs can provide you with an idea of the airplane's maintenance history and can suggest places to inspect as you look it over.

The AOPA's Aircraft and Airmen Records Department provides such a list. Also among its services to used-plane buyers is provision of an accident/incident report for the particular aircraft by registration number. This service will tell you if an aircraft has been banged up seriously enough to require a report to the FAA, although a clean sheet from the FAA is not a guarantee that the aircraft has been accident-free. The report is a way to check out a claimed damage-free history.

Between claims and/or assumptions and the truth there can lie a life-and-death gap which pilots must fill. That takes curiosity, knowledge, determination, and communication, even if we feel we are technologically out of our league. As Lee Gruenfeld relates, it means asking the shop, "Just what have you done?"

Two of my clients asked me to fly them from Jacksonville, Florida, to Herlong Airport, 30 miles to the south. A recently licensed pilot, I readily agreed and chose N797AX, one of the Cessna 172s in which I had taken lessons. It had just come out of a 100-hour inspection, and everything checked out fine in preflight.

The engine, still slightly warm from a test flight by the FBO's chief pilot, kicked over immediately and smoothed out at 1,000 rpm. While taxiing out to Runway 7 (all 8,000 feet of it), I noticed that the throttle was pretty far forward for the rpm I was holding, which caused me some mild concern. However, I thought back to a text I had read that every new pilot is certain his airplane is going to fall apart on his first few night flights, so I proceeded. Besides, I intended to shoot a few touch-and-goes before heading for Herlong.

The runup was flawless: engine smooth, magneto checks on the money, all gauge readings normal. As part of my own personal checklist, I always end the runup by pulling the carb heat and the throttle all the way back. This assures me that the engine will not quit on landing or power-off glides. The engine idled smoothly for the five or six seconds I held it back and easily returned to 1,000 rpm.

After waiting about four minutes to clear the wake turbulence of a departing DC-9, we started our takeoff roll from an intersection. It seemed to take a bit longer than usual to reach flying speed, but that could have been due to the weight of the second passenger; I was used to flying with just my instructor. We were airborne with no problems. However, a haze forewarned of impending ground fog, so I decided to head for Herlong immediately, drop off my friends and come right back.

Leveling off at 1,000 feet, I had my first real indication of trouble. N797AX is the 160-hp version of the 172 and picks up airspeed rapidly after leveling off from a climb. Since the tach usually reaches 2,600 rpm within a few seconds after level-off, I start pulling back on the throttle to prevent red-lining even before the airspeed builds up to cruise.

That night, however, the needle never indicated higher than 2,300 rpm with full throttle. A little worried, I requested a touch-and-go at Jacksonville, just to play it safe. I received instructions to extend downwind to clear a landing jet and turned base about five miles out. The tachometer held steady at 2,300 rpm, and I tried to figure out why. I ruled out carburetor ice and, in fact, decided to apply no carb heat; I wanted all the power the engine could muster, just in case.

I stayed high, and when I was sure I could glide to the runway, I pulled the throttle back and the nose up in preparation for dropping flaps, keeping a little power for the night landing. Then came the next surprise. I reached the end of the throttle travel but was still getting power. I could not reduce the power. I pulled back on the yoke to decrease my airspeed and dropped flaps as soon as I hit the maximum flap-extended speed. I could see that with a normal landing glide, I would reach the runway, except that I was maintaining altitude at landing airspeed.

As soon as we cleared the threshold, I made my decision. I killed the still-too-fast engine by turning off the magnetos, which was a mistake—I should have pulled idle/cut-off. I left the master switch on so I could have lights and the radio. With about 100 feet of altitude left, I contacted the tower and told them I was coming in with a dead engine; I landed dead-stick and came to a stop on the runway.

My passengers had no idea that anything was wrong until we climbed out to push the airplane off the runway. ("We just figured you always land with the prop stopped," one of them said.) Attempts to restart the engine had been futile.

I found out later that the mechanics had taken advantage of the inspection time to rebuild the throttle assembly and carburetor. The assembly came loose during my flight and the linkages did not seat properly, leading to the loss of throttle control.

What did I learn from this? Three things:

First, trust yourself. All those hours of training should have sharpened my senses to the signals the airplane gave off. My instructor once told me that in nearly every accident involving mechanical problems, the pilot had some indication on the ground of what might be coming.

Second, beware of a tendency to feel that major work on an airplane is reason to relax, because the plane has just received close attention. That is actually cause for extra caution because of all the handling and alterations.

Third, talk to the mechanics about the airplanes you fly. I want to know what has been worked on so I will know what to watch carefully. If the mechanic is too busy or is insulted (which has been rare in my experience), I just remind him that I fly the airplane, not he.

Cementing the Partnership

How is the gap between the concerned owner/pilot and the expert mechanic to be bridged? How can the pilot get the most out of the vital partnership not only the first time but whenever the shop services his airplane? Again, mutual consideration and communication make the spanning possible. The burden lies mainly with the pilot, who is like a patient bringing an ailment to his doctor: He must describe accurately what hurts him.

Mechanics often complain that pilots are vague or inaccurate in describing malfunctions, thus complicating the mechanic's job and leading to higher maintenance bills. Notes such as "Listen to engine in air" or "Brakes not quite up to par" mean little. Are the brakes stopping the plane, or aren't they? Are they pulling to one side? Is there too much pedal or not enough? Mechanics prefer listening to useless facts among which may be a bit of information that can lead to solving the problem. Unfortunately, the ability to recognize and interpret maintenance problems is not something that is taught in the private pilot syllabus. It comes with self-education and experience.

It involves steps we have described, such as reading up on your airplane's systems through the pertinent manuals. One of the things the books will teach you is how to operate the *whole* aircraft properly. Frequently, a mechanic's first reaction to a maintenance squawk is that the pilot doesn't know what he is doing—that the real malfunction is a "short between the headsets." And it does happen often that the equipment is not broken but is simply misused by the pilot.

When a legitimate problem does arise, you can make the mechanic's job easier, and perhaps reduce the bill, by doing some preliminary troubleshooting—experimenting in order to isolate a faulty mechanism. It usually is not hard to identify a total component failure. What bedevils mechanics and avionics technicians is the intermittent failure that can be so hard to duplicate on the ground. Troubleshooting will decrease the likelihood that a repair shop will have to resort to an expensive remove-and-replace strategy in an effort to find the weak link in a system. Generally, if a mechanic or avionics technician cannot identify a faulty component after two or three hours of troubleshooting, he may replace the most suspect unit and return the aircraft to service rather than run up a larger bill.

You have one advantage over the mechanic when you troubleshoot in that you can identify symptoms when the aircraft is flying, observing and noting its performance under varied conditions. The key to providing useful information is to take meticulous notes about everything you notice when you are troubleshooting an intermittent failure. Assuming the malfunction is not serious enough to ground the airplane, take the opportunity to make notes on the problem during several flights, so as to sample occurrences in various flight conditions.

If you are troubleshooting a rough engine, the mechanic will want to know a number of things: When did the engine run rough? On start-up, during the runup, in a climb, in cruise? How was the engine leaned? At what altitude? What was the power setting? Did you try carburetor heat? What happened when you changed the manifold pressure or rpm? Did you check the magnetos? What was the oil temperature, the cylinder head temperature, the oil and fuel pressure?

If the Number 1 nav is intermittent, ask yourself: Does it fail after the unit has warmed up? How is the audio quality of the radio? Does it work when other radios or electrical equipment is switched on or off? What navigation facilities were being used when the problem occurred, and what was the aircraft's altitude and orientation? Does the failure occur in precipitation? Has other, unrelated mechanical work recently been done on the instruments or airframe?

Suppose there is a glitch in the autopilot. In which mode (heading, navtrack, approach, altitude hold) does it manifest itself? At what airspeeds, altitudes, temperatures? Is there an oscillation in pitch or roll? Can you time the cycles and determine the degree of pitch or bank? The answers you supply to these and other questions should start the mechanic in the right direction, allowing him to rule out several possible causes of the malfunction.

Avoiding Trouble After Shooting It

After you have done your homework, it still may be valuable to invite your mechanic or avionics technician for a flight so he can try some airborne troubleshooting of his own.

When you have done your best to explain what is wrong with your airplane, you should monitor the work that is done on it. Many pilots fail to adequately supervise the maintenance performed on their planes and then are surprised by the bills they receive. Communicating your desires to your mechanic is the best way to avoid such shocks. If at all possible, get an estimate of what it will cost to get the airplane out of the shop. With such clarification between you and the shop, they won't have to call you for an okay every time something is to be done.

Sometimes they will have to call you, because the job becomes more costly than was first assumed. A lot of small tasks, such as drilling out screws or replacing nut plates, can suddenly balloon a half-hour job to one taking four or five hours. Pilots' special requests or unusual problems can legitimately hike costs. Such factors can make an estimate very difficult.

If you intend for the mechanic to call you for approval to proceed with more expensive repairs, you must be available at the other end of the line. If you can't be reached and the work can't go forward, your airplane will only clog up hangar space and shake up the work schedule of the shop. Desperation may lead the shop chief to go ahead with the work anyway.

You can make certain that, during an annual inspection, expensive work will not be done without your approval by participating in an owner-assisted annual. Lending a hand in an annual by turning screws and wrenching nuts and bolts also is an excellent way to learn something about your airplane, including maintenance requirements.

Some mechanics enjoy having owners assist in the annual, others do not. An owner-assisted annual is different from supervised owner maintenance, in which a mechanic signs off work performed by an aircraft owner. Unless you are performing preventive maintenance tasks allowed under FAR Part 43, a mechanic in all likelihood will not be keen to supervise your work. He may well charge for the time spent *constantly* watching you— as the FAR requires—at the same rate.

One way to ensure that your airplane will be repaired in the most expensive way possible to is communicate a sense of extreme urgency to the mechanic. If you say, "I absolutely have to have the airplane ready for a business trip on Thursday," the mechanic may assume that the cost will be no object to you. Avoid pressuring the mechanic into rushing. Have an alternate means of travel available. Some FBOs will give pilots whose planes are in for maintenance a break on rental or charter rates. Many delays in the maintenance process cannot be anticipated. Shops try to accommodate transient customers whose aircraft have broken down, and this "walk-in" business can disrupt scheduled jobs. Difficulty in obtaining parts, furthermore, can delay repairs for days, weeks, or even months, but unjustifiable waiting should not be tolerated. It's best to let the shop know when you want to use the aircraft again for an important trip. Often, the work schedule can be arranged to meet a reasonable deadline.

In the final analysis, simple courtesy and a proper respect for the mechanic's skill, intentions, and problems can lead to better maintenance. It's one thing to think defensively and to take reasonable steps to protect yourself against poor treatment, but hostility or displayed distrust are likely to inspire defensiveness in turn. Most shops do want to satisfy their customers and in an atmosphere of respect and amiability will seek to take good care of the aircraft left in their charge. By constantly looking over your mechanic's shoulder or criticizing his work, you do the opposite of gaining his good will.

It also pays to observe shop etiquette. Unless you have arranged with the shop to assist in an annual inspection, for instance, don't ask to borrow tools, and don't open the cowling just to save a few dollars. If you do open cowlings or access panels, you will be expected to close them. You can also sow confusion by disrupting the mechanic's methodical work flow, a sure way to cause oversights and mutually unwanted neglect.

Don't ask a mechanic to perform additional work just as he is getting ready to roll your airplane out of the shop. This can mess up his schedule and put him in a bind with other customers. What if you were one of those customers?

Pay your repair bills promptly. If you don't, the word will get around, and you will find mechanics treating your requests for fast, inexpensive work with the same casual attitude.

It can be a great feeling to know that you can trust the work and priorities of your mechanic and that he has a genuine concern for the health of your airplane and for your satisfaction. When you find a repair shop in which you have reasonable confidence, foster the relationship. Help out by being specific with your squawks, courteous in your personal treatment, and considerate of their requirements. You should expect no less from your ground support. After all, you always have the prerogative of taking your business elsewhere.

There is another vital dependency that pilots are heirs to—the faith they must place in their engines and the fuel that drives them. As we shall see, the human element again looms as a major factor, with the pilot often being the quirkiest element.

10
Fuel Mismanagement

It is no surprise to pilots that the foremost factor in general aviation accidents is weather. But it does come as quite a shock to many general aviation pilots that engine failures and malfunctions rank second only to weather as crash causes. There has long been a myth abroad that such problems are seldom encountered, that decades of experience and technological advancements have transformed engine failures from constant sources of apprehension to rarities. Not so. On the average, of every ten general aviation accidents, three are powerplant generated, and these usually result from human failure.

The dark side of the partnership between pilot and powerplant often begins on the ground, where safety can become precarious through error or neglect by mechanics and line personnel. A recent survey of NTSB accident investigation reports over a six-month period showed that out of some 410 sample *engine failure* accidents, 35 were due to improper or inadequate maintenance and inspection. In several cases, engine control assemblies were misrigged or not resecured during annual inspections. Deteriorated fuel and oil screens were not replaced. A mechanic's scribe, left in an engine compartment, punctured a hole in an oil cooler. A fuel selector was installed backward. Fuel and oil lines and an oil sump drain plug were not secured properly. A carburetor was misadjusted. Rags were left in a throttle body intake and in a fuel cell outlet. Fuel tank vent lines were crossed.

Pilots have a right to be appalled at such dangerous nonsense, but they need also to look to themselves, for their own lapses help to ensure that ground-support errors will lead to disaster. Airmen also have a way of causing engine failures all by themselves, as they violate discipline and ignore warnings until they discover themselves without fuel or a working engine.

In the sampling of engine failure accidents just mentioned, 116 of the 410 total were due to undetermined causes. Of the remainder, 158—more than half—were of fuel-related origins such as fuel starvation, exhaustion, contamination, and miscontrol. In this area more than any other—including faulty maintenance and repair—the partnership between powerplants and their users breaks down.

Alien Presences

If not from our first, then certainly from our second lesson as student pilots we are given the message that fuel must be pure as the driven snow—purer, for in fuel no water is allowed, zero. In the old days, some pilots may simply have kicked their tires then lit their fires, but most pilots were zealous in trying to keep the fire safe from being doused by water and other contamination in their petrol. Today's avgas is better protected than yesteryear's, but fuel contamination of various kinds still causes accidents and fatalities:

• The engine lost power shortly after the Beech Bonanza took off from a 5,500-foot runway. The pilot attempted to make a left turn back to the airport. According to witnesses, the bank angle during the turn was between 60 and 90 degrees. The Bonanza stalled and crashed on the runway, about 1,300 feet from the point at which it had begun the takeoff roll. The pilot and his passenger were killed in the accident. The NTSB found the Bonanza's fuel pump to be inoperative due to total blockage by particles of an unidentified black substance.

Materials such as sand, rust, paint particles, and even fuel additives and the wrong fuels have been known to strangle engines. The majority of such accidents involve water contamination—approximately 65 per year:

• The pilot was operating his Skylane on automobile fuel and had filled a storage tank on his ranch with 1,200 gallons of regular unleaded gasoline. He was taking off with his wife and daughter aboard when, at about 60 feet up, the Skylane's engine stopped producing power. The pilot was maneuvering the airplane to avoid contacting deep gullies when it stalled and crashed. The pilot was seriously injured; his wife sustained minor injuries, and his daughter escaped injury. NTSB investigators found that the storage tank was contaminated by water; a sample of fluid from the Skylane's carburetor bowl was found to be 95 percent water.

• Shortly after making an instrument takeoff in weather that included a 250-foot ceiling and one mile visibility in rain and fog, the pilot of a Cessna 310K lost partial power in both engines. He descended below the overcast and was apparently searching for a place to land when the 310 struck a telephone pole and crashed. The pilot and his passenger were killed. The seals within the fuel tank filler caps had deteriorated, and investigators found water in the fuel distributing systems for both engines.

The Purge Routine

We all know the usual preflight ritual: A small cup capable of holding only an ounce or two is used to drain each fuel tank's sump. In multi-engine airplanes, crossfeed lines and other low points in the fuel lines often are drained in the same way. The common practice is to draw two or three small samples of fuel, look briefly at the contents for signs of water or foreign matter, then dump the fuel on the ramp. Many planes are equipped with remote drain valves that allow fuel strainers and crossfeed lines to be purged of large amounts of fuel in a very short time. Fuel drained this way is usually left uninspected, to form a large puddle on the ramp beneath the airplane.

This is the way most water-contamination accidents begin. Part of the problem lies in the purging's being a ritual that is often performed by a pilot who is too anxious to fly:

• The manager of Troy Executive Airport, in Clawson, Michigan, arrived for work at 8:00 a.m. and checked the fuel sumps of the Cessna 152. He discovered a considerable amount of water. A student pilot arrived, hoping to fly the airplane, but the manager told him he would have to wait until the water was cleared from the tanks. After several samples were drained, no more water was observed. The manager allowed the fuel to settle between each draining. A mechanic suggested that the fuel system be drained through the 152's belly drain. This was done, and a final sampling of the wing tank sumps showed no further water contamination.

At this point, the owner of the airplane arrived. He wanted to take the 152 on a VFR business cross-country to Fort Wayne, Indiana, so the student's flight was canceled to accommodate the owner. The manager warned the owner that there had been evidence of a large amount of water in the fuel. The owner replied that he had a meeting set up and had to leave shortly.

The owner drained the sumps once again. Later, he reported, "I found some water, so I kept draining until I got fuel only. I then went to the carb fuel sump and found an excessive amount of water. I drained the water from the sump, and after taking four good samples, I continued my preflight check. . . . I again checked for water in both wings and the carb sump. I did not find any more water, so I elected to continue the flight."

The pilot performed a runup and then took off. Just after departing the traffic pattern, there was a drop in rpm. Over Unicom the pilot advised that he was having engine trouble and would be returning to land. During the turn back to the airport, the engine regained power; the pilot reduced the power and applied carburetor heat.

On final, the pilot realized that he was too high and fast for a safe landing, so he tried slipping the airplane with full flaps. But this was not enough to correct his glidepath. "I was half-way down the runway and still at least 300 feet too high and going 80 knots, so I decided to go around . . ."

The 152 climbed at full power, but during a right turn, the engine quit. The pilot realized that he would not be able to glide to the runway, so he planned to make a forced landing in a nearby parking lot. The airplane struck telephone lines during the descent and skidded to a halt in the lot, striking a parked truck and causing substantial damage to the airplane. The pilot was uninjured.

Investigators found no fuel in the carburetor float bowl, only water. The fuel strainer drain was checked, and it, too, was completely filled with water. All samples (totaling half a gallon) from the wing tanks were at least half full of water.

The NTSB ruled that the probable causes of the accident were the pilot's inadequate preflight preparation and planning and water in the fuel.

Although they think they do a good job, pilots either do not drain enough fuel to find any water, do not check the fuel coming from the strainer drains, or do not check the system for further contamination after finding some evidence of a problem in their samples. Many pilots who have suffered contamination accidents drained their sumps, found small amounts of water in the samples and then kept on draining the sumps until they received samples filled only with fuel. Textbooks say that this is a proper method for clearing a fuel system of water. However, most of the pilots involved in such accidents who observed water in their first samples "cleared" their systems using this method.

How the Stuff Invades Your System

There are three ways by which water can enter an airplane's fuel system. Storage tanks and fuel trucks may contain large concentrations of water. This water is often the result of careless handling, negligent testing, or improper refining.

When FBOs buy their fuel in large lots, such as by the tanker load, they must store it for long periods of time. Such long storage, especially in partially filled tanks and trucks, is conducive to the second form of water contamination, condensation. In high humidity, water droplets can condense on the bare walls of a partially full tank and then fall into the fuel below. The same is true for an airplane's tanks. The longer the fuel container is kept in a partially full condition, the greater the chance for condensation.

Leaking fuel-cap seals or fittings are the other main cause of water contamination, particularly in airplanes parked outdoors and exposed to rain. Worn, cracked or out-of-round rubber gaskets are the principal problem. Some fuel cap designs compound the problem—many airplanes have their caps slightly recessed below the surface of the wing. A pool of water can form above this type of cap.

Water Wings

We tend to regard untopped fuel tanks as "half full"; in view of the threat of water condensation, we are better advised to regard them as half empty and therefore dangerous, whatever one's reasons for leaving them so. Recently, when a wave of fuel thefts struck Chicago Midway Airport, the owners of a Mooney M20E made it a policy never to top off its tanks after a flight. One day during the preflight inspection, the pilot had the tanks filled to 42 gallons of their 52-gallon capacity. He drained the sumps and found no indication of water. Two hundred feet up on his climbout, the engine roughened and quit, forcing a badly damaging emergency landing. The gascolator subsequently was found to contain water, as did the fuel injector servo screen chamber. The right and left tanks both contained water. The servicing fuel truck showed no fuel contamination. Thwarting thieves thus wrecked the plane and endangered the pilot.

Put partially filled tanks, ambient moisture, and defective caps together, and another grim tale unfolds. The tale was lived and is related here by Rick H. Martin:

For two weeks, my Cessna 182 had been tied down at the Elko, Nevada, airport waiting for me to return and the weather to clear. I fly over to Elko every weekend from Salt Lake City to cover the community hospital's emergency room. As a noninstrument-rated pilot, I have to leave my airplane behind on occasion to take other means of transportation. A particularly bad bout of weather on this occasion had forced me to leave the airplane in Elko for two weeks.

The weather finally had cleared, and on a cold December morning, I prepared for my return flight to Salt Lake City. While having the engine preheated, I examined the aircraft and found extensive frost on the wings. After ensuring that the aircraft got a thorough warmup, I taxied it over to the Flight Service Station and parked it so that the wing surfaces received the maximum sun exposure.

According to the weather briefer, conditions in Salt Lake were 1,800 feet overcast and two and a half miles visibility in smog. The weather at Ogden, Utah, just north of Salt Lake, was 5,000 feet and five miles. It looked as though my destination would be Ogden, so I decided to have my tanks topped—the fuel required was 28 gallons. I returned to the airplane and began brushing the frost from the wings. To my surprise, I found ice beneath the frost—a solid sheet covering the upper surfaces, which the sun would have to thaw before I could remove it. I returned to the FSS to file a VFR flight plan to Ogden and to double-check the weather.

Returning again to the airplane, I drained the fuel sumps and performed the rest of the preflight inspection. I was ready, but the ice remained. My patience was worn thin, and I walked to the FBO to inquire about deicing equipment. With the ice removed, I performed the usual pretakeoff runup and departed for Salt Lake. As I climbed toward my cruise altitude, my spirits were completely restored when the Elko FSS called to advise me that the weather at Salt Lake had improved to 5,000 feet and three miles. It looked as though I would be able to land there after all.

The climb to 11,500 feet was uneventful. I established cruise altitude and began to lean the aircraft. I noticed the exhaust gas temperature fluctuating while I attempted to adjust the mixture. Within a few minutes, it settled down, and the engine was leaned for cruise. However, I noticed the EGT occasionally fluctuating; must be the gauge, I thought.

Suddenly, the engine quit. At first, I could not believe it had happened; there had been no drop in manifold pressure or on the tachometer. I quickly scanned all the gauges and switches. Everything was in order, except that the engine was not running. I attempted to restart: mixture in full, carburetor heat on. No luck; even after multiple attempts, the engine would not restart.

I began transmitting to Salt Lake City Approach that I was a Cessna 182, VFR to Salt Lake, and that it looked as though I would have to make an emergency landing on Interstate 80, east of the Knolls exit. I asked Approach for possible solutions I might not have considered. Their multiple suggestions had been tried already, with unsuccessful results.

At that point, I realized that I had to concentrate on flying the airplane. I was at 9,500 feet. I began the measures for a forced landing without power: fuel selector in the Off position, full flaps, mixture lean, and—after a final position and intention report to Approach—I shut off the electrical switch. Setting up an approach somewhat slower than that suggested in the manual, I chose a spot and made a full-stall landing behind a tractor trailer on the Interstate. I came to a full stop, and as there was no traffic behind me, I got out and pushed the airplane off the highway and into the roadside ditch.

Unable to raise any facility on the radio after landing, I examined the aircraft, climbed in and attempted a restart. To my surprise, it turned right over. With the help of some very kindly Utah Highway Patrol officers, who had been notified of the general area of my touchdown, I taxied the Cessna to a cross-over about a mile from the landing point and tied it down.

The next day, I returned to the airplane with a mechanic, whose examination revealed water-contaminated fuel, measured in gallons. An inspection of the gascolator revealed ice obstructing the flow of fuel to the carburetor.

Where had the water contamination occurred? I noticed no water during my preflight. However, the airplane had been parked for two weeks with the tanks partially filled. I should have known that water condensation can play a major role in contaminating an airplane's partially filled fuel tanks. In humid conditions, water droplets form on the walls of a fuel cell, then roll into the fuel. This water may not show up in fuel samples, because it can be trapped behind baffles or remain in suspension. But I did not know that.

Then I realized that it had been a stretch of IFR weather that kept the 182 grounded for so long. Moisture could have formed in the tanks or passed through leaky filler caps. Unfortunately, I never thought to include a check of the filler caps as a part of my preflight.

Had the fluctuation in the EGT been a warning? It will be in the future. My tanks now are topped after each flight, especially if my stay will be prolonged by cold, adverse weather. Also, I now use Ig-lo, an ethyl alcohol based drying compound, during the long, frigid winter months.

Water is heavier than fuel. This is why fuel drains are installed at the lowest points of a fuel system's components. The theory is that any water will collect at these low points and thus be detected and drained easily. But there are problems of which pilots should be aware. Water can remain in suspension above a tank's low point. Tanks with baffles and wet wings can trap water behind wing ribs and other internal components. Droplets of water held in suspension and water trapped behind baffles and ribs may not show up at all, if the typical fuel sampling procedure is used.

Can Sumption Be Done About It?

Obviously, the usual preflight procedure for checking fuel is inadequate, in view of the fact that water can hide in the system's nooks and crannies. Extra measures should be taken:

• Check the condition of your fuel caps and cap seals before each flight.

• Drain all sumps and drain fittings. Consult your pilot's operating manual to make sure no drains are overlooked. If your airplane is a Cessna 150 or 152, have a belly drain installed; this is the lowest portion of these airplanes' fuel systems, not the strainer drain. Take four samples of fuel from each drain and inspect them. Collect all fuel drained from the fuel strainer, crossfeed or transfer lines; do not allow the fuel to run out onto the ground.

• Rock the wings and then allow enough time (approximately five minutes) for the contents in the tanks to settle. This can help to dislodge any pockets of trapped or suspended water. If the airplane you fly uses turbine fuel, remember that the specific gravity of jet fuel is different from that of avgas; water takes four times longer to settle in jet fuel than in avgas. However, small amounts of water are less critical to the operation of turbine engines.

• Drain more samples from each fitting.

• If there is any evidence of water or any other contaminant, drain a large amount of fuel—say, a quart—from each fitting. If water is still present, you have reason to suspect a severe case of contamination. Consider having a mechanic drain the fuel system. Checking large quantities of fuel is the only sure way to detect contamination.

• Alert your fuel supplier and other pilots to the problem. Other airplanes may have been contaminated by a bad shipment of fuel or subjected to the same atmospheric conditions that may have caused condensation in your airplane's fuel tanks.

To lower the odds of water contaminating your fuel, these additional steps can be helpful:

Fly the airplane frequently. This keeps fuel from losing its volatility and prevents the trace amounts of water that exist in all fuels from coalescing into pure water. Top off the tanks after each flight. This prevents condensation. (Note, however, that some aircraft have fuel tanks that can expand when high temperatures cause fuel volume to increase, to the point that leakage occurs. Check with your mechanic to find out if your airplane's tanks can be affected in this way.)

If possible, hangar the airplane. This, too, minimizes condensation and keeps rain away from the fuel caps. Have a mechanic regularly check the condition of the caps to replace the seals before they can admit water into the fuel system.

It is also a good idea to check the condition of your supplier's equipment and the status of his fuel. Is the fuel supply near depletion? If so, condensation may have formed in his tanks or trucks. Fuel pumped from the dregs of a tank or truck often is contaminated with water and other foreign matter. Ask about the condition of the fueling equipment's filters and screens. Has any water been detected? Are the screens rusty? If they are, water has been in one of the fuel loads.

Avoid refueling from drums or other makeshift sources. In remote areas, this practice is common. In Alaska, for example, many water contamination accidents have been traced to unsealed drums and poor filtering techniques.

A mechanic's inspection of an airplane's carburetor bowl or fuel-injection plumbing also will detect water contamination. Airplanes that have been sitting outside for long periods of time should have these components checked—in addition to the checks just mentioned—for water or water damage. Water left standing in carburetor bowls, fuel lines, or fuel screens will cause corrosion of these parts. If the corrosion is left unchecked, the components will swell and crack, allowing corrosion products to enter the engine and causing fuel leaks. When temperatures drop and trapped water freezes, fuel lines and gaskets can burst.

Aircraft manufacturers sometimes recommend that concentrations of no more than one percent (by volume) of isopropyl alcohol be added to aviation fuels so that the trace amounts of water in avgas will not turn into ice crystals in freezing temperatures. However, this is a preventive measure only. Adding alcohol to an already contaminated system will have no effect.

The same holds true for Prist, an antibacterial agent designed to prevent the growth of cultures and organic residues that form in turbine fuels. Prist also will prevent fuel ice, but it will not eliminate preexisting pure water concentrations.

There are no shortcuts to detecting and eliminating water-contaminated fuel. Mechanics concur that extensive draining is necessary. Disposing of the drained fuel can be a problem, and your preflight will be extended, but to be safe, you must take your time and be willing to drain large amounts of fuel. The pilot who drains four ounces and goes on to the next step in the preflight may well be making a big mistake.

Jet Beset

Upon arriving at a Maryland airport, the pilot of an Aero Commander 500B gave a lineman his fuel order of 95 gallons. According to the lineman, "He did not specify what kind of fuel. My first impression from looking at the plane was that it was a jet aircraft." The 500B's twin Lycoming IO-540 engines are designed only for 100-octane low-lead aviation fuel.

The lineman had been on the job for only two months and had no prior aviation experience. He filled one of the 500B's tanks with 13 gallons of jet fuel, but as he did this, he "looked around and studied the plane. I wasn't sure what kind of a plane it was, so I stopped putting fuel in the plane." Another lineman told him to use 100LL, so he did—95 gallons' worth.

"I really didn't know what would happen to the airplane," the lineman later stated. "For some reason, I had in my mind the difference like between hi-test and regular and didn't think that the small amount of jet fuel would make any difference, and that with such a large quantity of avgas, it wouldn't really matter." The pilot, who had not supervised the fueling, hurriedly took off. Two days later, the plane returned to the same field. After a weather briefing, the 500B took off. Two minutes later, the pilot reported an engine out. Attempting to return, the Aero Commander crashed near the airport. Four persons were killed on impact. A fifth died five days later.

Investigators found that the aircraft's fuel was comprised of a mixture of 10- to 20-percent jet-A fuel and 80- to 90-percent avgas. The spark plugs showed damage from intense heat; melted aluminum was splattered on two of the right engine's spark plugs. An examination by Avco Lycoming revealed that both engines had been damaged by preignition. The engines' valves had been elongated by extremely high temperatures.

Other fatalities and several crashes have resulted from misfueling piston craft with turbine fuel. While it is tempting to mark linemen as the sole culprits, their mistakes are only part of a series of ways by which such a thing happens.

For instance, fuel truck drivers often do not understand the differences between aviation fuels or the meaning of the labels on their trucks. Also, at FBOs, fuel is stored in large tanks labeled according to their contents. But transient loads of different types of fuel may be labeled improperly. A tank normally used to store avgas may contain jet fuel on an irregular basis. If all fueling personnel are not kept up on the status of an FBO's tanks, there is a danger of misfueling.

Linemen, particularly inexperienced ones, are the next culprits in the distribution network. Without a knowledge of the differences between jet and reciprocating engines, the range of aircraft types, and the fuel requirements of each, a lineman is left to his imagination. There is evidence to suggest that linemen are often confused about the terms *turbo, turbocharged,* and *turbine*—which often are printed on cowlings or engine nacelles. Thinking that the *turbo* prefix refers to a turbine engine, they have fueled turbocharged aircraft with jet fuel or filled their crankcases with turbine-engine oil.

The Pilot's Checks

Finally, there is the pilot, who has the last chance to detect a misfueling. But first, the pilot must understand that jet fuel contamination of avgas is dangerous because it damages the combustion chambers of reciprocating engines. Second, he must take the time to supervise the fueling of his aircraft.

The defense begins with checking the labeling on the truck, tank, or pump and asking the lineman to verify the contents.

Next, observe the color of the fuel you drain during the pre-flight. Avgas with an 80-octane rating is reddish; 100-octane avgas is a light green; 100LL (low lead) avgas is a light blue; avgas with a 115/130-octane rating is purplish. Jet fuel is *color-less*. Mixtures containing avgas and jet fuel can be straw-colored or clear. To be safe, you should not operate your plane if your fuel sample is any other color than the one(s) recommended. Suspect fuel must be drained completely from the airplane's fuel tanks and lines. Jet fuel also feels greasier than avgas. It evaporates more slowly and has the odor of kerosene, its principal ingredient.

These properties of jet fuel permit a simple test to confirm its presence. Developed by the AOPA Air Safety Foundation, this test requires only a clean sheet of white paper and a medicine dropper. The test will detect fuel contamination levels as low as five percent. To perform the test, fill the dropper with a small quantity of fuel, then place a drop of the fuel on the sheet of paper. Try to make a spot of fuel about the size of a quarter. As the spot dries, hold the paper up to a light source and observe the perimeter of the spot. Pure avgas will evaporate from the perimeter inward, leaving the outer margin indistinct. After approximately one minute, pure avgas will leave no sign of a spot. Jet fuel, on the other hand, will leave a distinct perimeter, and the spot will evaporate only after several minutes have elapsed.

Applying decals to fuel filler parts indentifying the type of recommended fuel is one commonly used way to minimize the chance of misfueling. The General Aviation Manufacturers Association sells identification decals. Other identification devices are in the works. Still, pilot vigilance is the prime defense.

Fuel Starvation

Not only are pilots guilty of allowing "poisoned" fuels into their aircraft systems, they also frequently starve their powerplants of fuel that is available:

• While conducting a preflight inspection of his Mooney M20A, the pilot found the left fuel tank nearly empty and the right tank half full. He had the left tank serviced with 12 gallons of fuel before taking off but left the fuel selector positioned to draw fuel from the right tank throughout the brief, local sightseeing flight. According to the NTSB, the engine lost power due to fuel starvation when the pilot banked the airplane steeply to the right to enter the airport traffic pattern. The pilot attempted unsuccessfully to restart the engine by pumping the throttle; then he tried to land on the nearest runway, but the airplane touched down about 700 feet short. The pilot and his passenger sustained injuries, and the Mooney was substantially damaged.

• The 4,091-hour pilot of a Cessna 172M Skyhawk was on a pleasure flight over Georgia with two passengers, ages 10 and 11, who were sitting in the right front seat and sharing a seat belt. According to one of the passengers, they asked the pilot to "fly up and down," which he had done for them on previous flights. As the airplane was climbing, the engine lost power. The Skyhawk struck a powerline, crashed and burned, killing the pilot and one of his passengers. The other passenger was seriously injured. The NTSB said that the fuel selector was positioned on the right tank, which was nearly empty. The board included as factors sunglare and poor judgment.

Poor judgment, inattention, or absent-mindedness play large roles in accidents due to fuel starvation. It is hard to tell if the pilots' mistakes were once-only errors or habits that finally caught up with them. Perhaps the best way to suggest defenses against fuel-starvation mishaps is to indicate how they happen.

Fuel starvation involves a failure in the delivery of usable fuel to the engine. Inattention has led pilots to forget to switch tanks with no time or ability to effect airstarts. Some pilots fail to follow the proper power-loss emergency procedures; for instance, failing to activate auxiliary fuel pumps in switching tanks.

Many starvation mishaps stem from improper use of controls. Pilots take off with the fuel selectors positioned on near-empty auxiliary tanks, though the main tanks are half full. Pilots inadvertently position the selector between tanks while preparing to land, while other airmen pull out the mixture or primer controls trying to apply carburetor heat. Failing to deselect carb heat on go-arounds and leaving it on during takeoff cause crashes. Show-off pilots have pretended to stop the engine to scare or impress passengers and accidentally did stop it without being able to restart.

Defenses? Make no fuel-effective move—physical or mental—without considering its consequences or, in some cases, its sanity.

Flying on the Fumes

Among the nearly 300 engine-failure accidents with known causes sampled in the six-months survey we have been discussing, approximately 100 aircraft crashed because their pilots continued to fly them until they consumed all usable fuel. The pilots ranged from a 27-hour student in a two-seat trainer to a 15,000-hour ATP in turboprop twin. Why did these pilots fail to defend themselves and their passengers against a grim eventuality even when warned? According to the NTSB, many were "inattentive to fuel supply." Others had miscalculated the fuel consumption of their engines or misjudged the amount of fuel in their tanks. Some pilots made the mistake of trusting their fuel gauges, rather than keeping tabs on time, fuel burn, and supply. In a few cases, aircraft ran out of fuel after their pilots got lost or made lengthy flight diversions for weather. Fuel siphoned from loose fuel-tank caps prematurely depleted the supplies of fuel from two aircraft.

If there is such a thing as a "typical" fuel exhaustion accident, this might serve as an example:

• There was no fuel available at the field when the pilot of a Piper PA-28-181 landed after a three-hour VFR flight to pick up a passenger. His ultimate destination was 25 miles away, and he estimated that about one hour's worth of fuel remained in the Archer's tanks. He took off and began navigating by pilotage and dead reckoning. About ten minutes after takeoff, the pilot felt he was drifting south of his intended course and corrected to the north.

At his ETA, however, the pilot was unable to locate the airport. He contacted a local control tower, gave his position, and requested vectors to the nearest airport. The pilot later said that he advised the controller that he was extremely low on fuel. The controller said that the tower did not have radar equipment and recommended that he contact Approach Control. According to the pilot, he "had to wait" to contact the facility due to frequency congestion. After assigning the Archer a transponder code, Approach located it about two miles north of the pilot's intended destination.

Shortly thereafter, the pilot reported that he was still unable to locate the airport and that his left fuel tank had run dry. He was given the direction and range to another airport in the vicinity. The pilot spotted the private airstrip and attempted to land. However, anticipating that he was going to run off the end of the runway, he began to go around. The Archer was in a climbing left turn when the engine quit. The pilot and his passenger were seriously injured, and the Archer was badly damaged when it struck a barn gable and crashed. The NTSB's report noted that about eight ounces of fuel were found in the Archer's tanks. When asked by the board for recommendations on how the accident could have been avoided, the pilot replied that he either should not have attempted to continue the flight or should have flown to a nearby airport to refuel before proceeding and that he should have declared an emergency, because the ATC facilities he contacted "did not seem to understand that I was in a critical situation that was getting worse."

Optimism and Reality

When there is a firm chance that your fuel supply will become critical, you can't afford to take such things for granted as getting to your destination in the shortest time, getting the help from the ground that you want, not having to divert to an alternate airport, making it into the field on the first try. The one thing this pilot knew for sure was that he had less than optimum fuel. Everything else should have been secondary to the necessity of diverting early-on for fuel.

It seems that in fuel-exhaustion cases, the inexhaustible ingredient is optimism, as related by pilot William P. Krieter. After a series of problems with their newly overhauled Cherokee 180, Krieter and his wife were primed to get home to Compton, California:

. . . That morning, we had to wait for the fog to clear and didn't have enough money to fill the tanks (the FBO required cash). Eventually, we did get into the air, headed for home. The flight went well as we landed at Chico for fuel.

Error One: With full fuel, I estimated the 476 miles from Chico back to Compton to be well within range.

Error Two: I took the wrong highway out of Stockton and had to make a big dog-leg to get back on course.

Error Three: Near Porterville, both fuel tanks showed one-quarter, less than I expected. However, I figured that Compton was just within range, with a 30-minute reserve.

(Later, I found that because the engine had been recently overhauled and not broken in, its fuel consumption was 10 gph instead of 8.8, as the manual said.)

Error Four: classic press-on-itis. Passing Burbank, fuel consumption seemed to be running as figured, and I decided to go all the way. I had considered Murphy's Law several times, but I was still a nonbeliever. As Compton came into view, I began to expect engine failure at any time. Checking the pattern, we appeared in good shape, one aircraft on downwind, one on final for 25R. I called two miles straight in for 25L.

As I reduced power to 1500 rpm and began slowing to approach speed, I noticed a C-152 nearing the hold line. I became a believer. Something told me, "That 152 is not going to wait." It was one-quarter final for 25R. I reached for the mike: "Cherokee 39W one-half mile final Compton 25 Left."

The 152 began to roll as I replaced the mike. Go around? Fuel starvation, engine quitting over 152 or on climb out? No! Offset to 25R? Low-wing on runway rolling to stop, should be clear. Bank right, full flaps, bank left, where's the runway? More left. It's clear, good! Too high, too fast, nose up (don't stall), cut the power. Wings level, on center, touch down, 152 off left wing "never even saw me!" Runway half gone. Brakes. Flaps up! Okay, the fence has stopped coming.

Afterthoughts? The fuel tank in use had one-half gallon usable remaining, the other tank had one gallon usable. Never again will I try to stretch my range. This time, I was lucky.

The Wisdom of the Gauges

If our car's fuel gauge lies to us and we run out of gas, we roll to a stop and then we wait or walk, vowing to trust the damn thing less next time. If our airplane's fuel gauges deceive us into running out, we glide or fall and then . . . it depends.

We may vow never to trust the damn things next time, but why did we trust them the first time? Perhaps because in some ways we don't accept that airplanes aren't like autos. Pilot Robert M. Ross describes how dangerous such misplaced trust can be—on the up side and the down:

In my 1,000 hours of flying, I have enjoyed many safe and happy hours in the air, but there have been close calls. Two of the closest brought into sharp focus the importance of good fuel management and planning.

The first occurred one warm, south Texas summer day. I was flying a 12-year-old Mooney M20G that I knew well. My two passengers and I were heading home to Houston on a fishing trip that included multiple stops. My rough calculations indicated that I had not burned either tank's full load of fuel; however, except for the fuel-gauge readings, determining fuel consumption accurately was difficult because of our multiple takeoffs.

It was getting late, and I neglected to inspect my gas tanks visually. My gauges still read more than one-quarter on each side, and since the flight home was only about 45 minutes in good VFR weather, I felt confident in going. Nevertheless, something needled me to promise myself that as soon as one tank ran dry, I would land at the first available airport—regardless of where I was. This escape plan, in retrospect, turned out to be a lifesaver.

We flew up from Matagorda Bay to Houston. I had to drop some passengers off at Andrau Airport on the west side of town and then continue on to my home base at Hooks Airport to the north. After an uneventful landing at Andrau, I said goodbye to my passengers and taxied out for my final seven-minute flight home. Takeoff performance was excellent; I climbed to the south and then banked to the north, now only six minutes from home.

At that point, the engine sputtered slightly, and the manifold pressure began to fall. One fuel tank had run dry. I immediately switched to the other tank, and the engine sprang back to life. Being only six minutes from home, I was tempted to continue. But I remembered my promise to myself. The first available airport was Andrau, which was directly below my left wing. After momentary deliberation, I decided that a promise is a promise and that it is always better to be safe. My thinking was also affected by the fuel-gauge readings. The empty tank still indicated about one-quarter, as did the tank I was then on. I cut the power, reentered the circuit and landed without incident. At the gas pumps, when I opened the fuel tank, to my surprise no fuel was visible. To experiment, I restarted the engine and let it idle at about 1,000 rpm; it ran smoothly for about two minutes and then went dead. If I had not stuck with my plan, I would not have made it home.

Another, even more hair-raising incident occurred about a year and a half later. I had flown my Cessna 182 Turbo Skylane RG often during my eight months of ownership, and I felt very comfortable with its fuel-consumption characteristics. I was eager to take my young son on a long trip from Houston to Kitchener, Ontario—about 1,150 nautical miles. I planned to refuel in Indiana, probably around Evansville.

We left on a beautiful CAVU summer day with only the occasional cumulus cloud and south-southwest winds. I watched the lineman top off my tanks (88 gallons usable). Then I took off, climbed out of the Houston area, put on my oxygen mask and went to altitude, where brisk tailwinds helped maintain our 190-knot groundspeed. Time sped by as we flew north. Because the airplane was relatively new, I took it up to its maximum operating altitude of 20,000 feet to see how it performed.

Over Indiana, we had been airborne for about three and a half hours, and I knew that at the selected power setting, the airplane should have six hours and 20 minutes' cruise, with 45 minutes' reserve. I decided to continue and possibly stop at the south side of Lake Erie. At that point, the winds were still favorable, and, having used just a bit more than five hours' flying time, I supposedly still had a good hour and 20 minutes of fuel left before I had to hit my reserves. Kitchener was an hour and 20 minutes away.

But the gas gauges read mysteriously low, showing only about 19 gallons left; at my cruise consumption of 14 gallons per hour, that meant only one hour and 20 minutes of fuel total. However, during previous flights when I had measured fuel consumption, this airplane had flown according to the book; I therefore felt confident that sufficient fuel remained for six hours and 20 minutes of flight. Remembering the faulty fuel gauges in the Mooney, I tended to dismiss the low fuel gauge readings. Nevertheless, I formed an escape plan—to stay high and not begin the descent into Kitchener until I knew I could make it.

It was now dark. I had been flying for more than six hours and was approaching London, Ontario, about 40 miles southwest of Kitchener. I carefully noted where the airport lights were and gave serious thought to landing there, for my fuel gauges were now reading empty. However, according to the book, having flown six hours and five minutes, I should have had 15 minutes' more flying time before I hit my 45-minute reserve. At 160 knots groundspeed, Kitchener was but 15 minutes away. I proceeded.

Almost exactly halfway between the two cities, the manifold pressure started to fall. The gas gauges read zero. Terrified, I looked behind us to London and ahead to the visible beacon at Kitchener. Attempting to use all my wits, I decided it was best to continue to glide toward Kitchener—from 11,000 feet, I should just have been able to cover the 20 miles. As the fuel pressure dropped, I hit the auxiliary pump. The pressure came back up, and the engine came to life. Simultaneously, I realized that I might need power later, so, committed to a power-off glide while a tiny bit of fuel remained, I leaned out the engine and shut it down.

In the middle of the night, with a silent engine and the gear-warning horn blaring, I started my slow glide toward the airport more than 20 miles away. The glide seemed endless. My eight-year-old son was sound asleep beside me. I made every effort to wake him so that he could protect himself in case of an accident, but he slept through the whole thing. I tried not to panic, maintained an appropriate glide speed and kept my eyes fixed on the airport. Just in the front of the airport, there is a small river valley, which would have been an inhospitable place to land. I called the tower and told them that I was low on fuel and would be making a straight-in, downwind landing. They obligingly turned on the appropriate runway lights at full intensity. My descent was about 700 to 800 feet per minute. I reached circuit height just as I got to the airport. That meant that I had a "safety margin" of only a little more than a minute between landing at the airport and crashing. As soon as I thought I could make the airport, I put the mixture back in and turned the mags on. With a wonderful sound, the engine caught. I landed and taxied into the parking area, where the engine promptly quit.

After my knees stopped shaking and my legs would support my weight, I went over my trials. How could I have been so stupid as to endanger my airplane and our lives? Where had I gone wrong? From careful measurements of fuel consumption, I knew that the book was right. However, I had forgotten to take into account three vital factors: I had climbed and descended at altitude, going to 20,000 feet, both of which increased my fuel burn. At cruise, I was burning about 14 gph; 45 minutes' reserve at six or seven gph is only 6/88 or about eight-percent variation, for which I should have allowed, particularly with the empty gauge readings.

My most important error was in failing to look at my fuel tanks prior to takeoff. The Cessna is a high-wing airplane, and it is awkward to inspect the tanks visually. I had watched the lineman fill them, but the filler necks are extremely wide, and unless the fuel is absolutely right up to the top, the tanks can be missing a couple of gallons on either side. Although this amount usually is not significant, those two or three gallons on either side were the six or so gallons I was missing for my 45 minutes' reserve flying time.

I humbly relate these two embarrassing incidents to stress some important points. First, always make an escape plan. Second, always include as essential to any preflight a visual inspection of the fuel tanks. This cannot be overstressed. Even though the owner's manual and the gauges are quite accurate, they can be subject to small errors and should be cross-checked against each other. If they don't agree, err on the safety side by landing with enough rather than too little fuel on board.

Finally, fuel systems on small private aircraft need to be better. Electronic gas gauges cannot be relied upon totally, and there is no foolproof way of knowing when you are at your reserves. It is crucial to use just as much fuel as is safe, to get the maximum range; otherwise, you might as well carry less fuel and non-useful weight. We need a meticulously accurate way of measuring remaining fuel that is not subject to errors made in assuming consumption from a manual or in watching fuel or fuel-flow gauges. Until such precise instrumentation is available, it is very important to observe and cross-check quantities closely and to err, if at all, on the side of safety.

What Is Available

The most sophisticated fuel-quantity measuring system is the capacitance, which has no moving parts within the fuel tanks such as floats, rods, levers, and wipers. Instead, the difference in the conductive properties of fuel and air (fuel vapor) form the basis for measurement—the dielectric, nonconductivity principle. The system measures fuel by weight instead of gallons, and is thus more accurate. Sophisticated twins and jet transports use this best—and most expensive—system.

Most general aviation craft use the electrical quantity gauge found in cars. It relies on a float-and-lever principle, with an variable resistor providing the indication. Its advantages are flexiblity in location, multiple tank indications, easy replacement, and inexpensiveness. However, resistors wear out, rods are bent when the plane is not level, moisture within tanks corrodes or freezes parts—all sources of errors. Also, in full tanks the floats don't float until several gallons burn off, so that the gauge reads *Full* too long. Actually a crude voltmeter, the system measures electricity, not fuel.

Sight tubes and sight rods show positive fuel indications. However, sight rods in particular cannot be calibrated.

Most fuel exhaustion is accompanied by the gauges' denying it is happening or by pilots denying that the gauges can be wrong. Many accidents are caused by the pilots hoping that the indications were erring on the optimistic side.

Fuel totalizers and fuel-flow and -management systems help long-stretch pilots greatly, but whether he has them or not, the pilot must shoulder the management responsibility.

Fuel up and flight plan to meet *at least* the basic requirements: VFR day—fuel to first airport of intended landing plus 30 minutes' reserve at normal cruise; VFR night—add 15 minutes to the day reserve; IFR—fuel to first intended airport, then to an alternate, and then for 45 minutes at normal cruise power, with allowances for instrument approaches and delays. However, as the accounts we have seen show, life is not so simple. In fuel management, time is rarely on our side, but planning and monitoring by time and rate of consumption is our invaluable ally in the power struggle.

11
Briefing Obscured?

From year to year without fail, accident statistics demonstrate that the aviator's most ubiquitous and dangerous enemy is the weather, be he VFR-only or an IFR veteran. As he prepares his defenses against the vagaries of flight, the pilot must turn his attention foremost to the state of the atmosphere. What his scrutiny finds there should tell him whether he should make the flight at all and what courses to take, navigational and otherwise, to keep himself out of meteorological trouble. His main problem is, however, that unless he intends merely to churn up the local skies, he must make his plans without first-hand knowledge of what will lie ahead. He is dependent on others—men and machines—for the information on which to base decisions that he as pilot-in-command must make. He is involved in a critical and potentially dangerous partnership with some form of weather briefer, who or which will be safely on the ground when the pilot is airborne amid the volatile elements.

The main problem of weather briefing used to be that information was sparse or late. Today, satellites and other devices provide an amazingly expansive big picture and a host of details about changing events within it. For most airmen, the problem is in getting the specific information the individual pilot needs for his particular flight, presented so that he can digest and analyze it accurately. As it has been evolving, the briefing system has encouraged the pilot to be passive, as data is automatically fed to him. It is important for him to be an active and dominant participant in the process of finding out what he needs to know. Otherwise, he may come away satisfied from a briefing that is

essentially obscure because it is incomplete or doesn't make total sense.

Curiosity Saves

When it comes to weather briefings, pilots seem to fall into
one of two categories. One, call him Pilot A, believes that he
knows everything he needs to know about meteorology, according to the FAA's mind-set. After all, he studied hard for his
written exam(s) and learned enough to botch only two of the
ten-or-so weather questions. No matter; he did pass the exam.
He figures that surely he must know enough to be safe, and he
carries that "just enough" attitude—along with a blind faith in
things working out—with him into the briefing. He goes through
all the motions that he learned in ground school and from his
instructor, but he does not really know or care enough to get a
full and clear grasp of the weather situation. Often, he possesses
an eagerness to fly more than an intense and healthy curiosity
about what's going on up there and a shrewd outlook on what
he is told about it. He may hear and react, but he doesn't question; he doesn't *think*.

On the other hand, Pilot B exercises these latter qualities
when he is planning to fly and even to some extent when he is
not. He habitually studies the weather and its lore, going to as
many sources as he can. From his experience in the air and his
perceptions on the ground, he develops a sense of when forecasts tend to be true and when conditions make them suspect.
Just for kicks, he might wonder about the winds aloft or feel
like comparing the media's word with Flight Service's. It does
not take much nudging for Pilot B to dial the Pilot's Automatic
Telephone Weather Answering Service (PATWAS) or the FSS
even if he is not flying that day. He is particularly interested in
pilot reports. By constantly staying in touch with the huge network of weather information surrounding him, he comes to know

the usual patterns and realizes when a spell of bad weather is coming long before Pilot A does. By building this arsenal of knowledge and instinct, he will be able to obtain better weather briefings when the chips are down.

That is crucial, for by law, though pilots are dependent mainly on information provided by weathermen, they are themselves expected to be weathermen enough to make their own go/no-go and go-where, go-when decisions. In the briefing there may be a caution "VFR flight not recommended," but it is up to the pilot to concur—and many pilots fail to do that. (For a fuller treatment of this problem, see *Crises in the Cockpit.*) Many a pilot cheerfully copies synopses, readings, and forecasts that should stimulate caution but does not comprehend the warnings that lie before him. He waits upon the briefer to say "go" or "don't go," which isn't the briefer's responsibility, and either doesn't consider what portents lie in his notations or fails to ask critical questions.

The FAA claims that it is trying to make knowledge-gathering easier for pilots, but that isn't necessarily the result of a great many changes in the FSS system that have occurred or have been planned for in recent years. "Modernization" is the buzz-word, but the effects of various FAA schemes to automate, privatize, and economize the weather-briefing system remain open to question. The main concern not only of pilots but of conscientious people within the FAA is whether the specific needs of pilots will be met by such changes as FSS reductions and increased reliance on automated services and computerization. In other words, will the pilot get what he pays for from the government he pays for?

This controversy promises to be with us for some time, and in the meantime, pilots must develop defensive strategies to get what they need.

You begin by determining what you want to know, what sources of information will provide it, and what questions you must ask to get the answers. The briefing exists for *your* benefit and protection, and you are in your rights to get from it all the help you can.

A good briefing is methodical and thorough. How you approach it should depend on the purpose of the flight. A local flight in good VFR conditions may require only listening to the PATWAS recording. After checking the day's weather on radio or TV you will find that the information contained in the PATWAS will round out the picture very well. You will learn the synoptic situation, local surface winds, winds aloft, and hourly observations from nearby airports—all without tying up the FSS. A flight beyond the neighboring hills, however, will call for a more elaborate briefing.

The Preflight Process

Before you pick up the telephone or walk into the FSS, there is much that you can do to increase your knowledge of the effective weather. The Public Broadcasting System program, *A.M. Weather*, contains current aviation weather information. There are many other sources of weather information given on TV, which can put you a step ahead in your briefing. Newspapers are not of much use, because their maps and forecasts are almost always based on upper air observations made much too early.

The process—whether it is conducted in person or over the telephone—should begin with a look at the *synoptic situation*. This is the big picture, and the questions you need to answer center on the locations and movements of low- and high-pressure systems, fronts, and general areas of marginal VFR or IFR conditions.

Next, you should focus on the *current conditions* along your route. The emphasis here is on the reported weather conditions at your departure airport, airports en route, the destination airport, and the alternate airport (if your IFR flight plan includes a destination airport expected to have a ceiling below 2,000 feet and/or visibilities below three miles from one hour before to one hour after your ETA).

An examination of the current weather is not complete until you ask about hazardous weather. Sigmets (weather advisories concerning severe weather of concern to all aircraft) and Airmets (weather advisories concerning phemonema potentially hazardous to aircraft of limited capability) should be requested. Also, remember that current weather reports often mean little by themselves. Trends over the past few hours should be studied. Current conditions in areas experiencing the weather predicted to affect your route of flight should also be checked. A review of the winds aloft is another part of the review of current conditions, but you should know that winds aloft information is frequently dated (reports often reflect information that is ten hours old) and, therefore, inaccurate.

Even though they may not necessarily deal with weather-related information, Notams also should be checked. They cover late-breaking operational and safety news.

Other almost-current weather products include radar summary charts and GOES (Geostationary Orbiting Environmental Satellite) imagery.

A review of *forecast conditions* finishes the briefing. As with synoptic and current information, several different weather information products should be consulted for forecast information. These products should include area forecasts, terminal forecasts, low- and high-level significant weather prognosis charts, winds and temperatures aloft forecasts, route forecasts, center weather advisories, stability charts, freezing level charts, and severe weather outlook charts. Some sources, such as Notams and ATC delay advisories, give information concerning current and anticipated conditions.

Obviously, the information portrayed on weather charts cannot be easily visualized in the course of a telephone weather briefing. Since most pilots obtain their briefings over the telephone, this constitutes a major shortcoming. Until the days when real-time color weather imagery fills the screen of every pilot's or FBO's personal computer, the best we can do is to sketch our interpretations of weather chart information on a map of our own.

There can be other significant drawbacks to the telephone weather briefing.

The Briefer

FSS briefers are not meteorologists. They merely convey to pilots the information prepared by meteorologists of the National Weather Service. Meteorologists in the NWS's 52 Weather Service Forecast Offices prepare various aviation forecasts and synopses several times each day. Others in the NWS's National Meteorological Center prepare aviation weather charts. Still others at the NWS's National Severe Storms Forecast Center issue convective Sigmets and convective outlooks. Additional analysis and forecasting is conducted by the NWS's National Hurricane Center, National Environmental Satellite Service, and Weather Service Offices.

Flight Service briefers work for the FAA. Their job is to translate and interpret weather information. They can provide advice, recommend against VFR flight, and use persuasion to discourage flight into conditions they believe to be beyond the capabilities of the pilot or into conditions they believe to be patently unsafe.

The ultimate go/no-go decision is up to the pilot, not the briefer.

The briefer lives in a technical world that he sometimes does not completely understand. No meteorologist, he is a quasi-expert whose briefings must conform to government specs, as set down in his operating manual.

Briefers issue three types of briefings: standard, abbreviated, and outlook. Paragraph 502 in the *Airman's Information Manual* gives the checklist for standard briefings. Your briefer will follow these guidelines when he gives you a standard briefing. You should also follow this checklist.

Standard briefings are for pilots who have not received a previous briefing. In a standard briefing, the specialist should supply information concerning adverse conditions, synoptic weather, current and forecast conditions, winds aloft, Notams, ATC delays, and *upon request,* information on military training routes and military operations area (MOA) activity. You also must ask for Class II Notams (those covering special traffic procedures, changes in airport facilities and services and FDC Notams—i.e, those with regulatory impact) and for distant Notam (L) information. Notam (L) information is given local distribution only. Your departure FSS will have to telephone the FSS serving your destination airport to find out if any local Notams are in effect.

Abbreviated briefings should be requested when you need to update a previous briefing or need only one or two specific items. Regardless of the type of information a briefer issues under an abbreviated briefing, he is supposed to advise you if adverse conditions are present or forecast.

Outlook briefings are for those times when your proposed departure is six or more hours from the time of your briefing. The briefer is supposed to give you all available forecast data pertinent to your flight, but this briefing is for planning purposes only. Pilots should receive a standard briefing prior to takeoff.

If the briefer provides all the required information, you should have enough to make an intelligent go/no-go decision. But briefers have bad days just like the rest of us, and they may not willingly give us all the information we need.

If you are not satisfied with the briefing direction, you have alternatives. You can ask for more information from the briefer. You can ask for a "ring-through" to an NWS meteorologist for more in-depth information. You can call an NWS briefer directly, or you can hang up and try another briefer.

Step by Step

There is no single correct method to review weather briefing information. What we present here has been arranged to conform to the weather briefing sequence. For most pilots, this approach will be the best. Others will rely on their own methods. The essential thing is to have a strategy for evaluating weather information, to make your briefing as thorough as your flight warrants and to stick to your briefing plan.

Begin your briefing by telling the briefer if you intend to conduct the flight IFR or VFR. Then give him your N-number, type of aircraft, estimated time of departure, proposed route of flight, proposed altitude, and destination. This will help the briefer to efficiently assemble the information you will need. As you go through the briefing, make sure you cover each of the essential categories of knowledge.

Synoptics: the Big Picture

Though the *area forecast* is a forecast, it also serves as a concise tool for summing up—in plain-language abbreviations—the conditions over an entire region. Areas of anticipated thunderstorm activity, icing, and turbulence will be mentioned. So will ceilings and visibilities (expressed as VFR or IFR) and freezing levels. The area forecast also can be helpful for pilots who want a rough idea of cloud tops. At the end of each area forecast (code abbreviation: FA) is a 12-hour outlook for the region. There are six FA regions in the conterminous United States, plus Alaska and Hawaii.

The *weather depiction chart* presents a simplified record of areas of IFR and MVFR weather, frontal positions, and surface conditions at selected airports. Because of the chart's simplicity, many pilots find it the best source of general information. Station models show type of cloud cover, ceiling height, and visibility, if under seven miles.

Surface charts provide a synoptic view, but their station models are so cluttered and full of symbology that they can be hard to read. For those who apply themselves, though, much information can be obtained. Remember that the surface chart can be four hours old by the time you see it, so the weather conditions and frontal positions will not be current.

Constant pressure charts show pressure (and, therefore, wind) patterns at various altitudes. The winds shown on constant pressure charts are observed winds aloft.

If you see a well-defined trough on the 500 millibar (approximately 18,000 feet) or 300-millibar (approximately 30,000 feet) charts, it is a sign of strong jet steam activity. If the troughs extend deep into the continent, expect any underlying fronts or low-pressure areas to become especially intense. Compare these charts with the surface chart to see if the jet stream is "feeding" low-level adverse weather.

Constant pressure chart station models also can be used to make rough predictions of icing. If the temperature aloft is between 0 and −20 degrees Centigrade and the station model is blackened (indicating a 5-degree C or less temperature/dew point spread, which suggests clouds), suspect icing conditions at the charted pressure level.

Recorded telephone weather from a VRS (Voice Response System) or PATWAS provides both current and forecast conditions in brief, recorded messages. Hourly observations for selected airports along a defined route are given, plus a brief synopsis of the current and forecast weather. Another recorded service, which provides telephone access to Transcribed Weather Broadcasts (TWEBs) aired on certain navaids, gives much the same information. For local VFR flights not requiring exhaustive information, the PATWAS or TWEB service is a hassle-free means of learning all the weather information you need to know.

Finally, there are the television weather programs. PBS's

A.M. Weather and Cable Network's Weather Channel (in that order) are the best.

Current Conditions

Once you know the synoptic weather, reports on current conditions should come as no surprise. "Current," it must be said, is a relative term. In every current weather information product we are about to describe, there is a degree of lateness. Sometimes the information lag is ten minutes (surface observations), sometimes it is 30 minutes (GOES imagery), and sometimes it is five to eight hours (constant pressure charts for winds aloft observations). It is your responsibility to seek out, evaluate, and assign priorities to the most recent information.

GOES imagery is useful for viewing the cloud conditions over the entire United States. Storm circulation often is plainly visible. A comparison of consecutive GOES imagery will give you a stop-action view of cloud system movement. Since the GOES uses infrared sensing, only the coldest clouds (i.e., those with the highest tops) will be shown. Clouds nearer to the surface may not be as clear. GOES imagery is transmitted to FSSs every 30 minutes.

Sequence reports (code abbreviation: SA) are derived from hourly field observations made by FAA or NWS personnel. SAs contain information on cloud cover, ceiling, visibility, obstructions to vision, barometric pressure, temperature, dew point, wind, altimeter setting, precipitation, and runway visual range or runway visibility. Be sure to check previous hourly reports for such trends as decreasing visibility, lowering ceilings, or a close (less than five degrees F) spread between temperature and dew point. A close temperature/dew point spread indicates a high probability of fog. An hourly observation with an SP (unscheduled special observation) or RS (scheduled observation that contains special information) prefix should raise an alarm. One or more elements of the hourly observation that have undergone significant changes can bring about the "special" designation.

The *radar summary chart,* even though it is at least two hours old by the time you see it, is another almost-current weather record. This chart shows the location, extent, and height of major cloud systems. Thunderstorm movement is plotted, along with notations on precipitation, storm severity, and life cycle. Tops are also shown, but since small water droplets do not reflect radar energy, the cloud heights reported on the chart are often misleading. The actual cloud tops may be 2,000 or more feet higher than the values depicted. Areas enclosed in dashed boxes are where a severe weather watch is in effect.

Remote radar weather display imagery is available at those FSSs equipped with radar units capable of reproducing the weather radar imagery generated by the NWS's nationwide system of weather radars. This imagery provides the pilot with real-time radar imagery.

For *observed winds aloft* information, you must rely on the constant pressure charts. The charts may be several hours old, so the information will be dated. *Sigmets* and *Airmets* are issued upon first word of adverse conditions. The briefer should mention them in every type of forecast. If he does not, ask if any are in effect. Sigmets are issued for severe turbulence, severe icing, thunderstorms, and dust or sand storms. Convective Sigmets are issued for tornadoes, lines of thunderstorms, embedded thunderstorms, and thunderstorms with radar intensities of level four or greater. Be especially alert for mention of any severe weather watch bulletins. Expected conditions requiring a severe weather watch bulletin are severe thunderstorms with damaging surface winds with gusts of 50 knots or more, and/or hail ¾-inch or more in diameter, and/or tornado activity. Airmets are issued for moderate icing, moderate turbulence, sustained winds of 30 knots or more at the surface, widespread IFR ceilings and visibilities (below 1,000 feet and/or three miles), and extensive mountain obscurement.

Moving closer to real-time observations are Pilot Reports, *pireps,* which carry the code abbreviation UA. Pireps are in-flight reports submitted by pilots. If they are recent, if they report conditions along your proposed route and altitude, and if they contain useful information, they can be of great help in a briefing. They can confirm—or disprove—a forecast. They can also tell of unforecast conditions.

There is an additional consideration. Various airplanes behave differently under the same conditions. Moderate turbulence to the pilot of a Beech Baron can feel like severe turbulence to the pilot of a Cessna 152. Conditions producing light icing on a DC-9's airframe can cause severe accumulations on a Mooney. These distinctions are the result of variations in wing loading and air foil characteristics—not necessarily the reporter's experience level. Consider your aircraft's behavior under adverse conditions before taking a pirep at face value.

Always ask for pireps. Once in flight, submit them. They are the pilot's only input to the network data base.

To obtain current surface observations without going through a briefer, you can telephone certain airports' *Automatic Terminal Information Service* (ATIS) or *Automated Weather Observation System* (AWOS) frequencies for the late surface observations. This service is in limited use now, but it will be expanded.

Forecast Weather Information

The most specific forecast information is contained in the *terminal forecasts.* These forecasts (code abbreviation: FT) cover airports and other reporting stations, and pilots planning cross-country flights must check them. IFR pilots will need to know if an alternate airport must be designated on the flight plan (i.e., when the destination airport is forecasting ceilings and visibilities at or below 2,000 feet and three miles for one hour before

to one hour after the ETA) and if the alternate they have selected is suitable. An alternate airport must be forecasting ceilings and visibilities no less than 800 feet and one mile (for airports with non-precision instrument approaches) or 600 feet and
one mile (for precision-approach fields) *at the estimated time of
arrival at the alternate.*

Terminal forecasts use an abbreviated plain-language code.
The forecasts are issued three or four times per day (depending
on the location) and are valid for 24 hours. A six-hour categor-
ical outlook is appended to the terminal forecast; this gives a
very general outlook. Watch for amended forecasts. An amend-
ment, like a special observation surface report, indicates that
significant changes have occurred in one of more elements of
the forecast.

Make sure that you have received the latest FTs before your
departure. Otherwise, your forecast data may be up to five
hours old.

Forecast winds and temperatures aloft are another must-check
forecast source, since adverse winds can lengthen a flight and
deplete fuel reserves. The winds and temperatures aloft forecast
(code abbreviation: FD) is issued twice daily, in chart and teletype form. Since the issue times are 12 hours apart, it is important to maintain a healthy skepticism. Still, FDs can give a reasonably accurate portrayal of conditions aloft.

One useful technique is to cross-check the winds aloft forecasts with winds aloft observations on recently issued constant
pressure charts. If the forecasts do not correspond with the observations, you know that the forecast was inaccurate and that
conditions may not be as predictable as the briefer suggests.

In the icing season, temperatures aloft—together with radar
summary charts, terminal forecasts, surface reports, and pireps—can give an accurate representation of potential icing altitudes.

Winds and temperatures aloft forecasts are issued in a written abbreviation code, over teletype. There is a graphic counterpart. Forecast winds aloft also are given in chart form. The charts

show winds and temperatures with station models. The wind barbs are easy to read, and they quickly indicate the strength and flow of the predicted wind fields. The drawback is that precise wind directions are missing.

Significant weather prognostic charts ("prog charts") show 12-hour and 24-hour forecast conditions on a series of four map panels. Prog charts contain information on areas and types of precipitation, turbulence, and frontal activity, along with freezing levels, areas of expected IFR and MVFR weather and notations on the movement and intensity of low- and high-pressure centers. Two of the charts address forecast surface conditions. The other two deal with anticipated weather conditions from the surface to approximately 24,000 feet. The charts show conditions as they are forecast at the valid time of the chart. Because the prognostic charts are a longer-range forecast, they should be used for general planning purposes—not as the definitive word.

For planning a flight when thunderstorms threaten, there are some additional forecast products you should use. Take the trouble to ask the briefer for this information. Briefers may not have it at hand, but they can obtain it from their many sources. First, obtain the *convective outlook* (code abbreviation: AC). This outlook is issued twice daily by the National Severe Storms Forecast Center. It describes the prospects of severe and general thunderstorms for the next 24 hours. The areas of anticipated storm activity are identified and outlined by station identifiers. If the briefer does not have the convective outlook at hand, have him call up the information from the NSSFC by using the teletype request code RQ MKC AC.

The *severe weather outlook chart* is a visual counterpart to the convective outlook. The chart consists of two maps, one for 12-hour forecast storm activity, the other for 24-hour predictions. Each map has a line with an arrowhead. The areas of expected thunderstorms are to the right of the line and are outlined with hatched symbols. Tornado watch areas are plotted. Like the prognostic charts, severe weather outlook charts are for planning purposes only. The convective outlook gives a much more detailed, shorter-term look at areas of anticipated storm activity.

The *stability chart* is another helpful tool for analyzing the probability of thunderstorms. This chart shows the locations of stable, unstable, and neutrally stable air. These areas are identified by S, U, or O symbols. Unstable air contributes to thunderstorm development.

Before you file your flight plan—IFR or VFR—be sure that you have indeed gathered sufficient weather data upon which to plan sensibly. The briefing tools and the strategy for using them described in this chapter are good only if they are thoroughly used. They demand genuine mental effort by the pilot. They can seem intimidating in their complexity. If you are getting your briefing by phone, making sure that you are given the advantages they provide can create an oppressive sense of taking up a lot of the briefer's time—a sense some briefers encourage by an impatient manner. That is their problem, not yours. That should not deter you from asking all the questions you need to pose in order to recognize conditions that can affect your safety.

Most FSS specialists appreciate talking to a pilot who knows what he is doing. They can quickly "get into" the briefing process as they see the legitimacy of your concerns.

Keep asking, and do your best to visualize the building picture as you make note of what the specialist is telling you. Think in terms of what you will need to know at each stage of your flight—especially as conditions will affect both your ability to land where you would prefer to land and to keep your fuel situation healthy. You want to avoid unpleasant surprises. If deterioriation is in the air, it is best to face up to worst-case possibilities before you commit yourself to coping with their hazards. For instance, if your IFR primary destination is in real danger of going under, provide for alternates that promise to remain good and that you can reach without having to penetrate heavy frontal activity to get there.

When you have your information gathered and your plans made, you will then have to confront the actual weather and possibly revise your scheme. That is one of the necessary elements of command, which we will discuss in the following section. Still, having made the most of your groundborne partnerships before going should make the job of command easier.

Part Four
QUESTIONS OF COMMAND

12
En Route Decisions

When we take command of an airplane, we always carry with us a crew of one who has to be kept in check—that is the devil within us all, a flier who is capable of recklessness, stupidity, or simple rebellion against good sense and legitimate authority. As we plan our flights in our dens or living rooms, we tend to be conservative, thoughtful, cool-headed, and safety-minded. However, under the stress of a flight that is not panning out as planned, many a pilot has given in to the negative side of his or her personality. A flight is, after all, a series of decisions—some crucial, most small—to follow through as planned or to take an alternate course of action.

It is central to a sound handling of command responsibility to know when to be self-reliant and when to call on help—and to be able to judge if the help you are given will increase or decrease your safety. The two areas where such considerations come most to the fore are coping with deteriorating weather and being lost aloft.

As we shall see in two forthcoming incident accounts, knowing how to seek help and whether to trust it can call for the sensitivity of a diplomat and the sagacity of a Wall Street lawyer. First, pilot Don Bragg reports how a sudden weather change can jolt a pilot into seeking help from the ground:

It was my wife's birthday, and a long weekend trip to Reno was the perfect gift. We would stop at the weather station to get a preliminary briefing and then look over and load the airplane. At sunrise, we would leave Long Beach, stay east of the Sierra Nevadas and follow Highway 395 up the Owens Valley. Three and a half hours, and the two of us would be eating breakfast in Reno. The plan worked fine until we got the weather briefing. The high-pressure system was going to hold the good weather for the weekend—calm winds and good visibility. Our hopes for perfect weather soon were tarnished when we heard the phrase "early morning marine layer"—when the Los Angeles Basin looks like a bowl of potato soup, a VFR flight often will be delayed for many hours.

As we loaded the airplane, we noticed that the clear sky displayed more glitter than Los Angeles normally saw. The airplane was loaded, fueled, and ready to go. We didn't want to eat tomorrow's lunch at home. Fox Field, Lancaster, was only 25 minutes away, but it was outside the basin. We decided to spend the night there and escape the marine layer.

The engine purred, the sky didn't shake, and we thought that we could see a million square brightly moonlit miles. Time passed quickly—Lancaster didn't seem 25 minutes away. Didn't we just leave Long Beach?

"Twelve o'clock, just below the horizon, that has to be California City. Let's sleep there and be that much closer for tomorrow."

"That glow over the horizon, it has to be Bishop, and we'll be halfway. Now that we are already halfway, there is no sense in stopping." The airplane sounded good, the flying was the best possible. We'd sleep in Reno.

Sunday afternoon came too soon. We should have been in the air instead of packing suitcases. The weather briefing was the same one we'd had in Long Beach: more high pressure and severe clear. I asked about the western side of the Sierras, looking for variety, and learned that it was also clear. The only adverse report was "thin scattered" over the Tehachapi Mountains, a low range that sometimes has notoriously bad weather. We crossed to the west, over Lake Tahoe, and began following the VORs down the central valley. The last half of the trip was to be at night, which should not have been a problem, since the entire trip north had been made at night. Besides, by the time we were to enter darkness, we should have been able to see the glare from the Los Angeles power display.

The flight was peaceful and soothing. The moon wasn't quite as bright as it was on the previous flight, which made it easier to see the little lights of scattered farms. The instruments were all in their places. My wife had closed her eyes and was just beginning to sleep.

All at once, the windscreen turned white. My world ended three feet in front of my face! The shock lasted for what seemed to be several minutes before I realized that I was flying in cloud. Where had it come from? I still had 20 minutes to go before I was to reach the Tehachapi range.

As I began to calm down, I checked the gauges. My wings were level. My airspeed was the same. My altitude had not changed. This would be easy. All I had to do was to complete a one-eighty. Every book that I had read had promised that this would get me out. Carefully, I started to turn, and the turn was good. I didn't want to declare an emergency because I would have to confess that I was cloud flying, a definite VFR violation.

It is hard to judge time when you are in a foreign environment, but I knew that I already had spent more time in a northbound cloud than in the southbound cloud that I sought to escape. Now was the time to talk to someone! I had been listening to Bakersfield Flight Service for the past hour, so they were the logical choice. When I called, a cheerful voice responded. I explained my little problem. The problem suddenly grew when he asked, "Where are you?" I thought that I had a reasonable idea, but in reality, I knew that I couldn't have guaranteed my position to be correct within a hundred miles.

Flight Service then had me start a radio count so that they could get a fix on my position. While I counted, I turned on the DME, which, until then, I hadn't needed. After the count, I asked for the Bakersfield VOR frequency so that I could use it as a cross check on the VOR that I was navigating with. Flight Service answered with the frequency and also suggested that I talk with Center. I really didn't want to tell anybody else about my transgression, but then I realized that Center probably already knew, since my transponder was screaming 7700.

I have never found Center to be as respectful as they were that night. For the only time in my flight career thus far, they did not answer with "One-Eight Sierra, stand by." Instead, the controller asked me how much instrument flight experience I had. When I told him that I had three and a half hours as a student pilot, the voice on the radio replied, "No problem." Its doubtful tone, however, said, "Good luck."

The voice also assured me that I was showing on their radar. I offered that I should be 55 nm from the Bakersfield VOR on the 285-degree radial. When Center confirmed my position, I knew I had it made. The airplane was running fine, and I knew where I was. Their next question was the hard one: "What are your intentions?" My intention was to sink into a soft, low bed—but I hadn't thought about *where*. But then an airliner en route reported that Bakersfield was clear. I headed for the VOR.

The clouds should have been breaking any minute. It had been 40 minutes since I first had entered the cloud. As I closed in on my destination, I began to think that instrument flying was easy. Just as my lost confidence was returning, the drone of the engine was broken by a loud "crack!" Excess ice being flung back at us by the prop. Suddenly my wife noticed that her side window was no longer white, and I could see out my side window. Why was the windscreen still white? The truth hit hard: The whole airplane was covered with a layer of ice! We needed to find warmer air.

Slowly, I started to descend. I could see the lights of Bakersfield through the side window. I started to decrease my airspeed so that I could lower my landing gear and flaps. I knew that I was slowing down—so why wasn't my airplane slowing down? It *was* slowing, but the airspeed indicator was showing full cruise speed. I realized that the pitot tube was frozen! For the first time since I had entered the cloud, I understood what fright could be. I saw myself attempting to land at an unfamiliar airport, at night, with no airspeed indication and no vision to the front.

Nature finally cooperated as I continued to descend. The windscreen slowly began to clear. The airspeed indicator began to register when I was on short final. The landing was smooth.

After I shut down the systems, I thought about the two men I had talked with on the radio. I wanted to thank them. The man at Center was in a building with his radar, perhaps hundreds of miles away; the specialist at Flight Service was there on the field. I knew that the FAA would want my license, but this man wasn't the FAA; he was the voice that had been there to help. The FAA has never said anything about the incident, although they really couldn't add to the lessons that I learned that night. If I ever fly into a cloud again, I will turn the necessary 180 degrees—plus 5 degrees more. That night I must have been flying parallel to the cloud bank, and when I made my turn, my new course kept me in the cloud. Five more would have taken me across my old course into clear air. I also now keep my position accurately plotted. I also learned not to fly cross-country at night. Some of the route I took would be hard to land on by day; darkness would have made an emergency landing a losing gamble. Also, in my flying there are no schedules, no time limits. If I am late or the workload becomes too heavy or if weather threatens, *I don't have to go.*

Differences in Perception

There are some pilots about whom fate has decreed that they will taste in rich measure the burdens, limits, and triumphs of command early in their flying careers. Stephan P. Barnicle was introduced in quick time to emergency problem solving:

Ceilings were at 10,000 feet with 12 miles visibility, according to the Flight Service Station just over the hill at Bradley International, in Windsor Locks, Connecticut. On this side of the ridge, it looked even better; a great day for my first solo cross-country. Having been shut out by the weather three times before, my instructor and I both were anxious for me to complete this next milestone in my quest for the license.

My flight plan called for a leg down to Westerly, Rhode Island, and then over to Bridgeport, Connecticut, and back home to 4B9 in Simsbury, Connecticut. It was a lovely flight, which I had taken once before with my CFI as a practice run. The FSS, however, informed me that Westerly was under a blanket of fog that had blown in off the Sound. My CFI signed me off to Bridgeport and Bradley as an alternate, since skies were clear at both locations.

Within minutes, I was off—on my own for the first time, away from the familiar hills, towns and reservoirs that comprised the womb in which my knowledge and flight skills had been nurtured for the past several months. Soon, even the long ridge leading back to the familiar landing strip had shrunken into the landscape. After informing Flight Service of my departure and activating my VFR flight plan, a kind inquiry followed: "Is there anything else I can do for you?"

"Negative," was my confident reply.

"Then have a good trip, and don't forget to close your flight plan when you're back on the ground."

"Thank you," I replied. How refreshing it was to hear the people at the FSS speak in English! Truly on my own, I called on new-found skills to keep track of my progress across once-familiar terrain. I had driven that route so often in a car—how different could it be, from 3,500 feet?

Changing back to the departure frequency of Bradley's TRSA, which had me on advisories, I was informed, "Eight-Seven-One, you are leaving our advisory area, frequency change approved, squawk 1200." I acknowledged and tuned to the Bridgeport VOR, which is on the airport. I was right on the 210-degree bearing that I intended to follow in. How reassuring.

As my attention was held by such cockpit activities, not to mention reaching and maintaining altitude and establishing engine settings and directional control, I hardly noticed the decrease in visibility. At first, I chalked it up to gaining altitude. After all, I had been above 3,000 feet only three or four times, and never in haze. I assumed it to be normal visibility. I continued to follow the VOR signal, since I was sure that I was more than halfway to touchdown at Bridgeport.

As the flight progressed, my checkpoints became lost in the haze. I would have lost sight of the highway, which should have been to the west of me, if I hadn't stayed right over it. It was time to drop down below 3,000 feet. With only about ten miles to go, I assumed there would be plenty of air below. At 2,500 feet, the landmarks were clear. The airport should have been just ahead, but I couldn't see it. (It is large enough to be seen easily from that distance on a clear day, sitting out on a point, surrounded on three sides by water.) "How could I miss it?" I wondered, but all I could see was a light gray haze that looked more like fog.

Tuning in on ATIS, I learned that Bridgeport had a 10,000-foot ceiling, with a 4,000-foot scattered layer and 12-mile visibility. I began to wonder if I were at the right airport. Checking the ADF reassured me that I was on course. I should have been six or seven miles out, but ahead of me all I could see was blank sky. It looked like clouds all the way to the surface. I tuned to the tower, which was reporting 10,000, with 4,000 scattered and 10-mile visibility. What do I do? Do I turn back to Simsbury? I'm only minutes from the runway. It looks like clouds ahead, but I'm at 1,500 feet now, and the tower reports 4,000 feet scattered and *10-mile* visibility. That's twice as far as I am from them. I'm a novice—I guess I just don't know good flying weather when I see it.

As those thoughts rushed through my head, I suddenly ran into NOTHING!—everything was gone! The ground, the sky, up, down, everything beyond the nose and the wing tips was gone. I knew I was in cloud and totally on instruments. My initial panic reminded me of my classroom instructor's words, "When you fly inadvertently into bad weather, PANIC—*P*osition, *A*ltitude, *N*ature of emergency, *I*ntentions, *C*omply. Fly to the good weather." A quick 180 and I would be out of the soup and into better weather in short order.

It was time to ask for assistance. Calling the tower, I informed ATC that I was a student pilot on my first solo cross-country, five miles north of the airport with little or no visibility and no airport in sight. The controller told me that Bridgeport had 4,000-foot scattered and 10-mile visibility, except off to the southeast. Perhaps I should contact New York Center to verify my position. Several calls to Center produced no response. Tuning back to Bridgeport Tower, I heard two or three pilots reporting a 700-foot overcast layer north and east of the airport. The tower still claimed to have 4,000 and 10. Out from under this carpet of gray I saw another single climbing into the hazy sky. Dropping down to 700, I thought I might get in the same way that he got out. But at 700, the layer was still below me, although I dimly saw the city beneath it.

Time to go home, I decided. I wasn't flying into Bridgeport—I was not even sure of where I was. Retuning my OBS, I found that I was just west of the 030-degree radial that I wanted to follow back up north. As began to turn, my left wing pointed directly at Sikorsky's Heliport, so I was where I should be. I just needed to work back the way I came, figuring time checks in my head, since I had not planned out this leg of the trip. As I continued to monitor Bridgeport, ATC reported, "Bridgeport is below VFR minimums." It was good that I had not landed there, for I would have been stuck for the night.

The flight home was low and slow—few landmarks were visible. The ride was bumpy, the cockpit was hot, and I had done more flying than I cared to. Then the ADF went crazy. I was out of the range for the altitude. Now what? Nerves frayed, checkpoints gone, VOR out of range—Where am I? I wondered, almost panicking again. I decided to maintain my heading and hope that something familiar would appear. I checked the time; it seemed I should be getting close to home, but I could see nothing but trees and hills that all looked alike. I thought that I must have been west of my course, because there was little sign of population; the area east of my course was heavily populated. If I were on course, I should recognize some landmarks.

Just as I was about to lose hope, I saw a reservoir that looked familiar and just beneath it a church where I had once worked. "Home," I sighed. I was on the ground in a matter of minutes, the terror finally behind me.

But why the terror? How did I let myself get into this uncomfortable situation? Why didn't I establish contact with an FSS at the first sign of trouble? Most important, why did I let myself fly into weather beyond my understanding? One can never let his judgment be clouded by his desire to reach a location. Nor can one forget that the primary responsibility for the flight rests with the pilot-in-command. No matter what ATC said, I knew what I was seeing, and I should have stayed clear of it. And I should have remembered those helpful voices on the FSS frequency: They would have reduced my apprehension with positive suggestions for an appropriate course of action. That is why they are there.

This student pilot's confusion stemmed in part from his not knowing that visibility reports at airports cover the clearest semicircle on the horizon. The observer scans the horizon, picks out the farthest visible landmark and then determines the farthest visible landmarks 90 degrees to the right and left of the originally chosen landmark. The distances to these landmarks are then averaged, although the reported visibility is usually the maximum distance from the station. Essentially, conditions are reported that directly affect airport operations; additional data occurs in addenda. A few miles can make a difference between what pilots *at* and *near* the field see.

Decisions in a Disappearing World

The above account has elements of incidents that do not turn out happily. Here is a typical sequence of events: A private pilot with less than 500 hours flying time plans a long cross-country flight in marginal visibility or at night. He is in a hurry to get to his destination and is not as thorough as he should be; he treats any forecasts of possible IFR conditions optimistically. He takes off and, after flying for a few hours, realizes that he has lost track of his position. What is worse, he has run into the IFR weather the briefer had mentioned. What he knows of VOR orientation procedures vanishes as he begins to panic. With a minimal background in instrument flying, he is now on the gauges, lost and confused. Instead of taking any corrective action, the pilot flies on until he either runs out of fuel or flies into the ground.

Every year, there are approximately 20 fatal accidents that come under the "lost" category. In a sample period, from 1978 to 1980, there were 54 such accidents. Of these, 33 involved private pilots with less than 500 hours; all but ten were noninstrument-rated; 35 accidents occurred to noninstrument-rated pilots in IFR condtions.

In practically every case, the pilots failed to perform three important lost procedures: climb, confess, communicate.

Climbing not only will help you to keep clear of terrain and obstacles, it will give you a better vantage point to locate features identifiable on a sectional chart. A higher altitude also increases the range of radio transmission and reception. Whether to climb will depend on sky conditions, for entering a broken or overcast layer is asking for worse trouble.

Confess and communicate speak for themselves, although many pilots in trouble are reluctant to speak for themselves. We may recall the pilot who feared letting ATC know he was lost in cloud. Momentarily, at least, his license was more important than life. Command responsibility includes a willingness to do what may be inconvenient or uncomfortable but is necessary to survival. Good commanders are willing to "bite the bullet" and "take their lumps" in order to protect those in their charge. So rather than flying on, hoping that something recognizable will show up, admit your predicament to a FSS or an ATC facility.

Use the 121.5 emergency frequency if necessary—that is what it is for—and request help. Also, unless you are sure that panic will ensue, engage your passengers in looking for landmarks. A passenger's chance spotting of a town, a city, an airport, or a highway can be a lifesaver.

Pilotage, an Invaluable Option

Over the years, flying by pilotage has become neglected as more and more electronic navaids have filled our panels. Navigation is now high technology: Hop in, dial up this or that gizmo, and go, often with an autopilot to turn you into a passenger. But then one day, the lights go out and the needles fall dead or go nuts, and you, the pilot-in-command, are on your own with only the terrain, your sectional—you do have one, don't you?—and skills you may not have used since those long-gone few hours when your student ticket was new.

Being lost is a relative matter. It is one thing to be lost during the day over terrain that presents many identifiable checkpoints. It is another to be lost by dismal day or at night over mountainous terrain, where checkpoints cannot be seen at all and where a course error of just a few miles could have serious consequences. Before you take off—IFR or VFR—think about all of the possibilities should you lose track of your position or use of the electronic aids upon which you so greatly depend.

Pilotage is too often taught as a matter of preselecting a series of easily identifiable discrete features on a VFR chart and planning and flying a trip along that route. Simple in concept, but not often realistic in practice. What may look to be obvious from the charts may be anything but that in less than ideal visibility. If the sun is at the wrong angle or any of a number of other possibilities—say, snow-covered terrain—develop, "well-defined" ground features can disappear. Pilots have become disoriented trying to find VOR antenna domes, church steeples, antenna towers that are more prominent on the chart than on the landscape, railroad tracks long rusted or grown over, or drive-in theaters still active on the charts but long gone out of business and out of sight. Yet these pilots were in view of major towns or cities or other prominent reference points.

For navigation, a checkpoint does not need to be a finite point, and it is usually easier to find if it is bulbous. An airport at a city is a checkpoint, but so is the city itself, and it will be much easier to spot. Avoid choosing villages where two roads intersect—there are too many of them. Use small checkpoints only if there is something else in the big picture that gives the spot an unmistakable label: a major highway, a powerline, a distinctive body of water, and so forth. Large checkpoints are not good for monitoring groundspeed, but if you are trying to work out where you are, knowing your speed is less critical than locating yourself as quickly as you can.

Of course, Murphy's Law says that if your navaids malfunction, it will be when you are in a totally unfamiliar area with no identifiable landmark or checkpoint in view. Here, logic can help. Initially, your best bet is to steer a compass course as straight as possible in the direction you want to go, while you figure your next move. At a flown distance of 60 miles, even if you are five degrees off course, you will only be five miles off, and you generally will not be flying VFR with much less than six or seven miles visibility.

One of the easiest techniques for finding your way visually is to "box" your destination. Look for something on the chart that you cannot miss, such as a major highway (preferably one on each side of your rough course line). As long as you stay near this feature, it will be difficult to become disoriented. Add some prominent features that put a limit on your route and "box in" your destination, and the biggest part of the battle is won. Or you can just follow a nearby highway to that destination. Landmarks for this boxing technique will depend on the features peculiar to the region. Along the corridor from Boston to Washington, D.C., the only usable highways are four-lanes, divided. The smaller highways that might be prominent on a chart for Arizona won't show on these metropolitan area charts, because there are so many of them.

Cluttered features in some parts of the country can deceive any pilot. Central New Jersey is a notorious case. It is full of horse-training complexes, so the charts show several conspicuous track ovals—in fact, more than 50—a hopeless clutter.

As you get closer to your destination, the detail on the chart begins to help you pinpoint your airport's location. Use any helpful checkpoint, but do not make the absolute decision, in advance, as to what landmarks you will use. Learn to spot conspicuous landmarks on the ground and then find them on the chart—not the other way around.

If you must choose between striking off in a straight line across inhospitable terrain or taking a less direct, somewhat ragged course with good landmarks, choose the course with the landmarks. After all, even when you are using VORs, whether on or off the established airways, you probably are not flying a straight line. Landmark to landmark: The principle is the same, whether by pilotage or electronics.

The close kin to pure pilotage is dead reckoning, which is based on the principle that if you fly long enough at a certain airspeed and in the proper direction, you will arrive at your destination in the anticipated time. In the old days, compass, clock, and airspeed indicator—plus a sense of the wind—were the equipment needed, and fundamentally they still are. We now use directional gyros, but must keep them checked against the magnetic compass. If we fly the VORs without DME, we determine our groundspeed and therefore the wind by timing ourselves from omni (checkpoint) to omni. If you are IFR and your nav radios go out, dead reckoning becomes a critical recourse.

Locating by VOR

If you have working navaids but are lost, dial in the frequency of a nearby VOR station. You can select it from within the area on the sectional you are likely to be. It helps to fly high while you are doing it, for the higher you are, the longer the range of your reception. When you have identified the station, center the CDI needle FROM and note the bearing. If the needle centers at 090 degrees FROM, you are due east of that station. Now select another nearby VOR, preferably one on the same side of the first VOR as you, identify it and center the CDI needle FROM. Note the bearing. By drawing lines along the two radials defining your position, you can locate yourself at the point where they intersect. The procedure is simple, but be careful to identify the stations, select FROM indications, and watch out for a flag on the gauge, which would mean that a signal is not usable. Don't think only in numbers—090 degrees, 256 degrees—but also in terms of cardinal directions—due east, west-southwest. When you are located, plot a new course to your destination, starting either by flying to a VOR or intercepting a radial and proceeding from there.

When It All Seems Hopeless

In a worst-case situation, where you cannot receive a reliable VOR signal or identify any checkpoints, or when night or clouds are closing in, and you are low on fuel, there are two options.

One is to fall back on the three Cs. Once you have contacted a FSS or ATC facility, steps will be taken to identify your location and send you on your way to the nearest airport. If you have a transponder, this procedure is fairly simple. You dial in the code they specify and a controller can follow your progress.

Without a transponder, you will be given a direction-finder (DF) steer. For identification, you will be asked to key your microphone for five to ten seconds; DF equipment works by detecting the location of voice transmissions. Once the equipment locks onto your voice transmission, the specialist can give you headings to an airport.

The other option is a precautionary landing. This would be in order if fuel exhaustion or some other emergency situation—such as the approach of a thunderstorm—is imminent. Perform an approach to the landing site you select using a standard traffic pattern, complete with downwind, base, and final legs, and try to remain as cool and alert as you can.

The best way to avoid becoming lost is to exert your command judgment vigorously from the moment you begin to plan the flight. Demand of your navigator—you—that he have a navigation log with courses, headings, and ETEs for all checkpoints, with headings compensated for magnetic variation, compass deviation, and winds aloft. You as captain will be responsible for checking on Notams for VOR outages and other navigation-affecting changes. Last but never least, you will make sure you have adequate fuel *and reserves* for the flight you are planning. And if you keep safe principles in your mind as you plan, don't forget to fly by them as well.

Pilot James B. Freed discovered how lofty principles can be overwhelmed by the presumed needs of the hour and how such forgetfulness can turn against the guilty pilot and his kin:

I took my first flying lesson on my sixteenth birthday. Thirty-two years later—after college, medical school, and 110 hours of off-and-on instruction—I finally took my checkride. Balding, a little overweight, with four children, a wife, and a beautiful Cherokee Six, I finally did it. I remember the private pilot flight test. Preflight—careful and methodical. I found a small nick in the prop. "No, Sir, Mr. Examiner, we don't take off until this is checked." An hour later, we found an A&P who fixed the propeller with a flat file. "You can't be too careful," I informed the examiner. We flew, and I passed the test.

The examiner shook my hand and said, "Congratulations, you are a private pilot. You sure are a careful one."

The next day, I almost killed my sons, myself, and, quite possibly, some innocent motorists because of my carelessness.

We left Harrisburg, Pennsylvania, for Rochester, New York, that morning, the day after I got my license. After 110 hours, I felt ready to fly with my sons, just the three of us, alone. The boys and I had studied the winds aloft, Sigmets, pireps, and forecasts. We all agreed, "Nice and clear at five-and-a-half. Let's go to Rochester and watch Mary Sue (my daughter) graduate from high school." At the FSS, we learned that the weather featured 9,000 feet and 10 miles all the way to Rochester. Nick preflighted, and Steve double-checked. I did it again.

Level at 5,500 feet out of Harrisburg, but not for long. When the DME showed 30 miles from the Harrisburg VOR, we were down to 2,000 in heavy haze following the Susquehanna River to Williamsport, Pennsylvania. "Okay, boys," I said, "what's the first rule when flying VFR?" In unison, the boys answered, "Never run the scud." They were right—so down we went.

"But what about Mary Sue's graduation?" I consulted with my seven-year-old co-pilot. "Nick, we've got mountains on the left, mountains on the right, and what's that stuff up there?"

"Scud."

"Should we keep going toward Rochester?" I asked.

"Never run in scud," came back through the intercoms. Down at Williamsport and over to the FSS.

The gentleman at Flight Service was kind. He showed my sons the Teletype machines and the projection charts and gave them the facts. "Boys, the ceiling is 2,500 here. Is your dad an instrument pilot?"

"Not yet, but we've got to get to Mary Sue's graduation."

We hung around that FSS for three hours. At last the man told us, "Okay, things are clearing up. Ceiling is now 5,000 from here to Elmira and CAVU in Rochester."

We took off from Williamsport and were into heavy haze 20 minutes later. Out of 3,500 to 2,000 feet by Elmira. I thought, "Well, it must be local. I swore I would never be a scud runner, but I'll just stay between these hills for a little while." I also thought, "Do a 180; go back." But I couldn't go back because there just was not enough room to turn the airplane around between those hills. We were slowly getting lower. I swore I'd never do it. I had spent 110 hours training to be safe, sensible, prepared, and careful, and I was scud running at 40 feet agl! I almost hit a bridge, and just ahead I could not even see the highway.

I hit the three knobs to full rich mixture, full propeller, and full throttle, got off that road and went into the soup for the first time ever. The last thing I could see and recognize was a tree ten feet off my left wing. My trusty co-pilot and observer hadn't even twitched. Nick said, "Hey, Dad, it's dark outside!"

Scared to death, I rasped, "It's okay—maybe we aren't going to crash after all." And he said—God bless all seven-year-old co-pilots —"Okay, I'm going to take a nap now. I'm sleepy." From the rear of the airplane, my eight-year-old asked, "Are we almost there, Dad?"

I scanned the dials. A Cherokee Six shouldn't climb at 1,500 fpm, down to 1,000. Twenty-five pounds manifold pressure and 2,500 rpm. Can't see any cars or bridges, can't see anything! Time to call for help. Rochester Approach was on the Number 1 com. In as calm and quiet a voice as I could summon, I whispered, "Rochester Approach, Cherokee 56095." A kind, lifesaving voice replied, "Cherokee 56095, Rochester Approach."

As calmly as possible, I screamed into the microphone, "Rochester—I just got my license yesterday! I'm in the clouds—I don't have an instrument rating. Shall I call Mayday?"

A calm voice responded, "Well, can you fly straight and level?" "Yes."

"Continue on your present course and climb at 500 feet per minute?"

"I think so."

"Well, just do that, and in a few minutes I'll give you a nice surprise."

"Yes, sir. But, sir, you don't understand, sir. I'm in the middle of a dense cloud and I don't know where I am and I've got my two little kids with me and I just got my private pilot's license yesterday!"

And that nice controller said, "Where are you from?"

"Harrisburg, Pennsylvania."

"Is that right? I'm from Allentown."

"Well, I was born in Allentown." We chattered on, and he had me squawk and ident, and then he said, "Get ready—here comes your surprise!"

Thirty seconds later, I broke out of the tops at 7.500 feet into clear, bright, beautiful sunshine. I said, "Thank you, sir. I'm okay now, but could you tell me what do I do next?"

The voice said, "Just fly 360 degrees, and you'll get your big surprise." That was easy. I could see; clouds below and clear sky above. The kids were still sound asleep.

In about ten minutes, the clouds disappeared below. I could see from the ground all the way to heaven. Severe clear.

I landed at Rochester and immediately woke my crew.

"Dad, are we there now?"

I said, "Yep, let's go to the graduation. And clean up those candy wrappers on the floor."

My logbook for that day shows 25 minutes of actual instruments, and every one was spent talking to an air traffic controller. I don't know his name, but he saved three lives that day.

I have my instrument training now. I'll never have to run the scud again. But I won't forget how easy it is to fall into the trap. And whenever I talk to a controller, I'll remember—and when my boys learn to fly, I'm going to teach them to say, "Thank you, sir," and really mean it. And I'm also going to teach them—even if I have to tattoo it on their arms—"Fly! and learn to love the sky! But never— *never*—be a scud runner."

Successful command means keeping up our defenses against temptations to do dangerous things. These temptations are all the more insidious and compelling because they hit us by surprise. We plan the perfect flight—or at least near perfect—and then something goes down or something comes up, and we have to make quick, disciplined decisions. It isn't that it is easy to judge wrong—the pilots we have flown with in this chapter knew better and heard a still, small voice of reason even as they made the wrong move. It isn't all that easy to foul up; it's that we are so capable of it, in spite of ourselves. Our defenses are at times just not solid enough.

Is the reason that there are things our instructors don't tell us, or do we need *within ourselves* to keep preparing for command in the real world?

13
Command and the Real World

At the heart of command lies a chain of paradoxes: Command is both an absolute office, defined by written rules and honored custom, and a fragile thing in a real world the rules try to encompass; the status of command may not in reality be the power to control; the power to control may lie elsewhere—or nowhere. For monarchs and presidents, for Napoleon and Captain Bligh (and Captain Ahab, for that matter), for countless generals and executives, these contradictions have been agonizing facts of life. So are they, too, for pilots-in-command, from skippers of supersonic bombers and transoceanic clippers to lone captains of piston singles. For the airman-in-charge, the issue is that though captains propose, events may contrarily dispose— and the outcome usually depends on the wisdom and discipline each commander brings to his or her office.

The Federal Aviation Regulations lay down two essential principles of command: "The pilot-in-command of an aircraft is directly responsible for, and is the final authority as to, the operation of that aircraft." FAR 91.3 elaborates that "in an emergency requiring immediate action, the pilot-in-command may deviate from any rule" governing operations and flight rules "to the extent required to meet that emergency." The pilot may then have to account for the deviation. The point is that, under the law, command carries an ultimate authority balanced against an accountable responsibility to apply that power with proper regard for the rules and reality.

Usually, it is failure to achieve or maintain that balance that lies behind accidents attributed to pilot error. Defensive flying is dedicated to maintaining that balance, to retaining effective and safe command of a flight.

Pilots concern themselves with various threats to their command authority. Some of these threats are real, others are only perceived, and it is important to be able to distinguish between the two.

Among the perceived "encroachments" upon command prerogatives we have already discussed are those by ATC controllers, Flight Service and Weather Service briefers, and even maintenance personnel, people whose prescribed responsibilities, general expertise, or knowledge of the immediate situation invest them with leverage in affecting our command decisions.

Yet such intrusions really involve partnerships, which, when they work well—as they usually do—make flying safer and smoother than potential dangers would otherwise allow. It is, however, still up to the pilot-in-command to be alert, knowledgeable, judicious, and purposeful in exercising his command responsibility to keep these associations "honest."

Real threats to command authority—in the actual, physical sense that one may have command status over an aircraft but not a genuine control over the situation—are far more dangerous. Here, true command authority may be lost, but the weakened captain remains responsible and accountable for what he does or fails to do. In this gloomy realm of flying, we find pilots deviating hazardously from the rules and good sense. This is often a place of desperate adjustments or blind accommodations, a place of bizarre choices. Frequently, the pilots themselves create the emergencies.

As we have said, a flight is a series of connected decisions which begin with the first intention to make the flight. The devil that betrays us counsels decisions to cut corners and render ourselves defenseless against unawareness, "glitches," and varieties of panic. What we don't know can overwhelm us before we find out about it; it can pounce upon us too late to be warded off or remedied. One lethal unknown is the extent of our own limitations—or our incapacity to admit them to ourselves and others. As a result, we assume titular command of our aircraft, but we also wrongly assume we have command of the flight:

• After a Thanksgiving dinner with friends in California, the pilot of a Cessna 150L prepared for a 30-minute flight back home. He had a private pilot certificate and 87 total hours. It was nighttime, and dense fog was forming in the area. There is no record that he obtained a weather briefing, but he did talk with another pilot, who had just landed and who, upon learning that the Cessna pilot was not instrument qualified, advised him not to take off. The Cessna pilot replied that he could see the moon through the fog and would climb straight ahead until he was on top of the fog layer. He told the other pilot that he had left the Cessna's master switch on, depleting the battery charge, and asked for assistance in hand-propping the airplane. The other pilot declined, but a service attendant helped with the job. The pilot lost control of the airplane on takeoff. The Cessna crashed nose-down and right-wing-low at a high rate of speed. The pilot and his passenger were both killed in the crash.

Weak Links in the Command Chain

Blind overreaching stretches the chain of situation control beyond the breaking point. New pilots often do that, and retribution often comes swiftly, as it does for pilots who are experienced enough to know better but are not sufficiently in command of themselves to defend against overconfidence.

It is rare when an accident can be ascribed to one factor, to one decision in the series, to one link in the chain of command dispositions. Still, the chain can withstand only a few weak links—which ones, who can know? (There is truth in the old saw that a pilot who does not discover at least one mistake or learn at least one lesson during any particular flight is not paying attention.) Too many weak links, or a bad enough weakness in one, and an accident occurs.

Consider the crash of a commuter airplane in Vieques, in August 1984. There were three weak links in the chain: an aircraft loaded beyond its weight-and-balance envelope; contaminated fuel; and a commercial pilot who had neither the training nor the experience required by regulations to conduct the operation to which he was assigned.

Vieques is a small island off the southeastern coast of Puerto Rico. At the time, air service to the main island and to St. Croix, Virgin Islands, was provided by Vieques Air Link (VAL) with a Piper Cherokee Six, a half-dozen twin-engine Britten-Norman Islanders, and one three-engine Britten-Norman Trislander.

On the morning of August 2, one of VAL's pilots flew a short, round-robin charter flight in one of the Islanders. He was 20 years old. He had joined VAL four months earlier, after earning his commercial certificate and instrument and multi-engine ratings. He had logged about 500 hours when he joined the airline. The total included six hours of multi-engine time—in a Piper Twin Comanche used in his training for the rating. In four months with VAL, he added 200 hours, including about 180 in the company's multi-engine planes. He was pursuing a flight instructor's certificate and had already started boning up for his airline transport certificate exams.

After returning to Vieques, the pilot taxied the Islander to the fuel pumps, where it was serviced with 60 gallons of fuel, 30 in each wing tank. The Islander was scheduled for a flight to St. Croix. At about the same time, the company's Trislander also was refueled.

Earlier that morning, a check of the fuel storage tank by a ramp inspector for the Puerto Rico Ports Authority had shown one and a half inches of water at the bottom of the tank—an inch more water than had been in the tank when it was checked the day before. The weather at Vieques is usually clear, but the island does experience occasional rain showers and thunderstorms. The island had been drenched by a heavy shower the previous night. More than two inches of rain had fallen, and it is believed that some of the water seeped into the fuel storage tanks. According to procedure, the tank was supposed to be manually purged of water whenever the level exceeded one inch. However, both the Islander and the Trislander were refueled before the tank was purged. An FAA inspector later filled two soft-drink bottles from the Trislander's tanks, and he estimated that the liquid was 75 percent water.

While the Islander was being refueled, the young pilot was assigned to fly the airplane, with eight passengers and some cargo, to St. Croix. Later, there was considerable debate as to whether he was qualified to conduct the flight. VAL contended that the flight technically was a VFR, on-demand air taxi flight, which could be conducted by a pilot with a commercial license. The NTSB and the FAA determined that it was a commuter flight and should have been assigned to an ATP. (It is interesting to note that VAL previously had been granted an exemption by the FAA, allowing it to use non-ATP-rated pilots for commuter operations. In its petition for the exemption, the airline said that the requirement for ATP pilots would create economic hardships for the company, as well as disrupt essential air service to Vieques. That exemption, however, had expired, and further petitions by VAL had been rejected by the FAA.)

It is not known whether the pilot realized, when he accepted the flight, that the ATP who originally was scheduled to conduct the flight had refused to take it. According to investigators, the ATP "detected major discrepancies between the airplane's proposed load and the load given to him on the manifest." The captain's skepticism initially was aroused when he walked by the Islander. He normally could walk under the airplane's horizontal stabilizer; but that morning, he found the stabilizer of the loaded airplane level with his forehead. When he challenged the weight-and-balance computations, he was assigned to another flight, and the young commercial pilot was asked to fly the Islander to St. Croix.

Reconstruction of the actual weight and balance of the Islander involved some guesswork by investigators. According to the factual report of the accident, weight-and-balance documents for the airplane were falsified. (For this and other alleged misdeeds, the ATP certificate of the airline's director of operations was revoked by the FAA.) However, after expending considerable effort to compile a true account of what was loaded into the aircraft and where, investigators estimated that the Islander was from 120 to 410 pounds over gross weight, and its center of gravity was beyond the aft limit on departure.

There is no conclusive evidence that the pilot checked the Islander's fuel or its weight and balance before taxiing out for takeoff on Vieques' 2,500-foot Runway 9.

Three weak links were about to doom what, otherwise, could have been an uneventful flight. The pilot was relatively inexperienced in multi-engine aircraft, and he did not even come close to meeting legal *minimum* requirements to conduct the flight. There was water in the Islander's fuel tanks. The aircraft was overweight and tail-heavy.

The airplane had climbed about 200 feet and was turning left for a crosswind departure when the left engine lost power due to the water-contaminated fuel. The NTSB said that the pilot did not execute the emergency procedures prescribed for handling an engine failure. Witnesses saw the Islander in a nose-high attitude, losing altitude. The airplane began to porpoise and then abruptly banked steeply to the left and crashed into the water in a near-vertical attitude, killing all aboard.

Could a properly qualified pilot have handled the emergency? Could *this* pilot have handled the engine-out if he had been better trained or if the airplane had not been overweight and tail-heavy? What would the outcome have been if the water had been detected and removed from the fuel?

Questions emerge here for all pilots. Have you established a personal program for recurrent training? Would you know what to do in an emergency in any aircraft you fly? Do you always check weight and balance and fuel? Above all, do you see these measures as part of your responsibility as pilot-in-command?

Is Currency Proficiency?

Just as governments cannot legislate morality, they cannot dictate proficiency—both these things must be exercised by the person himself. Not surprisingly, the world's major airlines go beyond regulated currency guidelines in policing the proficiency levels of their pilots. The commander who falls below the mark swiftly falls from left-seat favor. For other civilian pilots, quality control still rests in the FARs, in the checkout policies of some insurance-goaded FBOs who keep an eye on aircraft renters, and in the personal dedication of the pilots themselves. But dedication to what? In airplanes, mere zeal can kill:

• This pilot had 1,200 total hours on his commercial, instrument, and multi-engine tickets. An instructor flew with him in his Aerostar on two occasions, and later reported:

"He came to me approximately one week prior to our first flight, stating that he wanted me to fly with him to evaluate his flight performance prior to a trip he was planning to take the following week. I flew with [the pilot] on two occasions. . . . I found [the pilot] considerably deficient with respect to engine-failure emergency procedures. During both flights, I reviewed engine-out procedures with him and found weaknesses in his aircraft attitude, altitude, and directional control (both VFR and IFR), when the simulated failure occurred. Also, he displayed a lack of familiarity with the manufacturer's engine-out emergency and systems-securing checklists. With respect to IFR (with hood on) departure, en route, and approach procedures, [he] displayed numerous piloting and navigational deficiencies. The most serious problem areas I observed were his slow instrument scan and instrument approach planning. While turning, he consistently overbanked the airplane, exceeding a standard rate turn, especially during VOR radial and localizer intercepts. I was especially concerned with the overbanking, as he would then let the pitch attitude decrease, resulting in a loss of altitude.''

The instructor's statement concluded, ''I made recommendations to him concerning his future operations with the airplane. He told me he was planning to fly to the Bahama Islands in the following weekend. In response, I recommended that he make the flights under VFR conditions *only*.''

The day after receiving this advice, the pilot—accompanied by his wife—flew the Aerostar from San Diego, California, to San Antonio, Texas, operating on an IFR flight plan. At San Antonio, the pilot fueled his airplane, obtained a weather briefing and then filed an IFR flight plan for a trip to Lake Charles, Louisiana. The weather at the time was ceiling 2,200 feet overcast, visibility 10 miles. Pilot reports indicated that the tops of the overcast were at 8,000 feet.

The pilot took off at 2:25 p.m. and was issued a clearance to climb to 15,000 feet. Then his clearance was amended to maintain 5,000 feet; then the pilot was given a vector and instructed to resume his climb to 15,000. During the climb, ATC issued the pilot several additional vectors. Twelve minutes after instructing the pilot to maintain 5,000 feet, San Antonio Departure Control attempted to contact him, but he failed to respond.

Several witnesses who observed the airplane in flight stated that the engines started ''cutting out'' and that it nosed over, entered a spiral dive and crashed. One witness stated, ''I heard a small plane rev its engines twice as if it were doing aerobatics. . . . I turned to look in the direction of the plane's noise in time to see a blue-gray plane come out of the clouds, nose down and crash into the pasture approximately a mile from where I was standing. There was an explosion on impact and flames leaping higher than the trees.''

Much of the wreckage was destroyed by fire, but investigators found no discrepancies in the Aerostar's powerplants. Toxological studies showed no physiological incapacitation of the pilot or his wife. The NTSB found that the probable cause of this accident was the pilot's attempting an operation beyond his experience or ability level, improper IFR operation, and spatial disorientation.

An even more distorted assumption of command is exemplified in this incident, which is not nearly as unusual as might at first seem:

• This pilot was a corporate president, age 59, private certificate, 2,008 total hours, 543 in the Cessna 421B. Without obtaining a preflight weather briefing or filing a flight plan, the pilot—along with four of his employees—boarded the Cessna on a flight from Hampton, Virginia, to Charleston, West Virginia. The 421B took off at 6:33 p.m. in VFR conditions.

At 7:52 p.m., the pilot contacted the Charleston FSS to request the latest weather. He was advised that the most recent information, an hour old, for Charleston was ceiling 1,000 feet overcast, visibility one and a half miles in fog, wind 060 degrees at six knots. The pilot reported no difficulties.

At 7:58 p.m., the pilot contacted Charleston Approach to say that he was 36 miles east of the airport and would be landing there. A controller repeated the latest weather observation. The pilot then asked if he could be worked in for what he called an "IFR landing." The airplane was radar-identified and then given vectors for a straight-in ILS approach to Runway 23.

The Cessna followed a United Airlines Boeing 737 on the approach. Twice, a controller advised the pilot to reduce his speed because of the Cessna's proximity to the airliner. At one point, the pilot said that he was "down to a hundred" and would slow up it up a little. Two minutes later, Charleston Tower told the pilot, "Reduce [speed] as much as feasible—you're just three miles behind a United jet." The Cessna pilot then reported passing the outer marker. He was advised that the jet was on a 1.5-mile final. There were no further transmissions.

The Cessna crashed into a steep, wooded hillside just inside the outer marker. The pilot and two passengers were killed. The two rear-seat passengers survived with serious injuries.

Witnesses on the ground and the surviving passengers said that the engines sounded normal prior to the crash. The passengers said that there was no turbulence. The accident investigation turned up no mechanical defects; the ILS was within specifications; wake turbulence was ruled out; and a pathological exam disclosed no pertinent information.

The pilot's qualifications showed that he did not possess an instrument or multi-engine rating and had not held an airman's medical certificate for six years.

A former company pilot said that the Cessna pilot was good in VFR but was "a little scratchy" in instrument conditions. Although a professional pilot normally was assigned to operate the Cessna on business trips, the company's current professional pilot was not asked to make this trip.

The NTSB determined that the probable cause of the accident was the pilot's attempting an operation beyond his experience or ability level and improper IFR operation. The brief carried the notation, "Crashed 1,000 feet below glidepath."

The Ahab Syndrome

Arrogant commandatorial forays into the forbidden have caused a variety of accidents, many weather-related and others involving the strapping on of airplanes and committing oneself to operations beyond one's knowledge or experience. Such pilots resemble Captain Ahab, in Herman Melville's *Moby Dick*. Ahab, fired with zeal, determination, and a sense of possessing supreme power and righteous stuff, launches himself into a struggle against an overwhelming foe that may well destroy him and his crew. Ahab does not tell the crew about the actual conditions of their voyage until they are committed. Did the Cessna captain ever tell his passengers that he was taking them into unknown weather conditions, which might be worse than he was qualified to handle and in an airplane he was illegally commanding? His command authority was only a stupid deception. His sense of command responsibility was nil.

All pilots must look carefully to maintaining true proficiency, but instrument pilots particularly must avoid flying Ahab-like into problems they are inadequate to handle.

Here, rock-bottom currency is virtually skeletal: FAR 61.57 says that no pilot may act as an IFR PIC unless he has, within the past six months, passed an FAA-administered instrument competency check; or logged at least six hours of actual or simulated IFR flight (half may be in an FAA-approved flight simulator), and performed at least six instrument approaches (all of which may be flown in a simulator).

Legal VFR currency is just as meager: Three takeoffs and landings every 90 days; at night, three night takeoffs and landings every 90 days. Beyond that, pilots—IFR and VFR—must pass a flight review every 24 months—usually a casual exercise.

As guarantors of safety, such standards by themselves are unacceptable. For instance, regarding accidents that occurred in 1979 and 1980, the NTSB blamed 94 pilots as allegedly unqualified or not proficient—and this includes those who complied with 61.57; 32 of these accidents occurred in IFR conditions.

Why do presumably well-indoctrinated, intelligent pilots plunge in over their heads? Ego is often to blame. They share with Ahab a burning faith in the power of their will to triumph over conditions and time. They delude themselves that their instrument skills will never become rusty, that recurrent training is unnecessary. The truth is that such skills degrade rapidly, far more than the required "six-in-six" can repair. The delusion may be fostered by successful flights "on the edge" until that flight is made when skill and luck run out.

"Self-taught and self-certified" pilots follow the same pattern. Often, they ease their way into illegal IFR operations and/or aircraft for which they are not rated, determining to be cautious, careful, conservative. But the kind of Napoleonic mentality that seduces them across the line of legality shoves them across the fatal line of caution. When two such mentalities occupy the same airplane, this can easily happen:

• Two pilots and their wives departed Owensboro, Kentucky, in a Cherokee Six at 5:30 p.m. under VFR conditions, bound for a basketball game in Lexington. After the game, at 8:40 p.m., friends drove them back to the airport, encountering dense fog on the way. The pilots commented that they hoped there would be no fog at Owensboro on their return flight. They also refused an invitation to stay the night.

The pilot and his passengers took off at approximately 9:36 p.m. in VFR conditions. No flight plan had been filed, and there was no record of a weather briefing.

The flight progressed without incident until 10:33 p.m., when the co-pilot advised Evansville, Indiana, Approach Control that the flight was encountering clouds and fog at 2,000 feet, 25 miles out of Owensboro. The co-pilot requested vectors to the Owensboro VOR and later asked for an ILS approach. Twice, the pilots were asked if they wanted an IFR clearance. Each time, they rejected the idea. They were told to maintain VFR. They reported no further difficulties and did not declare an emergency. They were provided vectors to intercept the ILS at 10:42 and were told to advise Evansville Approach when the airport was in sight, since Owensboro Tower was closed for the night. At 10:44 p.m., a voice identified as the co-pilot's was heard to say, ". . . put that thing on." No further communications were received. Radar contact was lost four miles south of Owensboro's outer marker. The airplane crashed in a pasture 12 miles from the airport. All four occupants were killed.

An examination of the wreckage showed no evidence of malfunctions, and toxicological studies showed no drugs, alcohol, carbon monoxide, or any other souce of crew incapacitation.

Both men were licensed pilots. The pilot in the left front seat was not instrument-rated, but had a private certificate and 412 total hours, 130 in type. The pilot in the right front seat had obtained his instrument rating two years earlier but had kept no records of his flying time. A friend of the pilot-in-command told NTSB investigators that he had "flown with [him] in [his] aircraft before." He said that it was "common knowledge that [he] would conduct operations that were over his head."

The NTSB ruled that the probable causes of this accident were the pilot-in-command's attempting an operation beyond his experience or ability level, his continuing VFR flight into adverse weather conditions, and spatial disorientation. Contributing factors were listed as inadequate preflight preparation and/or planning, a low ceiling, fog, the lack of a weather briefing, and weather conditions slightly worse than forecast. Weather conditions shortly after the time of the accident were ceiling 400 feet overcast, visibility two miles in fog.

One also has to wonder about the co-pilot. We cannot know, but we can wonder if, at some point, he may have assured the pilot that fog would be less of a problem since the co-pilot was instrument-rated—albeit nowhere near current. Such braggadocio has led other airmen and passengers to grief.

The Bligh Complex

Captain William Bligh, a highly able seaman and an officer sadly fated to be made famous by the mutiny aboard his ship, H.M.S. *Bounty,* had the negative trait of assuming a more lofty perch of command than was reasonable, at times refusing valuable offered help. Pilots can be that way, too, and allow an "I'd-rather-do-it-myself" approach to command to rob them of useful advice. Such pilots see themselves as operating on a level somewhat higher than their airplane (and crew)—until they are brought down by their ignorance or stubbornness in refusing "crutches."

Pilots carry such a Bligh Complex with them when they are solo as well as when accompanied. When alone, they mentally declare their supremacy over and independence from checklists—refusing to admit that in the air, crutches can be beautiful.

Checklists are important. At the very least, they can save a captain from embarrassment. At best, they can save his life. There can be no rational argument against using them, certainly not that the pilot is above them. Consider that an aircraft as seemingly simple as a Cessna Skyhawk has more than 100 items on its checklists for normal operations, and each item is there for a reason overriding a pilot's mental roulette.

Among the the 200-plus items on the normal procedures checklists for the Piper 601P Aerostar, there is one item that could have saved a pilot's life a few years ago, had the item been heeded. But before discussing the accident that claimed this pilot's life, a bit of history is needed to understand the chain of events and the working of attitudes that led to the mishap.

The pilot was a hard-driving and successful businessman. He began taking flying lessons in 1967, at the age of 41. After earning his license, he traded in his Piper Cherokee 140 for a Comanche 260. In 1970, with 800 hours in his logbooks, he took a multi-engine flight test in a Piper Twin Comanche. The day of the test turned out to be a long one for him. After his single-engine emergency procedures initially were found unacceptable by the examiner, the pilot flew with an instructor, who recommended him, again, for the rating. Later that day, the pilot retook the multi-engine flight test and passed.

A similar scenario occurred two months later, when the pilot took a flight test for an instrument rating and was busted for poor navigation and instrument-approach techniques. He took the test again a few weeks later and passed. Meanwhile, he began training in a helicopter. After 12 hours of dual instruction, he was approved for solo flight. A month later, he sustained serious injuries (a fractured shoulder and pelvis) when the helicopter he was flying struck a pole and crashed.

The pilot purchased the Aerostar 601P in January 1984. At age 58, he had accumulated about 2,500 hours of flight time, and during the next four months, the pilot logged 105 hours in the Aerostar. Of the total, 60 hours were dual instruction (the NTSB report contained no information on the type or quality of the instruction he received). In March, the pilot attended an Aerostar transition program at the Piper Training Center, in Vero Beach, Florida. The program at the time comprised two days of ground school and at least two hours of dual instruction. Although the pilot already had logged dozens of hours in his Aerostar, he did not do well when it came time to fly with one of the center's instructors. He was refused a transition certificate.

Following are excerpts from a report by the Piper Training Center instructor who flew with the pilot:

He said he had about 85 hours in the plane since he bought it but that he had never really done a preflight before, except to check the oil. . . . During the climb I noticed that he was very heavy-handed on the controls, and the airspeed was constantly varying between 130 and 160 KIAS, and the rate-of-climb varied from 200 to 2,000 fpm. . . . I talked him through a V_{mc} demonstration, but he seemed confused. . . . When I reminded him to add full power [to go around], he would push the throttles all the way forward and overboost the engines. . . . Throughout the whole procedure he seemed confused, and he slowly responded to my prodding. . . . When he put the flaps down we started climbing 2,000 fpm, and I had to remind him that we were trying to descend. . . . The landing was a little bit long, and as we rolled out (at high speed) we started veering to the left. He was putting in full right aileron to correct but didn't use the rudders. We started sliding nearly sideways on the runway, so I took over the controls and explained to him that the ailerons don't work on the ground. . . . I had to say 'go around' three times before he reacted, and by that time we were 50 feet over the runway threshold. He first retracted the gear, forgot the power and flaps. . . . He seemed bewildered. We were low, slow and misaligned with the runway, so I took over and landed.

While taxiing back to the ramp, I asked him if he knew a CFI who was familiar with Aerostars, so he could work with him. He didn't know of any near his home, so I recommended that he return to Vero Beach to fly with one of Piper's instructors. I told him that we have three flight instructors and one of us is always available, just to call before he comes.

The pilot never called, and there is no indication that he sought out an experienced Aerostar instructor after returning to his home in Washington, D.C. But shortly after attending the transition program, he had his airplane modified with a Machen Superstar I conversion package, which includes lower-compression pistons, new turbochargers and controllers, new fuel pumps and vortex generators on the vertical stabilizer. The conversion boosts the power rating of each engine from 290 to 325 horsepower.

In April 1984, the modifications were completed, and the pilot picked up his airplane in Lancaster, Pennsylvania. He was briefed on the modifications and the changes to operating procedures. He then went on a short cross-country flight for a demonstration of the power settings and the airplane's new fuel monitoring system.

After the demonstration, the pilot obtained a weather briefing and filed an IFR flight plan to Marco Island, Florida. Evidence suggests that his state of mind before leaving for Florida was not good. The pilot had told one person that he felt uncomfortable and nervous; another witness recalled that the pilot's hands were shaking. It was close to 3:00 p.m. when the Aerostar took off with the pilot and his son aboard. There was no significant weather along the route of flight. Ceilings in the Lancaster area were between 4,000 and 5,000 feet, with cloud layers to above 20,000 feet.

One of the items on the "after takeoff" checklist advises

that the fuel boost pumps should be on while climbing above 10,000 feet. The reason for this item is to ensure sufficient fuel pressure in the engine-driven pumps. At altitude, internal pump pressure can deteriorate if the boost pumps are not on, and the engine-driven pumps can cavitate and starve the engines of fuel. The NTSB believes that the pilot never turned on the boost pumps even though this is advised on the "takeoff" as well as the "after takeoff" checklists.

Fifteen minutes after takeoff, the pilot reported to Washington Center that he was climbing from 17,000 to 18,000 feet. Shortly thereafter, he radioed, "Mayday, lost engines, lost engines, dropping fast." The pilot then lost control of the airplane. ATC radar data show that the Aerostar descended at an average rate of 9,700 fpm. Several people saw the airplane before it hit the ground. One witness said that, after descending through the overcast, the airplane pulled up violently. The right aileron separated, and airplane rolled, inverted, and crashed, killing both the pilot and his son.

The NTSB listed seven probable causes for the accident. First was the pilot's failure to follow the checklists. This was the first link in the chain of events that led to the crash. Turning on the boost pumps probably would have prevented the accident. "Once dual engine failure occurred, the demanding situation exceeded the pilot's capabilities," said the board.

While it is likely that this pilot could have saved both his life and his son's by using his checklists, a deeper menace faced them. Checklists are an invaluable memory crutch, but they cannot serve as props for inadequate experience and proficiency. This pilot's history reveals that he was at the edge of his personal proficiency envelope most of the time, that he refused the intensive help he really needed, and that he was capable of—as he did on this flight—launching himself and another human being even though he was unsure of himself. He showed both the arrogance of the overconfident—remember his lack of preflighting thoroughness—and the bewilderment and nervousness of the inept, hardly the qualities of command.

Some nervousness before flying is not unusual in itself and is, in fact, healthy in stimulating and focusing our powers of concentration. At such times, however, we may be apt to hurry through procedures and overlook details, hence one value of checklists. Memorizing and retaining the hundreds of items on normal procedures checklists is beyond most pilots' capabilities. Any pilot who thinks he does not need such a "crutch" is deceiving himself. The records are full of checklist-related accidents occurring in virtually every flight phase and to pilots of all levels of experience. However, crisis circumstances virtually dictate that we memorize checklists for emergencies in which a pilot has little or no time for anything but swift, correct action. The wise captain determines and continually reconfirms what is appropriate and works accordingly as part of his regular flight preparations.

The Decisiveness/Flexibility Axis

As pilots-in-command, we can control events only up a point at which we must be able to respond to them in order to survive. Retaining true command authority over both airplane and situation demands remaining within the realm of reason and reality. That means being willing to replace one objective, however desirable it may have been, with another that has suddenly become more pressing—such as pushing on to a destination being replaced by simply landing safety. The following incident reflects the essentiality of this capability:

Air Illinois Flight 710, a Hawker Siddeley 748-2A, was behind schedule when it arrived in Springfield, Illinois, on October 11, 1983. The captain and first officer stayed aboard the aircraft while it was refueled. They had one more leg to fly, a 45-minute hop south to Carbondale, Illinois, the captain's home. Except for a few scattered thunderstorms, the weather did not look too bad: cloud bases at 2,000 feet, tops at 10,000 along the route. Carbondale was reporting 2,000 feet and two miles with light rain and fog. The flight crew was experienced. The captain had logged nearly 6,000 hours, with more than 3,000 hours in the 748, a large twin-turboprop commuter aircraft. The first officer had logged 1,700 of his 5,000 in the aircraft.

The captain was known to drive himself and his equipment very hard. In his determination to meet schedules, the captain would fly too close to thunderstorms, rather than deviating from course, and would operate the aircraft beyond airspeed limits to make up for lost time, said pilots who flew with him.

It is not hard to imagine the anxiety the captain must have experienced as he taxied for takeoff, 45 minutes behind schedule. Yet his ordeal was only taking form—in a tiny glitch.

The glitch began in the left generator. A banding wire broke, allowing the conductor bars to be lifted out of their mounts to rub against the rotating field coil. The friction caused the generator's drive shaft to shear. The left generator failed on takeoff; but for some reason, the first officer isolated the right generator and its busbar from the aircraft's electrical system. (The reason for this mistake never will be known. Investigators postulated that since there had been many squawks against the right generator, the first officer may have been anticipating its failure. The investigators concluded, however, that the flight crew's knowledge of the Hawker's electrical system and published and normal emergency operating procedures was inadequate.)

The right generator was producing 27.5 volts, but the first officer's attempts to get it back on line were unsuccessful. (Investigators believe that a malfunction within the switching unit was a fault.) The Hawker's electrical system was being powered solely by two nickel-cadmium (NiCad) batteries.

The captain reported a "slight electrical problem" to ATC. When asked if he intended to return and land at Springfield, which was above VFR minimums, the captain said no. He merely requested a lower cruising altitude and that ATC "keep an eye on us."

The first item on the emergency checklist for dual-generator failure called for immediately shedding all nonessential electrical loads by isolating two of the three main busbars. This was accomplished by the first officer seven minutes after the left generator failure. However, the captain ordered the first officer to reconnect the busbars so that the passengers would not lose their reading lights. He explained that he did not want to "scare the [heck] out of the people."

According to British Aerospace, the manufacturer, if load was reduced to 70 amps as prescribed in the emergency procedures, fully charged batteries would provide at least 30 minutes of power. The flight crew did turn off some nonessential equipment, but not enough. The Hawker's inverters, fuel boost pumps, and pitot-heat system were left on, and the weather radar system was operated for about ten minutes. A detailed analysis by investigators indicates that load on the batteries was reduced only to about 110 amps. The NTSB said that the flight crew may have been falsely reassured by indications that the batteries were maintaining a steady, high voltage. The board believes that the pilots did not realize that, unlike lead-acid batteries that lose their charge gradually, a NiCad battery maintains its rated charge until it is nearly depleted.

The Hawker lost battery power about 40 miles north of Carbondale, leaving the flight crew with only their airspeed indicators, vertical velocity indicators, the magnetic compass, and the first officer's altimeter. The aircraft had been cruising at 3,000 feet. The captain informed the first officer that he was going to descend to 2,400 feet and asked him to "watch my altitude."

The aircraft crashed, killing all 10 people aboard, near Pinckneyville, Illinois. The NTSB believes that the flight crew may have lost control of the aircraft, since the Hawker hit the ground in a descending right turn at about 200 KIAS. The board determined that the probable cause of the accident was the captain's decision to continue the flight to Carbondale, rather than return to Springfield after losing the aircraft's generators.

This accident tragically illustrates the importance of being able to evaluate your alternatives objectively and of knowing your aircraft's systems. In its report, the NTSB put it this way:

Most, if not all, pilots are motivated to complete their flights as scheduled; however, when the successful continuation of the flight is threatened by either environmental conditions, a mechanical malfunction, or both, the motivational drive must be tempered with good judgment. The major tempering factor is the pilot's knowledge of the environmental conditions along the route and the capabilities of the airplane's damaged system or systems. Based on this knowledge, the pilot must decide to either continue to his destination or to divert to an alternate airport.

Who Commands What? What Commands Whom?

What do pilots actually command? People? For the most part, no. The overwhelming majority of general aviation pilots-in-command do not lord it over crew members (excluding passengers) but over parts, systems, switches, knobs, buttons. We give orders to blindly accepting, obedient equipment. Were a working crew member suddenly to conk out, we would know what was lost in the way of functions and help. The same must apply to our equipment: When that becomes sick, we must be able to recognize the symptoms early, have remedies in mind, and be able to work around the loss of functions.

For many pilots, automatic systems often become "indispensable" companions, workhorse crew members. We command them to handle jobs, and they do them well—often better than we—and therein lies a danger that we will allow the things we command more authority and responsibility than they should have.

• Thirteen years ago, a Delta Air Lines Douglas DC-9 crashed into a sea wall during a late-morning ILS into Boston's Logan International Airport. During the approach, the visibility deteriorated rapidly as dense fog moved in over the airport. An aircraft preceding the DC-9 had landed at Logan after the flight crew spotted the runway when their aircraft was only a few feet above the ILS DH. The crew of another airliner, which flew the ILS after the DC-9, conducted a missed approach. During this time, the RVR decreased from more than 6,000 to about 1,600 feet. The transcription of the DC-9's cockpit voice recorder tape showed that about 20 seconds before impact, the captain told the first officer, who was flying the approach, "You better go to raw data, I don't trust that thing." Safety Board investigators believe that the captain was referring to the aircraft's flight director system.

The system had been the subject of several maintenance squawks by pilots who had flown the DC-9, and it had been replaced six times within the four preceding months. However, investigators found no evidence that the system was working improperly during this approach. Rather, the system was not providing the information that the flight crew was expecting. The flight director mode-selector switch had inadvertently been placed in the go-around rather than the approach mode. The NTSB noted that the flight crew had considerable experience flying aircraft equipped with a Collins flight director system and had only recently begun flying the DC-9, which had a Sperry system. Full clockwise rotation of the mode selector switch for the Collins system programs the flight director for the approach mode; the same action programs the Sperry system for the go-around mode.

The NTSB determined that the DC-9's crew became preoccupied with the questionable information that was being provided by the flight director and did not use other sources of information to monitor their altitude, heading, and airspeed. The admonition "go to raw data" came too late.

The increasing automation of flight control, navigation guidance and energy management functions, and the impact of automation on aviation safety has become a source of controversy, especially in view of several accidents—air carrier and general aviation—involving the relationship between pilots and machines.

An NTSB report published in November 1984 states that in most cases, automation does not really reduce workload but changes its nature from active control to task-monitoring: "There is convincing evidence, from both research and accident statistics, that *people make poor monitors.*" A NASA study has shown that participants actively controlling a dynamic system detected failures in the system sooner and more accurately than while monitoring an autopilot that was controlling the system. "These results were attributed to the fact that in the manual mode, the participants remained in the 'control loop' and benefitted from additional proprioceptive cues derived from 'hands-on' interaction with the system." The NTSB report cites accidents in which crews erroneously set or missed failures in their equipment.

Beyond pointing out the potential for pilots to relax their vigilance while relying on automated systems, the report stressed concern about the potential for loss of pilot proficiency, especially when a pilot is suddenly forced to fly a profile manually that he has habitually left to the autopilot. By consistently dropping from the control loop, he encourages rustiness.

Recent studies suggest that there may be a limit at which the efficiency and safety of an operation is optimized by systems automation. Beyond that limit, automation may jeopardize a pilot's ability to conduct the operation successfully. It is up to the pilot to determine his own limit. An autopilot with roll control and heading select may be perfect for some pilots; other pilots may need full-dress flight management systems.

Whatever else they can do for us, however, machines cannot relieve us of our responsibility to monitor closely both airplane and situation. And that returns us to the paradoxical factors— authority versus responsibility, flexibility versus control—that govern command. As we do with the forces that govern flight, we must exercise them in varying degrees and states of balance as real-world circumstances dictate. Yet there is a core of authority, of command discipline, that the pilot must maintain within himself. This is the weight that stabilizes the balance, and it must not be compromised. This discipline can be relinquished neither to machines nor to institutions. Call it intelligence or instinct for survival or whatever, it is our best reward for paying the dues of care and courage on every flight. We have seen the fates of airmen who neglected it.

Still, flight is not only a world of machine-, weather-, or institution-wrought circumstances. Its equations are not only physical but personal, and that, as we shall see, can be among the most daunting challenges for pilots-in-command and those who fly with them.

14
Left Seat, Right Seat

However large the airplane, its cockpit is a very small place. In the air, when personal considerations begin to affect a flight, there is usually no place to go for cooling off or a change of scene. If his co-pilot or a passenger presents a problem, the pilot-in-command must deal with it. At times, *cockpit* can be strikingly apt nomenclature. Yet the cocoon-like cockpit is usually a place of warm camaraderie and mutual support, in which "politics" is nonexistent or benign.

The atmosphere inside the cockpit or on the flight deck is usually what the PIC makes it. As always, he must weigh and balance authority and responsibility, flexibility and control. The dynamics of personality may also affect the conscientious co-pilot or alert passenger if the things start to go wrong. From the right-seat perspective, other, usually unspoken, questions may loom large: Is the pilot more jealous of his authority than correct in his judgments? Is the co-pilot more accommodating than is safe, or is he too pushy and the commander too flexible? In the throes of a crisis, these issues can be layered with confusion and the constant need to make the right decisions, whoever ends up making them. Underlying these matters is the relative healthiness of each person's objectives and priorities as well as the perennial question of how much authority and control a PIC should relax or relinquish in seeking help, and when to do so.

A situation that has often created such a test features skies full of fiery thunder. Within a thunderstorm or under the dire threat of one, even a highly experienced pilot-in-command can feel very small and alone, though a flight crew may be there to help him. Terribly unsure of conditions, he may well turn to ground observers for advice and regard their words not only as lifesaving advisories and instructions, but as commands.

When atmospheric conditions are right for convective activity, pilots often call upon ATC controllers to spot thunderstorms and provide guidance around them. These services are helpful to pilots using their eyes or their airborne weather radar to avoid thunderstorms. However, there are limitations to the capability of ATC radar to detect such storms and to the ability of controllers to provide reliable navigational guidance, try as they may to help. A pilot who relies *exclusively* on ATC to keep him out of thunderstorms is asking for trouble. How much so is indicated by an accident that involved an experienced pilot flying a pressurized piston twin several years ago. The circumstances could easily be repeated today:

During his preflight weather briefing, the pilot noted that the weather radar aboard his Beech Duke was inoperative. A cold front moving into the area was forecast to bring scattered thunderstorms, with tops ranging from 35,000 to 40,000 feet. The forecast indicated that the storms would be embedded—that is, the pilot probably would not be able to maintain visual separation from them. The pilot, who had more than 3,000 total hours, including more than 300 hours in the Duke, filed an IFR flight plan and took off about two hours later with five of his employees aboard the airplane.

During his initial contact with ATC, the pilot advised that his weather radar was inoperative and asked if the controller's display was "painting" any weather along the route. Advised that there appeared to be weather about 30 miles ahead, the pilot requested a vector around the weather and was told to maintain his current heading, 110 degrees. A few minutes later, the heading was changed to 090 degrees, then to 080, which, the controller said, "will take you north of some weather, and then you should have a clear shot, once you get by that." He then handed the Duke off to another sector controller.

According to the accident report, that next controller assumed that the Beech was landing at a metropolitan airport in his sector. (At this time, the Duke was well north and east of its flight-planned route.) He cleared the pilot to descend to 10,000 feet. The pilot, who previously had been cleared to climb to Flight Level 190, questioned the instruction. Realizing his mistake, the controller advised the pilot to continue his climb to Flight Level 190. The pilot then requested and received clearance to Flight Level 230.

Despite the confusion that occurred during the initial contact with the new controller, the pilot did not advise that he was maintaining a heading assigned previously to guide him around the weather. Did he assume that, during the hand-off, the first controller advised the second that the Beech had requested such guidance? Or did he assume that the heading assigned by the first controller would, indeed, take the flight north of the weather and that further assistance was not necessary, at least for the time being? Nothing in the accident report serves to answer these questions or indicate why the second controller did not advise the pilot that there was an area of heavy precipitation ahead of the airplane.

About ten minutes after initial contact with the second controller, the pilot, in garbled transmissions, reported that he had lost control of the airplane, which was on fire. Accident investigators determined that the Duke broke up after it entered an intense (level-five) thunderstorm and fell out of control.

The NTSB found these probable causes of the accident: It determined that the pilot attempted operation with known deficiencies in his equipment (the inoperative weather radar) and exceeded the design stress limits of the aircraft (he lost control). The board observed as well that thunderstorm activity and turbulence also were responsible for the crash.

Contradictions Under the Law

A federal court heard a suit brought by relatives of the accident victims against the United States government and came to a different conclusion, finding the government 90-percent responsible; it had "failed to carry out the assumed duty . . . to provide vectors around the weather." Ten percent of the responsibility was laid on the pilot for not confirming that the second controller knew he needed vectors around the weather.

Clearly, ATC cannot be relied upon as the sole source for weather avoidance, nor can a pilot assume that on a hand-off, all the details of ATC services and circumstances concerning the flight will be transmitted from controller to controller. ATC is neither in a position to control conditions nor to "command" an airplane to safety; the pilot remains responsible. The *Air Traffic Control Handbook* specifically states that the "primary task of the ATC system is to prevent a collision between aircraft operating in the system and to organize and expedite the flow of traffic." Other services, so says the book, are "limited by many factors," involving traffic and frequency congestion, radar quality, controller workload, "higher priority duties, and the pure physical ability to scan and detect those situations that fall in this category." In other words, the controller may be as much in the dark as the pilot. However, the *Handbook* also says, "The provision of additional services is not optional on the part of the controller, but rather is required when the work situation permits."

Such requirements and guidelines present both the controller and the pilot with a Catch-22 situation: The controller must provide additional services, if he is not too busy attending to the primary tasks of coordinating traffic flow and assisting with collision prevention. Yet when the weather is bad and pilots have the greatest need for the controller's services, the controller's workload rises exponentially.

Most controllers rise to the occasion, despite the difficulties, with professionalism and dedication, but they are hindered by their radar's being designed to track aircraft, not weather. The system is programmed to provide enhanced depictions of traffic and to inhibit returns from extraneous objects, such as water droplets. Displays of weather on the controller's plan view display are computer-generated. The weather displays consist of slash marks, which connect areas of similar reflectivity, and of *H*s or plus signs denoting areas of heavy precipitation.

The system provides very little useful information on precipitation intensity. The slash marks identify areas of precipitation less than five inches per hour; the *H*s or plus signs, areas with five inches of rainfall per hour or more. In the ATC lexicon, the former is considered light; the latter, heavy.

Efforts are underway to improve ground-warning capabilities. One plan is to provide a display of weather phenomena derived from Doppler radar either over the controller's plan view display or next to it. In the meantime, assistance from ATC should be considered a tool for weather avoidance, but a tool that may not be available whenever you need it, and one that cannot do the job alone. Knowing this should help pilots in avoiding the temptation to place themselves "in the hands" of others, expecting them to assume control and authority over the flight.

Advising and Consenting

Because experience, demonstrated skill, and knowledge are currencies of such great value in aviation, pilots who feel *relatively* poorer than others in these qualities can be subtly intimidated into making dangerous decisions. Those "others" may include the "old barnstormer," the veteran "long-distance ace," or the "grizzled bush-pilot" image types who haunt some airports, always ready to offer advice, imply criticism and generally awe their greener colleagues. Under their spell, the unwary pilot may be seduced across the line between listening to advice and being unconsciously "commanded" by it.

Pilot William E. Moore's experience now includes such an encounter. Moore was flying a Cessna 172XP from Portland, Oregon, to Lincoln, California. As he reached the Cascades, the weather took a turn for the worse:

By the time I reached Madras, Oregon, less than 80 miles from home, the towering cumulus I had seen earlier had become three full-fledged, anvil-topped, angry, black thunderstorms. One lay southwest between Mt. Jefferson and the Three Sisters—relative bearing about eight o'clock. The second appeared to be between my position and Mt. Hood—bearing 11 o'clock and perhaps 25 miles. The third and largest storm was dead ahead about 30 miles and so immense that, as I proceeded northward, it seemed to blot out the entire sky. Dust clouds clearly were visible as its gust front swept the desert floor. The Dalles and the sea-level route through the Cascades at the Columbia River Gorge were behind this storm, perhaps even under its monstrous canopy.

The only reasonable thing was to land at Madras and wait. By now, it was late afternoon.

Thirty minutes after my landing, a Cessna Cardinal appeared, inbound from the west. As the pilot alighted, I strode over to inquire where he had come from. "Portland," he said, turning to point to the space between the 11,000-foot peaks of Mt. Jefferson and Mt. Hood. "We came right through there, 'bout 7,500 feet. A few clouds in the pass, but once you're through, there's just some scattered stuff to the west."

He was a craggy old graybeard with weathered, leathery features and clear blue eyes that inspired a feeling of trust and confidence. We chatted about the route and the terrain elevations in the pass; whether it would be better to try sneaking through underneath or flying VFR over the top. While we talked, the storm in front of Mt. Hood moved eastward a few miles, and the pass between the mountains seemed a bit less threatening, though I had never flown it before. "Well, I guess I'll go take a look, at least," I said.

"You'll make it," the graybeard said. And with those reassuring words to ease my apprehension, I took off, climbed to 8,500 feet and headed northwest.

As I approached the higher terrain of the Cascades, well-centered between Mt. Jefferson and Mt. Hood, which are situated about 50 miles apart, I could see the up-sloping rampart of clouds beneath and head of me, typical of the orographic lifting effects of a westerly flow and moist, unstable air at the surface. More troubling, however, was the other layer of clouds above and ahead of me. I was flying into an aperture between cloud layers. I continued to press ahead toward this aperture, straining to see what was beyond. I was abeam Mt. Jefferson, just entering below the higher cloud layer, when suddenly I was engulfed in a blinding rainshower.

In panic, with the rain sounding like machine guns pelting the aircraft, I began to execute a 180 to the left and immediately found myself heading directly toward a cloud, the mountain completely obscured behind it. Aborting the 180, I banked and turned gently back to a westerly heading, finding myself now clear of the deafening rain in a wonderland of white. I had the feeling that I was flying into the mouth of a huge, white cave with white, puffy stalagmites of cumulus rising from the floor to the ceiling. There was plenty of room to maneuver; the tops of the floor layer were around 6,500 feet, and the bases above me were about 9,000, but the cumulus stalagmites kept easing me farther southwest.

I tuned in the Portland and Newberg VORs alternately on my one radio and guessed that I should be somewhere south of Portland. Those "scattered" clouds the old graybeard had promised should be showing up any time. Once, as I picked my way around cumulus pillars toward a more northerly heading, I saw another aircraft, a DC-9 I thought, descending several miles to the west through the open space of my white prison. After a few more minutes on a northerly course, I contacted Portland Approach, whose airspace I thought I must be near, and explained my situation. "Would you like an instrument descent?" they asked. "The ceiling here is 4,000 feet and overcast."

"I'd rather not. Are there any holes reported anywhere?"

"Turn right to 340 degrees. There are some breaks in the clouds reported near Pearson Airport."

Just then, I saw below me a lovely hole, perhaps a mile in diameter with, of all things, a runway directly beneath it. In the meantime, the layers of my prison had converged ominously in the north and east. I slowed to V_{fe}, lowered the flaps, banked into a steep turn and spiraled down through the hole at 80 knots to find that Troutdale Airport, my home base, was the owner of the runway I had seen through the hole.

"You'll make it": famous last—or nearly last—words that are akin to "I do it all the time" as would-be impressers of the impressionable. Another pilot who found that he had relinquished too much authority is Larry J. Duthie. He in mid-trip took on a co-pilot or co-captain, who remained in another plane:

I had spent nearly a month on vacation doodling around Alaska in a Cessna 170, enjoying some of the best flying of my life. The weather had been excellent, but as I headed south toward home, a low overcast stopped me at Fort Nelson in northern British Columbia near the Yukon. The next morning, it was obvious that the weather would be a problem again. The sky was dark and overcast. The Canadian weather briefer at Fort Nelson's airport was equally discouraging. The field was VFR with good visibility under a heavy stratus layer at 1,500 feet, but the layer extended south, where ceilings lowered until, about 100 miles down the Alcan Highway, the clouds touched the road and became fog—with light snow, according to a trucker's report.

As I received that disheartening briefing, another pilot hovered nearby and asked a few questions. He then began filling out a flight plan and asked if I was VFR, too. I nodded dejectedly. "Mind if I tag along with you?" he asked. "I've a bum radio." "Sure," I told him. "I'm going to hang around the airport a few hours and hope the stuff to the south lifts a little."

My companion was an Alaskan bush pilot who was headed to Seattle. He was flying a Tri-Pacer, and he saw no reason to wait. The weather, he insisted, was good enough for flying. "Why, you ought to see what we fly in all the time, up near Nome," he said. It was not long before my caution disappeared and a sense of adventure took charge—the vacation spirit.

Ah, sweet adventure! I, too, filed a flight plan. The bush pilot would lead and navigate, while I would fly his wing and handle the radios. he leveled off at 1,000 feet and began following the Alcan Highway south.

The first half hour, we scudded along under the clouds and maintained a comfortable clearance with the ground. The terrain, however, was rising, and, 15 minutes later, it had worked its way up to us until we were only a couple hundred feet above that brown ribbon of dirt road. Time to turn back, I thought. Instead, the bush pilot headed southeast to follow a little valley. The land dropped away from us for a while, giving us flying room. But a few miles later, the valley disappeared, and the forested terrain resumed its upward squeeze.

Snow began to smack the windshield. At first, it came in occasional wet spatters, but it quickly progressed to a steady snowfall, which began to adhere. I rocked my wings, waved and pointed back over my shoulder, where flying conditions were not so mean. The bush pilot slogged ahead.

I'll never know how much longer he would have pressed on, but I initiated the 180. I rolled out on the opposite heading and was relieved to see that we had switched leads. I felt slightly more comfortable with him on my wing. Changing leads did not stop the ice, however. It continued to pack onto our unprotected aircraft. I hoped to take us back through the valley to the highway and then fly along it to an airstrip identified on my Canadian chart as Sikanni Chief.

The icing continued. With treetops less than 100 feet below, there was no way to descend out of it, and climbing was out of the question. We were trapped—sandwiched between a layer of ice-making clouds and airplane-rending forest. The real fear hit when my airspeed indicator began to fluctuate, then unwind. The pitot tube was iced. I also could see ice building on the wing struts and, worse, the wings' leading edge.

A thick crust of ice covered my windshield and sealed off my forward view. I would have to dead reckon to Sikanni Chief by peeking out the side windows. By my calculations, we still were 40 miles from the nearest airstrip, so I was surprised when my bush-pilot friend broke off and swooped down toward a group of buildings. For the first time that morning, I was delighted. He was on base leg to a short, muddy patch. He had spotted an airstrip near a truck stop.

That approach and landing are the only aspect of that day's flying I'm not embarrassed about. The final had to be made in a slip, for I could see nothing through the front windshield. The short field required a slow approach, but the ice load meant my stall speed was higher. With no reliable airspeed indication and with the stall-warning sensor buried under rime, that really was a moot point. It was seat-of-the-pants time.

I kicked the slip out at the threshold of the miniscule strip, planted the main gear and peered out the side window, braking hard and concentrating on avoiding a ground loop. I sloshed to a stop in a deep puddle at the other end. Standing nearby, next to his own frosty airplane, was the bush pilot. He was grinning. We'd happened upon an uncharted private strip.

When a Puppet's String Runs Out

To relax one's defenses and surrender to a fool's game of follow-another-leader can be stressful enough, but many pilots face command decisions under the more troublesome circumstance that their leaders on the ground pursue them into the cockpit to impose decisions properly left to the PIC. Here, the worst kind of personal pressure can be brought to bear, for an ignorant or callous boss can force a pilot to balance good safety judgment against the loss of his job. Such equations frequently have led to fatalities, for which the pilots were held accountable. How starkly brutal can be the circumstances surrounding a pilot's relinquishing command to—or having it wrenched from him by—someone not charged with flying or, in this case, even riding in the airplane is illustrated by a recent accident:

• A young commercial pilot was assigned to fly a Cessna 182P on a charter flight from Richmond, Virginia, to Hilton Head, South Carolina, and back to Chesterfield, Virginia. He had 750 hours; although instrument-rated, he had logged only ten hours in actual instrument weather and was not qualified to conduct an IFR air-taxi flight as pilot-in-command.

VFR weather forecasts concerning the flight were pessimistic, and the pilot flew to New Bern, North Carolina, to recheck, landing at New Bern about 2:30 p.m. He was advised that Richmond was reporting a 2,200-foot overcast and three miles visibility. VFR conditions, with occasional ceilings of 1,000 feet overcast and three miles visibility, were forecast for Richmond.

However, the Flight Service specialist cautioned about a possibility of thunderstorms along the pilot's route of flight.

After relaying this information to his supervisor in Richmond, the pilot was told that the company would dispatch a Piper Aztec and an IFR-qualified air-taxi pilot to New Bern to pick up his passenger and fly the passenger to Chesterfield. After about an hour, the pilot again telephoned his company and was told that the Aztec had not departed from Richmond and that the weather was still VFR there. According to the NTSB, "the pilot reportedly was encouraged to proceed."

He and his passenger left New Bern in the Skylane at 3:55 p.m. and stayed between 1,000 and 2,000 feet agl to remain below an overcast. "Even so, moderate rain showers were encountered for about 30 minutes," said the NTSB. "The pilot considered landing at Rocky Mount [about one third of the way to Chesterfield] but was encouraged by orange sky as he traversed the area."

The Skylane soon was traveling above heavy ground fog. Upon reaching the Chesterfield airport, the pilot decided that he could not land there due to the fog. He contacted Richmond Approach and requested an instrument clearance into Byrd International Airport. The controller reported that weather conditions there included a 200-foot ceiling and one-half mile visibility in fog. "The pilot verified that he was instrument-rated and IFR-equipped and requested information regarding any known VFR conditions at airports to the west of Richmond. The pilot was told to expect vectors for the ILS Runway 15 approach to Richmond, but no information regarding VFR airports was provided."

The Skylane's glideslope receiver was malfunctioning, and the pilot missed the ILS approach. "He indicated that he wanted to fly westbound 'to try to get out of the stuff,' " the NTSB said. Another pilot reported that VFR weather conditions existed at Farmville, Virginia, about 52 miles west, and the Skylane pilot elected to go there.

"At about this time, the pilot's supervisor was granted permission to visit the tower and began to question the shift supervisor regarding the status of the Skylane,'' the NTSB said. ''He reportedly advised ATC personnel that the Skylane should not be vectored westward to an area where weather conditions could not be confirmed and suggested another approach to Richmond. It is unknown what influence [the supervisor] had with tower personnel. However, the aircraft was vectored back to Richmond despite the pilot's request for vectors to Farmville.''

The NTSB also notes that the pilot accepted ATC's offer of a combination localizer and airport surveillance radar approach to Runway 33 at Richmond. By this time, the weather at Byrd was below minimums for the approach. The pilot's supervisor told ATC personnel, said the NTSB, ''that they must tell the pilot that he would have to descend below the MDA for the approach to see the field.'' At 5:50 p.m., the ATC tower supervisor transmitted to the pilot, ''In order for you to see that runway, you're probably going to have to descend below your minimum descent altitude.'' The supervisor also advised the pilot that the weather included an indefinite 100-foot ceiling.

''At about that time, the passenger observed trees and screamed for the pilot to pull up.'' As the pilot added power, the Skylane's right wing struck a tree. ''The pilot said he experienced control difficulties but was able to complete a 340-degree left turn and to roll out on the tower-suggested inbound heading. Shortly afterward, the pilot observed the approach lights, proceeded inbound and landed on Runway 33.''

The Skylane was substantially damaged in the crash, but the pilot and his passenger escaped injury. The NTSB determined that the probable causes of the accident were improper IFR operation by the pilot and inadequate supervision of the pilot by his supervisor. The board said that ATC's issuance of an improper instruction to the pilot (to descend below the MDA) was a contributing factor.

That the pilot and passenger escaped injury pales before the jeopardy in which a series of decisions and a complex of attitudes placed them. That the pilot relinquished his authority over the safe conduct of the flight to ATC and his supervisor is clear. That he was held responsible for the consequences of his actions is also clear. Unclear is the relationship that enabled the supervisor to dangerously manipulate the flight through ATC. The fact that it could happen is appalling, and it underscores the point that in his own defense, the pilot had to look to himself— to his knowledge of his options, his limitations, and what his better judgment was telling him.

Confrontations between junior pilots and their bosses do occur. Recently, a case reached the United States Circuit Court of Appeals involving a co-pilot who was fired by his airline's chief pilot for refusing to make flights he regarded as unsafe although the captain insisted on going ahead. In firing him, the chief pilot had said that ''a co-pilot should keep his eyes open and his mouth shut.'' The president of the airline had confirmed the chief pilot's action.

The co-pilot sued the Indiana airline under a state law that provided damages to ex-employees discharged for fulfilling a statutorily imposed duty—in this case, a duty imposed on pilots by the FARs. The court noted that if the pilot had a duty not to fly an airplane with inoperative items and if he was discharged for fulfilling that duty, he allegedly has a claim of wrongful discharge under Indiana law *(Buethe v. Britt Airlines, U.S. Court of Appeals, Seventh Circuit, December 11, 1984)*. A blow struck for holding to the straight and narrow.

Rights of Passengers

Every PIC is responsible for the safety of his passengers, be they family, friends, colleagues, or casual acquaintances. In the close confines of a general aviation aircraft, we become especially attuned to discomforts, physical or emotional, our passengers may suffer. We may even consider them a reflection upon our flying, and there is a danger that our concerns about our passengers' immediate well-being can adversely affect our command judgment. Pilot James J. Newell relates such a case.

His was a sight-seeing flight from Long Island MacArthur Airport to the Hudson River and back in new-pilot Newell's Skyhawk with two friends who had never before flown in a lightplane. The forecast led the pilot to expect only a few bumps in a sky of scattered clouds and ten-mile visibility:

. . . The aircraft approached the Connecticut shoreline after a 10-minute hop over Long Island Sound; however, we also were approaching the now-broken layer of cumulus that, as forecast, lay at 3,500 feet. We slid under the deck. A light chop began buffeting our aluminum capsule, nothing a pilot would get worked up about. However, my right-seat passenger looked a little strange. He belched out one statement, "I don't feel very well." I suggested that he relax and try to ignore the minor jolts. To my misfortune, his condition worsened, culminating in a brief scene of vomiting. As I prepared to turn the airplane around, he told me that he felt better and that we should continue. My rear-seat passenger also pressed me to proceed to our destination, so I continued to the Hudson, our intended point of return.

I realized that my increasingly ill passenger was breathing heavily; evidently he was upset by the continued buffeting at our new, lower altitude. His face took on a strange paleness, his fingers began to turn yellow. Sensing that he was hyperventilating, I tried to make him breathe into a bag. Then he hit me with the bomb. He informed me that he had a blood disorder that had not flared up in years. He needed oxygen or he would pass out. I screamed, "Why didn't you tell me about your blood disorder?" He came back with, "You never asked."

Helpless to cure him, I tore out my sectional and flew toward Danbury (Connecticut) Airport. Trying to ease his discomfort, I opened all the vents and a window. In an effort to reach the airport before he passed out, I declared a medical emergency to obtain a priority landing clearance. My rear-seat passenger tried to comfort my ill right-seat passenger as I concentrated on navigating to an unfamiliar airport.

When the runway was in sight, I dropped flaps and settled the Skyhawk in to a landing. Later, after my ill passenger was released from the hospital, the doctors told me he had suffered from hyperventilation.

Never again will I take for granted that everyone is made to fly. My mistakes had been, first, that I failed to screen my passengers more carefully for medical problems; second, I mistakenly had let my passengers pressure me into compromising my first instincts of passenger safety; finally, I did not realize fully that a comfortable flight for the pilot might not be that way for the inexperienced passenger. New and experienced pilots must shake the exuberance or the complacency involved in their flying habits to meet the responsibilities of their passengers' safety and well-being.

Though your passenger may be in pain or suffering anxiety, it is vital to safety to adhere to the rule, *fly the plane first*. Pilots have been known to forget that all the way to their doom. To spare their passengers worry, pilots have refused to take emergency measures or call for help, though the flights were in peril. Others have courted disaster to avoid embarrassment. Our passengers fly with us on the rock-bottom faith that we have the skill and intelligence to exert proper command and control over the flight, even in an emergency. To do that, we must put the fundamental safety of the flight above everything else, including our *image* as pilots, the conveniences that flying is supposed to provide, and even the immediate comfort of the passengers themselves.

Blunders on the Right

When we fly with other pilots, be they crew or passengers, intra-cockpit dynamics can take many forms, which in a crunch can be dramatic. We fly together because we share an enthusiasm for and an involvement with flying. How we fly and what we know about it in significant part defines us for our fellow pilots, whichever seat we may ride. Many pilots unfortunately place as much value on their image as pilots as on the reality of their skill and experience, and their need to enhance that image can show up in socially unwelcome and, more important, hazardous ways. Unwanted helpfulness is a common way by which right-seaters make their "value" felt. For the PIC, it can be a problem:

Pilot J. H. Grosslight was making a trip in his Cessna 182 to Fort Lauderdale with, as he describes him, "a colleague and longtime flying buddy." A stop was planned for Cedar Key. . . .

. . . Halfway to Cedar Key, I decided to call the nearest FSS to obtain the local surface winds, since Cedar Key does not have a reporting system or Unicom. I cannot recall the exact winds that the station reported, but I do remember that they were somewhat from a northerly direction at 15 knots or more. The winds would not be directly down the runway, but landing should offer no problem. As we neared Cedar Key, Dick, my co-pilot, commented that I might as well descend for a straight-in approach to Runway 5. I did not respond but noted his suggestion and began the descent. We had not been flying very high. Now our ride, which had never been smooth, even over the water, got rougher. No doubt about it, relaxation was not possible now; it was one of those gusty days.

By now, I had Cedar Key and the runway in sight. As I approached the field, I did not proceed straight in, as suggested, but decided to circle the field to look it over once. As I made the turn around the field, I saw a twin taking off from Runway 23, opposite my intended landing. I was confused. The twin's direction of flight did not coincide with the surface wind report from the FSS and with my general impression of the wind direction. But I was delighted with my good judgment in circling the field and commented, "Why is he taking off in that direction?" Dick looked at the windsock and said that we still should land as planned, on Runway 5.

I was busy flying. I had flown with Dick many times and knew that his judgment was sound. I did not check further. All previous information confirmed a northerly wind, and it added up—two pilots, several wind verifications and only the discrepancy of a twin taking off in the opposite direction.

I proceeded on my planned approach. As I made a turn to enter a crosswind leg for Runway 5, I discovered that I was farther right of the field than I expected. With a bit of fighter-pilot style, I S-turned toward the field and flew around to line up for final. Even though the approach required some quick maneuvers to get back on course, no signals got through to disturb my confidence in landing comfortably in the planned direction. As I slowed down, Dick expressed concern that the airspeed was a bit low. I increased the airspeed; the stage was set. For the past several months I had been practicing landings—short field, flaps, no flaps, wasting no runway, landing at low speeds in order to save rubber and making the first turnoff at my base airport. After all, I had been reading landing technique articles in *AOPA Pilot* and felt I should be proficient.

The airstrip at Cedar Key is asphalt, 50 feet wide and 1,800 feet long. I touched down well into the runway. (What happened to all my practice?) Somehow, I seemed to be moving too rapidly, and the end of the runway was approaching much too fast. The runway ends in the bay—all water, not deep, but very wet. I immediately went for the brakes and found that Dick had stomped on his brakes, too. The opportunity to add power and go around was quickly lost—no time to tell Dick to get off the brakes.

We were at the end of the runway. I had read of a technique for a situation such as this. I jumped hard on the left brake and shoved in the throttle. We ground-looped almost 180 degrees and stopped in the sand between the runway and the edge of the water. We suffered only a blown tire as damage.

Some of the local people came out to assist and told me that my mistake was not rare—I had landed downwind. The pilot of the twin knew what I did not know. The scenario—downwind, short strip, a bit too fast, a short and poor approach, and a fellow pilot on the brakes—resulted in a state of embarrassment. From now on, I will be the sole pilot in command, even when one of my flying buddies sits in the right seat. *I* will check the windsock when I circle the field, and *I* will determine the airspeed; and no one else will touch the brakes or other controls unless I command or am unable to command.

It is best to work out with your co-pilot beforehand how you will share the chores of the flight: who will handle the radios, the navigation, the flight controls. If the co-pilot is a fidgeter who loves to "make sure" the settings are right, a gentle word of discouragement is in order, for such people have been known to switch frequencies, squawk codes, altimeter settings, and DG indications erroneously with confusing results. Over-eager co-pilots also disconcertingly get ahead of the pilot as he goes through the pre-takeoff checklist or in subtle ways suggest that he is not as thorough as he should be. Such intrusions are sources not only of confusion but of distracting irritation. It is up to the pilot to discourage them.

The Right-Seat Perspective

Before the decision to fly together is made, the parameters of the flight should be clear to each person involved. The weather and the aircraft to be flown should be carefully evaluated. A cross-country flight in a Cessna 172 in freezing rain is not a good place for a flier to become acquainted with a co-pilot who is a relative stranger. The pilot/passenger must assess his own limitations and determine if he wants to have them extended by another pilot. He should also be sure that the PIC has no unspoken demands or responsibilities for the guy in the right seat to fulfill. Then the pilot/passenger must accept the fact that there is only one PIC. The military, airlines, and some corporate flight operations leave no question as to who is PIC. His control is absolute, and there are explicit regulations and procedures that cover his actions in the cockpit, as well as those of the crew he commands.

General aviation fliers are not usually accustomed to multi-pilot operations beyond those with instructors. Even between good friends, the basic rule should be that the pilot/passenger will perform only those chores specifically requested by the PIC and won't accept responsibility that he can't safely handle.

Offering advice and criticism, unless it is asked for, can damage a pleasant cockpit relationship. Yet what if the pilot/passenger begins to feel genuine doubts about the PIC's ability?

To fly with someone else in charge means putting one's faith in him, and that is not a decision to be made lightly, as pilot/passenger Robb Mark discovered one evening:

I was to be flown from Pal-Waukee Airport, near Chicago, to a small grass strip near Rockford, some 50 miles away, to pick up a friend's Cessna 150. The trip would be short, but by the time Steve, the 150's owner, and I were ready to leave, it was obvious that it would be near dusk upon our arrival at the unlighted field. Considering the huge trees that surrounded the runway at our destination, Steve said that he would rather drop me off at Rockford where I could catch another ride, rather than risk landing at an unfamiliar field with darkness approaching. I smiled as Steve announced his unwillingness to complete the trip, but then he was only a private pilot with some 90 or so hours, and I was an instructor with nearly 1,500.

The sun was nearing the horizon when Steve let me out at Rockford. On the ramp I spotted one of the roughest-looking Tri-Pacers I had ever seen. Its pilot informed me that he was to be my taxi for the five-minute flight to the grass strip.

I gave the bird a quick once-over, raised an eyebrow skeptically over its appearance and then climbed in. "Let's get going," I said. I knew that the approaching darkness wouldn't be a problem if we wasted no time in getting off.

Airborne again, I could see just how beautiful a midwestern sunset could be. With the streaks of pink against the now-graying sky, it seemed almost peaceful looking.

My mind returned to matters of the moment as Jack, the pilot, announced our arrival over the strip. In the air, things still looked rather light, but as I looked at the ground, I became aware of just how dark it was becoming. I mentioned uneasily that perhaps we should go back to Rockford and return to the strip by car, but with a casual wave of his hand, Jack assured me that he was experienced at this sort of thing. Sometimes the person with more experience must take control of a situation. It made sense, so tonight was my turn to be the student.

The plan had been to fly over the top of the strip until someone on the ground turned on some auto headlights to aid our approach, but as I gazed out the window, blackness spotted by an occasional streetlight was all that I could see.

Jack looked over at me and smiled as he turned base for what I still believed to be an imaginary runway. Returning his smile rather weakly, I began to think that we should call the thing off—but then, he was more experienced than I.

We were now on final, and as we approached closer, I could see the lights of a car—one car! My eyes moved quickly to the altimeter, and I saw that we were but 200 feet or so from the ground. Another quick glance out the window, and I was aware that the silhouettes I saw against the sky were the huge trees surrounding the field. But the tops were now above us.

Sweat was pouring from my brow, and, with just one set of lights on the ground, my depth perception was almost nil. If I didn't do something quickly, Jack and I were going to be tomorrow's headlines, so instinctively my hand went for the throttle. "No!" Jack shouted as he yanked it back to idle. The airplane sank immediately. We hit the ground so hard that I was convinced my life had but a fraction of a second left.

When I realized that I wasn't dead, I looked out the window to see if the wheels were still attached, but I couldn't see the gear for the darkness. We rolled to a stop at the end of the runway. Not waiting for the engine to die, I jumped out and sighed with relief over surviving this insane trip.

The little voice of caution inside my head had tried to tell me that the trip was foolish, but I had refused to listen. Never—never again was I going to let another pilot, experienced or not, place me in a situation that my common sense tells me is dangerous.

As I spoke later with Jack about the state of my nerves, I asked just how much time he did have logged. "Oh, let me see now," he said as he scratched his head, "must be about 70 or 80 hours by now." "Jack," I said, "how many times have you landed at this strip at night?" "This is my second," he replied with a big grin. "How'd I do?"

Possession of an aircraft ignition key is no indication of a pilot's qualifications to command the aircraft. The competency of a close friend may be a known factor, but it is wise to be wary of the new guy on the line who issues a "let's get acquainted" invitation to fly in his plane. He may even be making a reunion with a machine that he hasn't flown in months. "Thanks, maybe later," is a safe, courteous response.

If time permits, check with the local FBO or with mutual friends to gain some insight into the pilot's ability. Casual conversation and an exchange of experiences with him can provide more clues. Directly stating your uneasiness about flying with a stranger may net an understanding soul who is willing to show you his logbook and certificate. The pilot who regards an open expression of concern as a personal insult is providing his prospective passenger with a clue to stay clear. An unobtrusive watch over the pilot's shoulder as he preflights may offer more information about his sense of responsibility and the airworthiness of his airplane. It is foolish to assume that a failure to preflight means that it was done earlier. Asking beats any amount of rationalizing as time comes to leave the ground.

Once you are aloft, the first priority of everyone is safety. If circumstances become hazardous, the pilot/passenger should not remain silent if the PIC is failing to act wisely; then the co-pilot's skills make him a preferred occupant, even if the pilot is a peer and a friend. Denny Komes relates how important that can be to keeping both the friendship and the friends alive:

My friend, Jim, who lives in the San Francisco Bay area, had invited me to go flying with him. Jim and I had logged about the same number of hours and had about the same number of years' experience. Because of the difference in weather conditions between the Bay climate and that of my home in the Midwest, I accepted on the basis of my being strictly a passenger enjoying the scenery and snapping a few photos.

Jim rented a Cheetah and checked the weather, and off we went. The weather was to be VFR, with scattered clouds and some fog along the coast. Apparently, this was not abnormal, for Jim did not seem concerned. So I chose not to worry, as I know that the coastal weather patterns are substantially different from the Midwest, as two Bay Area vacations had demonstrated.

Jim said we should head toward Monterey, and, if it were fogged in, we would try to fly up toward Half Moon Bay. As we headed toward Monterey, it became obvious that we would be restricted by fog, so we turned northward toward Half Moon Bay, following the shoreline. There were clouds ahead, and my friend felt that we could slip in under the overcast, so we dropped to 500 feet off the deck. The Cheetah purred along nicely for about 20 minutes; then everything turned gray. Fog! Jim looked at me and said we were going to have to make a 180 and get out of the soup. I agreed, for neither of us is instrument-rated.

He started into a standard-rate left turn, and I looked outside for a break in the fog. Suddenly, the engine sounds changed. I glanced at the T-group of gauges and saw that we were descending at 1,000 fpm. My heart was in my throat. I grabbed the wheel and began easing it back to arrest the descent and set the airplane up for a climb. As soon as I could talk, I looked over and said, "Jim, what are you doing?"

"I don't know what happened," he said. "I *guess* I got confused, but I have it now." We continued to make the 180. I glanced at the heading indicator and then at Jim and realized that we had passed the 180-degree course reversal by about 45 degrees and that Jim was totally confused and lost.

I took over the controls and told him that I had the plane. He released the controls and looked very relieved. Now I had some planning to do. Where were we? What was around us? First, of course, I had to fly the airplane and be sure we could clear all obstacles. I turned the Cheetah to a heading of 090 degrees, knowing that we would head toward land. I started a best-rate climb, confident that I would be able to clear the hills and clouds at 5,000 feet, as the tops had been around 4,500 when we took off. I knew that anything could happen, but I had to have a plan to follow. Fortunately, within a minute or two, we broke out of the clouds and were again in beautiful VFR.

Later, on the ground, I asked my friend what had happened, and he said he didn't know—he had just become disoriented. He had not flown under the hood since primary training and never in actual IFR. Now, when I ride with someone else, I check the weather myself and stay abreast of everything.

When Mutiny Is a Must

If the PIC deliberately jeopardizes safety, the pilot/passenger should at least voice his concern. It may be hard for a 50-hour pilot to cough up the words to the 5,000 hours' worth of aviator in the left seat, but that kind of directness may help to bring the airplane back to earth in one piece. One hopes that calm reasoning will do the trick, for the cockpit is not a place to argue or engage in fisticuffs. Certainly, a decision to physically wrest control of the aircraft from another pilot must be considered a last resort.

Yet sometimes there is nothing for it but to take such action. When two experienced pilots are involved, the personal situation can be dicey, but as in this case related by Randolph S. Diuguid, when the commander falters and the *physical* situation becomes desperate, the co-pilot may have no choice:

It was another working day. We left Dallas Love Field, headed for Wichita Falls, Texas, with a load of six passengers, including the president of the company. The weather was good in Dallas, cleansed by an evening of storms that had canceled our flight the day before. Our itinerary called for a stop in Wichita Falls to drop off the president, then on to Perryton and, from there, back to College Station and on into San Antonio that night. The aircraft was a new Super King Air 200B. Both crew members were experienced pilots of 15 years and combat veterans. It was April 2, 1982.

The route was one we had flown at least a hundred times, sometimes three times a day. The weather was severe clear in Dallas, but I had been watching a weather system on the West Coast as it moved eastward. The lowest altimeter setting to hit the California coast in years was wreaking havoc, with floods and rain; even the space shuttle had been sent around for more orbits. The weather had my attention, but the captain seemed unconcerned. The landing in Wichita Falls was VFR, but the winds were 44 and gusting, with a dust storm on the horizon.

We feathered the left engine, and the president and another passenger deplaned. After escorting them off the airplane, I checked the weather at the FSS. I asked for briefings on El Paso, Amarillo, and Perryton, Texas—our destination. The briefer was cordial as he ripped off the printout and handed it to me, mentioning the strong winds and dust with a chance of tornadoes. As I was going out the door, he said, "Son, Perryton's runway is 36/18. How are you going to land with a 76-plus-knot wind out of the west?'' ''I'm just the second-in-command, sir!'' was my answer.

As we taxied out of Wichita Falls, I tried to brief the captain on the weather. With a karate chop to the air, the captain said, ''Checklist! We're going anyway.''

I clamped the weather printout on the fold-down and started the checklist. On takeoff, the winds were so strong that the captain needed both hands on the yoke, and I had to reach over and bring the gear up—something I had never needed to do. The dust already had closed down Wichita Falls—it was covered with a deep brown layer.

At 24,000 feet, the air was smooth, but we were not out of the dust. At 26,000 feet, we were on top.

En route, I checked the weather and handled the radios. The captain was flying the airplane. He had read the weather strips but showed no reaction. On the radio, from the ADF and from Flight Watch, I was getting a story that didn't sound good.

Flight Service was calling it severe. An area Sigmet for tornadoes was issued for the area centered around our destination and into Kansas. Winds of 100 mph were already clocked and reported below 9,000 feet. On the ground, the weather had turned disastrous—trucks blown off the highway, a restaurant roof blown off, a cinder-block wall blown down in Amarillo, killing workers. Visibility was zero due to the dust— everything was black. The National Guard had been called out to help in the disaster. Still, at 26,000 feet above the din, the air was smooth.

I was writing all of this down and clipping it on the weather board. The captain remained unruffled. Other airlines—Continental, Southwest, United, and Air Midwest—were turning back. Alone, we were pressing on into the battle with the wind.

I was trained to fly into the Valley of the 600 and hold my tongue. In Vietnam, I had done just that. But this was different. Before my landing briefing and checklist, I had to ask the captain, ''What do you intend to do?''

''We'll shoot the approach,'' the captain replied.

''With 100-mph winds?''

''We'll take a look.''

''And what if we don't see Perryton?'' I asked.

''We'll shoot a missed approach.''

''Where will we go? Look at the fuel. Besides, this stuff is almost to Dallas by now.''

"We'll go to Kansas," he said.

From 16,000 feet, it was a rough ride. It was the worst I had experienced, but the worst was yet to come. Perryton had winds out of the west at 74 knots. We could barely see the runway through the dust, and we were shooting sideways. A mile out, as the passengers were yelling, "No! Don't land," I took control of the aircraft and started the missed approach. As the gear came up, one of the passengers passed out; the rest were still shouting. The captain did not resist my attempts to save us. We turned back toward Liberal, Kansas.

The climb back to 5,000 was difficult through severe turbulence. I could not reach the panel. I had trouble dialing the radios; I got nothing but static in my attempt to reach Garden City. The wicked witch of the west was loose, and I saw her for the first time. I didn't know that twisters were touching down across the panhandle into Kansas. Whole towns and dozens of people were dying. Our passengers were hugging each other and praying.

At 7.2 miles out, the autopilot intercepted the localizer ILS 35 at Liberal, Kansas. It now was black as night; the radar was solid red. The flying dust mixed with rain. Both pilots were on the controls, with the autopilot in the turbulence mode, trying to keep the aircraft level. We flew through the DH and, at about 50 feet, I saw the ground, slant range, through the mud-spattered windshield. We had keyed the approach lights, but it was bumping so badly that we did not know how many times we had keyed them. Finally, the lights were there, and both of us hooked the airplane to land on Runway 30, into the wind. We slammed down, and the King Air rolled about 50 feet. The airplane was coated in a half-inch of mud—blowing mud.

When we landed, the wind at Liberal was clocked at 76 knots. The wind was knocking over dumpsters; at the airport, airplanes were flying while in their tiedowns. The storm killed more than 100 people as it moved across the United States. In Paris, Texas, as the system moved east, a tornado wiped out 22 square blocks and killed more than a dozen people. We had indeed flown through the heart of a killer. I had heard of Texas dust storms, but no one ever had told me about blowing mud.

But we did live to tell this tale. The passenger who passed out was hospitalized for deep trauma. The aircraft received a compressor wash, but no other inspections were made. I left the company soon after. The captain still is flying in Texas.

In 1982, more than five aircraft, including a King Air, came apart along the route we flew in the area known as "Tornado Alley." In all cases, severe weather or tornadoes were forecast or involved. The attitude of the particular company involved in my incident—"There's no need to check the weather, we're going anyway"—contributed to the pressure on the captain to exercise bad judgment on a route that, while familiar to him, had tremendous severe weather potential. In at least five cases, this same lack of prudence proved to be fatal.

It is a grievous thing when command must be taken from a pilot. If it happens in the cause of survival, no betrayal is involved.

True command is a trust that must continuously be met and justified, for the other occupants of the plane have a vested interest in how the flight is guided. In those cases when the pilot loses control and/or his sense of responsibility, mutiny, sadly, becomes a must. Fortunately, such events are rare.

Unfortunately, not as rare are incidents in the small space of the cockpit when pilots-in-command are undone by betrayals as lethal and grievous as any personal and undeserved mutiny may be. It is here that command may be at its most fragile, for it is here that the pilot may be both alone and disastrously impaired—by his own doing, as the next chapter shows.

15
Pilot Impairment

Pilots can betray themselves, and because they usually do so with good intentions, they are the most difficult agents to defend themselves against. Most of the time, most of us effectively maintain the defenses we have discussed in this book, although we must constantly keep them in mind. Yet we often neglect ourselves, the most important part of that triumvirate of flight factors—the aircraft, the environment, the pilot. Not only do we not defend ourselves against personal impairment, we may even deny a need for it.

Stress and the Pilot

Pilot error is a wonderfully convenient way to explain accidents, but just what does it mean? What causes trained and presumably responsible airmen—some highly experienced—to commit errors and let their guard down? As human factors research has addressed itself to analyzing aviation accidents, we have begun to recognize that "pilot error" may only describe a symptom, not a cause. In looking at factors that cause errors in technique and judgment, we find that stress ranks high.

Stress is the body's reaction to any stimulus that disturbs its equilibrium. The stimulus (stressor) can be unpleasant or pleasant. Being fired is stressful; so is being promoted. For each person there is a stress level that allows him to function optimally. Too much or too little stress causes diminished performance and can lead to social or physical problems. A person suffering a stress imbalance may become argumentative, hyper-critical, and reclusive. He may feel exhausted, restless, inse-cure; he may suffer from insomnia, sexual dysfunction, and viral illnesses. Unchecked, such imbalance can cause acute depres-sion, high blood pressure, headaches, backaches, rashes, and stomach problems. Alcohol and drugs only worsen the problem.

Some stressors, in declining order of influence, are: the death of a spouse, divorce, marital separation, the death of a close family member, personal injury or illness, getting married, job dismissal, marital reconciliation, retirement, a change in a fam-ily member's health, pregnancy, sexual difficulties, business readjustment, a change in financial status, changing one's line of work, taking on or foreclosure of a sizable mortgage or loan, changing job responsibilities, a child's leaving home, outstand-ing personal achievement, changing living conditions, revising personal habits, and making changes in one's work conditions, residence, recreation, social activities, or eating and sleeping habits. In short, any alteration that evokes an emotional re-sponse, however hidden. The defense-minded pilot must ques-tion if he is under such stress that his performance will be af-fected, and if he brings his emotional responses into the cockpit.

Flying creates stresses. Sitting in a noisy, vibrating, often dry cockpit for long periods is highly stressful. The complexi-ties and implied dangers in the cockpit make their contribution, as does exposure to ozone, cosmic radiation, and consumption of caffeine and nicotine.

Here is a case of stress-induced error:

• A 35-year old captain had been promoted to chief pilot of a commuter airline, a position that did not suit his nonassertive style. He was under constant management pressure and com-plained that, while bearing great responsibility, he lacked au-thority to make changes. He and other line pilots were openly and intensely criticized and threatened with firing. The weather had thwarted his efforts to train new pilots—there was a large turnover—and the line's most active season was near. When he made his last flight, this pilot was showing symptoms of stress imbalance in chest pains, breathing difficulties, loss of appetite, and apparent exhaustion and preoccupation.

His 39-year-old co-pilot had recently joined the airline and was having trouble. Used to single-pilot operations, he found it hard to adapt to crew-coordination procedures. Captains he flew with noticed that on instrument approaches in the line's Twin Otters, he fell behind the aircraft, chased the needles, and allowed excessive descent rates.

The two pilots had completed the first leg of their scheduled flight; neither was keen to continue in poor and deteriorating weather. They had detected an unusual vibration, apparently in the left engine. After discussion, they agreed to continue. (A pilot recently had been fired for canceling due to weather, and others had been threatened with firing for aborting over mechanical problems.) The co-pilot may have been apprehensive, because it was his turn to fly.

As the Twin Otter neared its destination, the weather went below minimums for the NDB approach. One of the pilots told ATC that though they would shoot the approach, they would probably miss it and require clearance to their alternate. The plane crashed a mile short of the runway. Of the 18 people aboard, only one, a passenger, survived.

The NTSB cited failure to arrest the aircraft's descent at the MDA as the probable cause and determined that the pilots could not have had the runway environment in sight at the MDA. The board could not establish why minimums were broken, but it held that the pilot's chronic fatigue and the co-pilot's anxiety seriously compromised their performance. (The NTSB cited company pressure on pilots of the line to complete their trips, even by busting minimums. The line is now defunct.)

Preventing and Managing Stress

Each person must determine how much stress he can handle and find ways of avoiding or managing an overload. Assertiveness—knowing when and being able to say no—is one key. Also:

• *Work hard, play hard.* Relaxation and recreation are important. Regular changes of pace keep stress in balance, as do meditation and biofeedback. Simple solitude in a *quiet* environment (not a cockpit) is also beneficial.

• *Exercise.* A regular program helps to ward off physical stress symptoms. Some psychologists hold that exercises that increase the body's oxygen circulation—jogging, jumping rope, walking, bicycling, swimming—are best.

• *Take control.* Schedule your time carefully, avoiding procrastination, a stressor. Challenge yourself by pursuing short-term and long-term goals.

• *Eat right, sleep right.* Regular, balanced meals are vital. Avoid alcohol, caffeine, and other drugs. The average person needs one hour of sleep for every two awake, in regular patterns (retiring and waking at the same times daily).

• *Avoid closed-loop, negative thinking.* Worrying or harboring angry, irrational thoughts raises one's stress level. Positive thinking and talking out problems with a caring person are essential to stress management. Be good to yourself.

Many pilots fly to relax and relieve stress. Pilot Herman L. Meltzer relates how problems can invade the cockpit sanctuary:

"Don't fly when you are emotionally upset." In my 25 years as a senior Aviation Medical Examiner, I must have given that advice a thousand times, yet I never thought it important until circumstances showed me that flying and agitation do not mix. Having flown for 25 years, I have, like all pilots, developed a few bad habits. I have become so accustomed to flying short trips for recreation that I became like people who operate automobiles by opening the door, starting the engine, and going.

One morning, after a sleepless night, I was perplexed with personal problems. Financial anxieties, resentment, and self-pity were mulling through my head as I drove 21 miles to Logan County Airport, pulled my plane from its hangar, and took off. I don't remember preflighting or running it up. I had no destination in mind; I just wanted to forget my problems. I chose to go to Bloomington for coffee—about 30 miles. Looking at the gauges, I saw that I had forgotten to check the gas. The left needle was on empty; the right tank showed one-fourth full. I decided to fuel at Holt Strip, ten miles away. No sweat.

That field is a north-south grass strip 2,600 feet long with a powerline at the south end. The wind seemed calm. Several planes were parked at the south end, so I chose to come in from the north. In my sizable experience with such fields in 1,400 flying hours, I had never had trouble. But as I turned base, I saw that I was too high and applied full flaps. Flaring, I saw that I was going to overshoot, so I poured on the coal to go around. A Cessna 150 doesn't like go-arounds with 45 degrees of flaps and nose-high trim. I retrimmed, gingerly dropped the flaps and just skimmed over the powerline. (I had approached downwind on a hot day, and the 150 floated like a glider.) I was perplexed over my first aborted approach in years.

On the second try, I did the same thing, only as I started to flare, I realized that I was lined up with the alfalfa patch next to the runway and was again going to overshoot. I went around, and though I felt no anxiety, I couldn't fathom what was happening: "Am I going nuts or having a stroke?" On the third try, I made a strong, conscious effort to wake up and fly the airplane. I finally landed without trouble.

What had done this to me? Trick winds, density altitude? It was several days before I realized that in my emotional state, ruminating on my problems, *nobody was flying the airplane.*

Nothing Personal

A pilot who carries personal problems, or a need to rush, into the cockpit invites distractions from the moment-to-moment alertness that flying demands, so that the pilot takes the plane for granted. There are, of course, distractions that come with flying, and the pilot must manage them. Studies show that the pilot who can handle any intrusion and still fly flawlessly is virtually nonexistent. When other chores intrude, essential work, including holding altitude, attitude, and heading, suffers, but only slightly, if the pilot knows how to incorporate:

- performing checklists
- looking for traffic
- monitoring radar
- looking for airports
- dealing with systems malfunctions
- communicating with ATC
- studying approach charts
- intercrew conversations.

Distractions can be anything from bees in the cockpit to buzzings of an intercrew dispute. Any diversion is dangerous if the pilot focuses on it too much. This usually results in altitude deviation, though straying from one's route, penetrating restricted airspace, flying unstabilized approaches, taking the wrong clearance, and nearly missing other aircraft also occur. They are typically explained away as "pilot error"—small help. If no clearer explanation for fatal errors can be found, distraction may be it. Sometimes there is a clue in communications. A Cessna 170A crashed on climbout, for example, as the pilot responded to the tower's warning about escaping fuel; a MU-2P crashed when its pilot fixated on a faulty compass.

The Super in Superpilot

In single-pilot operations, the potential for distraction-caused blunders is higher than for multi-member crews, which also are vulnerable. Pilot training is geared to adaptation to a high-input environment requiring a constant division of attention. The pilot's scan must become fast and balanced to provide information from inside and outside the airplane. Emergencies and malfunctions demand close attention, but more often, minor things that go wrong cause serious problems because they divert attention from primary tasks. For example, a door pops open, so the distracted pilot lands gear-up. One DC-8 crew depleted its fuel while troubleshooting a gear-extension problem.

A World of Weariness

• The novice pilot (107 hours) had worked his normal shift in an oil field, rented a Cherokee PA-28-181 and flown a companion to Colorado City, Texas, where he landed downwind on his third attempt, with little runway to spare. Against advice to wait for morning, he insisted on flying to Memphis to beat a cold front and because he liked night flying. He also declined to top off because he was in a hurry and had sufficient fuel for Texarkana, where he would refuel. He received no briefing and filed no plan. The cold front was along his flight route. Most Arkansas and Louisiana airports were reporting IFR.

He boarded his wife, five-year-old son, and three-year-old daughter and departed at 6:20 p.m. At 8:37, he asked the Shreveport FSS for the Texarkana weather. The report was an indefinite ceiling of zero feet, sky obscured, and visibility one-half mile in fog. The best weather was at McAlester and Ardmore, Oklahoma, and at Pine Bluff, Arkansas.

On reaching the Texarkana area, the Piper circled an hour above the clouds. At 10:25, the pilot told the Fort Worth ARTCC that he was lost, in IMC, not instrument-rated, with about 15 minutes' fuel. He was vectored to the Texarkana Municipal Airport and was seen on radar to be over the field at 10:49. There was an indefinite ceiling of 200 feet, sky obscured, with a half-mile visibility in fog. The pilot said that he could not see the runway lights and then that he could and was "turning around."

At 10:52, he reported being out of fuel, and radar contact with him was then lost.

The plane was found in a heavily wooded area 1.5 miles northwest of the airport. The pilot and his wife and son were dead; the daughter was seriously injured. The NTSB cited continuation into adverse weather and becoming lost and disoriented, with fuel exhaustion also named. Contributing factors were the pilot's attempting an operation beyond his experience or ability, a low ceiling, fog, and pilot fatigue.

Here were familiar causes: compulsiveness, macho complacency, inexperience, the fatiguing grind of a full day—and fear. A noninstrument pilot in deteriorating weather is likely to suffer acute stress, which accelerates adrenaline secretion. When the energy supplied by adrenaline is depleted, severe fatigue follows. Flying in darkness is also wearying, and the visual monotony exacerbates the day's residual fatigue. At night, hypoxia occurs as low as 5,000 feet and causes fatigue. The accident may have begun to happen before the pilot boarded the Cherokee for his first flight of that long, last day.

Dr. William Lipsky is an ex-military and current commercial instrument-rated pilot connected with the space shuttle program. His experience offers a medically expert, intimate account of the exhaustion process at work, hour by hour:

While a flight surgeon at the USAF School of Aerospace Medicine, I frequently was called upon to lecture about acute and chronic fatigue, the peculiar demands of night flying, and multiple-factor accidents. Preaching good practice isn't enough.

I planned to fly my new T-tail Piper Lance II from Galveston to Linden, New Jersey, on the Lance's first real shakedown. The night before my departure, hospital emergency work prevented my getting my usual four to six hours' sleep on the shift. I missed dinner and managed but a 45-minute nap before heading home to shower, pack, check my plans, and head for the airport. To save time, I went without breakfast. Takeoff was early in the afternoon, and the four-and-a-half hour first leg was easy. As I refueled, I knew that I was late and probably would not reach Linden before midnight. The route forecast was clear, but I refiled IFR, grabbed a soft drink, cake, and some cookies and preflighted the aircraft.

After liftoff, Departure could not identify me: "November 36292, reset your transponder code." Sure enough, I had failed to reset my transponder after clearance delivery. I mumbled a reply and set the correct code; seconds later, "Contact." I set up for cruise climb, only a trifle concerned that I had missed such an elementary checklist item. Dismissing it with a shrug, I settled down for another uneventful flight. As landmarks began to fade in the dark, so did my excitement and exhilaration. Fatigue set in, the effect of nearly 24 hours without decent food and nearly 36 without sleep.

I set a course into a VOR and watched the CDI needle wander several degrees off course before I corrected it. Realizing that my flying was deteriorating, I shuddered at the idea of a dead-stick night landing in the Appalachians. I also noted that over the Virginia mountains, the CDI began to hunt and seek. I switched the autopilot from Navigation to Heading, which corrected the situation, as I could play one VOR off the other, splitting the error difference to track an acceptable course— at least for a while. My concentration wandered. I usually insisted on centered needles, but I now found myself two, three, sometimes five degrees off course before correcting. I would wonder why the Lance wasn't tracking on the autopilot and then remember it was in the Heading mode. I would correct to course, and the whole process would be repeated.

Southwest of Washington, D.C., I began to have trouble understanding the information on my VORs. I watched the digital course and radial data but neglected the CDI indications. As I wandered right of course, the readout indicated I was left, so I turned farther right, compounding the error. As I puzzled over this, I was handed to New York Center, who said that I was two miles from the centerline and should return to course.

I double-checked the VORs separately and then against each other. There was less than one degree of disparity! Yet the readout indicated that I was three degrees east of course. The CDI said to correct to the left, but that disagreed with my digital data. In my fatigue, I forgot which data was primary and secondary, so I deviated farther right. I knew that I was making a fundamental interpretational error, but I was so tired that, even with paper and pencil, I couldn't figure it out. Finally, I admitted to myself that I needed help. I asked Center for a vector to the centerline, and they obliged. Mumbling about VOR trouble, I began thinking about the approach to Linden.

I could not believe my predicament: I could not navigate in perfect VFR weather because of fatigue and hunger. I called Center again and admitted that I was having trouble with my navigation; I requested vectors to the IAF. It was 11:30 p.m., and Center was not busy. As they vectored me, I set the NDB approach frequency in the ADF, but soon realized that I was having even less success understanding the ADF. I did understand that the needle was lined up with my direction of flight. I was unsure of the mode to which the ADF select switch should be set. My assets were now down to a sound engine and unlimited visibility. I twice meticulously went through the checklist to give myself a fighting chance to make it down safely.

Soon it would be over, I thought. A simple VFR approach, pattern, and landing. No. When you are tired, confused, and on the back side of the power curve, nothing is simple. I did not count on Linden's being buried among city lights, highway lights, and factory lights, all brighter than the airport lights. I asked Linden Unicom for the strobes, was assured they were on, and could not see them. I knew that Linden was but five miles south of Newark International, whose airspace I wanted to avoid. I was three quarters of the way to Newark before I spotted my error. I made an immediate 180, instantly saw the strobes and made a hot but uneventful landing.

The corollary to get-home-itis is get-there-itis. I could have killed not only myself but innocent bystanders. My errors were caused by a lack of professionalism: I would never operate in that physical state, so why did I think that I could fly in that condition?

Acute fatigue is short-lived and common and results from poor sleep or diet, strenuous exercise, excitement, continuous performance of repetitive tasks, or prolonged concentration. Small amounts of coffee, tea, or cola may temporarily dispel acute fatigue, but after an initial two-hour burst of energy, these stimulants lose their effectiveness, as do candy, cakes, cookies— refined carbohydrates. Fruit and protein snacks are good, but not as substitutes for meals. After two hours, the fatiguing aspects of flying—noise, vibration, poor visibility, the intellectual labor in IFR work—wear heavily on pilots.

Chronic Fatigue

This long-term condition usually is the result of weeks or months of stress and takes its toll while being less physically intense than acute fatigue. The victim usually continues to perform without proper rest, nutrition, or recreation, unaware of his true condition. Professional help may become necessary to break the damaging behavior pattern in which sleep is needed but won't come, a balanced diet is needed but appetite is lost, relaxation is needed but the sufferer cannot relax.

The inflight signs of fatigue reflect loss of energy and skill. The pilot accepts lower performance standards, becomes irritable and blames the airplane, the weather, or—a favorite target—the System for his mistakes. Or recognizing his errors may lower his self-esteem and confidence until he accepts whatever happens. A breakdown in the instrument scan is typical. The pilot's eyes concentrate on movements or objects in the center of his visual field, neglecting the periphery, which helps to explain the many fatigue-related landing accidents. In calculating, reading charts, and other tasks, the sufferer's attention span is short, and he is prone to confusion and errors such as missing radio calls or forgetting things from frequency assignments to lowering the gear. His nervous system responds sluggishly; his reaction time is longer and his reactions and judgment are imprecise. Priorities are confused and situations lose their proper perspective. Decisions are late in coming. The PIC in fact loses control of his command, yet he may believe and insist that he is on top of things and flying well. He may defend himself with hostility, while he suffers increased sensitivity to physical discomforts such as burning eyes, shortness of breath, sweating, heartburn, constipation, and, when he does get to sleep, nightmares.

The Demons of Drowsiness and Illness

Accident statistics reflect only a hint of how many pilots sleep at the controls. Usually, it takes those who know such pilots' habits to reveal this about them. Some pilots are known to plan to sleep while the autopilot flies; others drop off from the effects of solitude, noise and vibration, monotony, and fatigue. Just knowing that everyone else in the airplane is dozing can lull a pilot into drowsiness that leads to a crash.

Sleep deprivation accompanies many airborne operations. Businessman-pilots who spend their nights in various beds from city to city get insufficient rest. Time zone changes and altered eating schedules disrupt the body's internal pacing, or circadian rhythm, adversely affecting performance. Such disturbances, including jet lag, can take two or three days to overcome.

Violent illness is more debilitating still and can suddenly lay a pilot low, as happened to airman Steve Nieman:

I vomited into my oxygen mask. It happened so quickly that I inhaled part of the retch back into my throat, choked, and threw it up again. Just as another wave of sickness wrenched my stomach, I ripped the mask off my face and helplessly watched as the control column and instrument panel became a blurry brown. The metal yoke became slippery, and I had to fight to control the twin-engine mailplane. I was alone, and no one was going to help me down through the one-and-a-half miles of atmosphere.

It had started as I was loading my Cessna 310 around 6:00 p.m. for a weeknight run from Ely to Elko to Reno, Nevada, and back. I had felt the slightest touch of nausea, but I shrugged it off as something I ate. Besides, I was hundreds of miles from home base, and even if I flew back, the 310's owner was not qualified as a backup pilot. If I didn't fly, the Post Office wouldn't pay, and our reliability percentage would lower. When I signed for custody of those mail sacks, so I believed, it was up to me to do practically anything to deliver them on time. So I climbed northwest out of Ely for Elko, heading for the Ruby Mountains, arguing that I had eaten too much dinner. A Tums or a carbonated drink would help, but I had neither, and I convinced myself that an eight-hour layover in Reno would allow enough rest to settle my stomach.

Adding more sacks in Elko took enough time for me to realize that I was sick, maybe with a touch of the flu—but how bad? With the night's winds, Reno was just one and a half hours away. I could press on, take it easy, finish the job, and then refuse the return flight if I did not feel better. I took off into the expiring pink light on the horizon.

I had made a miserable decision. Each mile seemed to stretch longer as I felt worse. I climbed to the 10,000-foot MEA as gingerly as I dared, but the higher I flew, the more claustrophobic my condition became. For help, I slipped the oxygen mask on sooner than usual and opened the valve. I took huge gulps, hoping the oxygen would heal my feverish body.

I crossed the Battle Mountain VOR 54 miles down the road, feeling as if I had flown 540. The MEA bumped to 12,000, and I began to doubt that I could stay conscious at that altitude. The sky had been clear, but ahead was a tall obstruction smothering ground lights and stars. Reno was reported 600 overcast and one, in moderate snow. The obstruction was the eastern edge of that system, burying my destination and maybe me.

After emptying the contents of my stomach all over the cockpit, I knew I could not continue. It was going to be tricky enough surviving a 5,000-foot descending 180 landing at Battle Mountain. I chopped the power and started coming about, still vomiting, my body racked by hot and cold flashes. My vision tunneled, and I began to feel faint. I was startled to see the instruments showing a 60-degree bank and the airspeed building toward red line in the turn. It had been as if I were in a dream, not in a fatal episode. Now I was convinced. I forced myself to concentrate—pitch up, slow down, steady, don't lose it now. Center was calling, and I canceled IFR to divert to Battle Mountain. This was unusual, and Center knew something was wrong. So as not to admit that the only pilot aboard was disabled, I assured them I'd be okay and switched to Unicom.

I carefully flew a normal pattern and at last heard the tires on the runway. I rolled to the end of the runway and stopped, engines running. I mustered what little strength I had and taxied toward the only light on the field, a trailer next to an old building. I shut down, at last feeling safe.

I ached and felt so drained that I could not move and decided to sleep in my seat. A man came toward me, obviously uneasy at approaching this dark, freshly shut-down plane from which no one was emerging. He climbed onto the wing and looked at me through the side window. I could only gesture toward the door. When he opened it, the sight and smell must have answered most of his questions. He helped me down and into the trailer. What a fool I had been, almost cutting short my life.

Flying aggravates physical illness. Altitude and oxygen don't cure ailments, so the preflighting rule for airplanes—either whole or no-go—should also apply to the pilot.

The Pilot at Altitude

• Night had fallen when the Piper Turbo Arrow took off from Taos, New Mexico, westbound for Las Vegas. The pilot airfiled an IFR plan and was cleared to FL 200, as he'd requested. His route was via Farmington and Grand Canyon. Soon after the Arrow was established on course and altitude, ATC realized that the pilot was in trouble. The following partial transcript of the conversation between him and ATC indicates the rapid and progressive deterioration of his abilities to think and fly:

"Are you deviating now? I show you turning southeastbound."

"I show myself going direct to Grand Canyon."

"I show you turning eastbound. You have made a left turn and are heading southeastbound."

"Oh."

"What is your heading now?"

"Heading is two-four-three."

"I show you tracking eastbound on a heading of about zero-niner-zero now."

[*No response from pilot.*]

"Check your oxygen. Are you receiving oxygen?"

"That's affirm."

"Your compass . . . your navigational equipment is not functioning right, or something. I show you in a left turn now."

"I show us going zero-four . . . two-four-zero."

"What is your visibility? Can you see the ground?"

"Say again?"

"Can you see the ground now?"

"Uh, two-thirty-seven, uh, hundred, uh, from Tuba City. And I am heading, uh, my two-four-zero."

"You are evidently not receiving your oxygen supply. I am going to try a lower altitude. Descend and maintain one-five thousand. Do you copy?"

"Descend, uh, one-five-zero."

"Check that you are receiving oxygen."

"Affirmative."

"Roger, are you descending now?"

"Affirmative."

"What is your altitude now?"

"Two-zero-zero."

There were no further transmissions from the pilot. The Turbo Arrow, which had an autopilot with altitude-hold capability, continued to circle at FL 200, about 60 miles southwest of Farmington. An Air Force C-130 was given vectors to rendezvous with the airplane. The crew could see no one aboard the Arrow, and they could not raise the pilot on the radio. The airplane was airborne for nearly three hours before the engine exhausted the fuel from the selected tank (the other tank was full). It began to descend in shallow spirals that alternated left and right. The pilot survived the crash but sustained severe facial lacerations and damage to his spinal cord.

Hypoxia and improper use of oxygen equipment were cited as probable accident causes. During a portion of the flight, the pilot had used supplemental oxygen, but instead of wearing a mask, he had merely placed a supply tube in his mouth. Evidence showed that the oxygen supply had been depleted and the flow valve on the oxygen cylinder had been turned off while the Arrow was still airborne. At altitude, the pilot could have remained conscious for only about ten minutes thereafter.

At 25,000 feet, there is the same percentage of oxygen in the atmosphere as at sea level, but there is much less atmospheric pressure to force sufficient oxygen into our lungs. At 10,000 feet, each inhalation gives us only two-thirds the oxygen molecules available at sea level, and only half at 18,000. Less oxygen per breath means less for oxidation—burning—of food to produce heat and energy. Unless we use supplemental oxygen at higher altitudes, our bodies become starved. At 45,000 feet, it takes only nine to 15 seconds for the average person to pass out with inadequate oxygen; at 30,000, one to two minutes. Charts show about 30 minutes of effective performance at 20,000, but a trip in an altitude chamber will demonstrate that people show signs of hypoxia long before that. Thin air is like thin ice—if offers little support.

Hypoxia symptoms are not easily recognized. Unless a pilot is aware of and expecting them, he may feel excellent and in control. He may calculate badly and copy erratically and illegibly while his fingernails turn blue and he stares dumbly at the panel, but he may still insist that all is fine.

Hypoxia can be caused by poor transportation of oxygen through the body or by the body's inability to use it. Drugs, alcohol, and tobacco aggravate the condition. One cigarette lowers the oxygen content of the blood and raises the apparent altitude of a person at sea level to nearly 7,000 feet. More smoking adds altitude to cabin altitude in flight. Excessive smoking can cause such *hypemic* hypoxia. Anemia, donating blood, and carbon monoxide poisoning have the same effect. Poor blood circulation brought on by excessive *g* forces or long periods of positive pressure breathing of oxygen (necessary above 25,000 feet) can cause *stagnant* hypoxia. Nor is oxygen a remedy for the *histoxic* hypoxia suffered by a hungover pilot. Only detoxification over time can restore normality, so shrinking from drinking is the only defense. One drink raises one's personal altitude by 2,000 feet. Poor nutrition, obesity, fatigue, illness, and poor general physical condition also affect our susceptibility to hypoxia.

Threatening conditions can differ from day to day and from individual to individual.

The Air Force requires its pilots to use oxygen from 10,000 feet up and from the ground up at night, for lack of oxygen can hinder night vision, including color perception and peripheral acuity. The FAA recommendation of oxygen use from 5,000 feet at night is conservative and should certainly be followed. The FAA's oxygen requirements begin with flight crew in unpressurized aircraft flying between 12,500 and 14,000 for more than 30 minutes. Above 14,000, oxygen is required for the pilot (or minimum crew) for the entire flight. Above 15,000, it must be provided for passengers. If the aircraft is pressurized, above FL 250, a ten-minute supply is required for each occupant. Above FL 350, at least one pilot must use an oxygen mask if the cabin exceeds 14,000 feet. (If two pilots are at the controls, quick-donning masks are sufficient below FL 410.)

Hyperventilation, or overbreathing, is brought on by emotional stress, fear, or pain, and it can cause the loss of carbon dioxide, causing symptoms like those of hypoxia. At the onset of hyperventilation, check your oxygen supply if you are using it, or start using it. Then slow your breathing rate by talking or singing aloud or by breathing into a paper bag to help restore the body's carbon dioxide balance.

A problem pilots and passengers often face in moving through varying temperatures is ear blockage. If pressure in the middle ear is not equalized during ascent or descent, pain ensues. Normally, air flows to and from the middle ear and the back of the throat through the Eustachian tube. Swallowing, yawning, or chewing gum aids this process in climbs or descents. If you have a cold, an allergy, or an infection that blocks the tube, the pressure may not equalize. Especially if you suspect ear problems, avoid rapid descents. If you tell ATC you have someone with an ear problem aboard, they will try not to descend you too quickly. If the pressure does not equalize, close your mouth, hold your nose, and blow, to force air up the tube and into the middle ear. (This maneuver is called the Valsalva procedure.) You may have to do this often on the way down. Nose drops can clear the tube, but overuse reduces effectiveness.

Use the Valsalva procedure frequently after a flight in which you have taken 100-percent oxygen for a time, for the middle ear absorbs pure oxygen, a cause of future trouble. The procedure can also clear a blocked sinus.

Gas Attacks

At high altitude, you may develop toothaches and gastrointestinal pain. As you climb, gas is trapped and expands. Toothaches, which indicate abcesses, cavities, and new root-canal work, usually disappear as you descend (especially if you are flying with a dentist). Stomach pains can be relieved through belching and another similarly resonant and therapeutic method.

Gas bubbles formed by nitrogen when pressure on the body drops sufficiently do not vanish as easily. *Decompression sickness* is similar to the release of bubbles in soda when the cap is removed. The bends, sometimes experienced by divers, is caused by nitrogen bubbles forming around large joints, such as knees and elbows. It usually does not occur below 25,000 feet. Keep an affected area immobile and do not massage it. Decompression sickness calls for 100-percent oxygen and landing. The symptoms may lessen or disappear when you are lower, but do not climb again. Check with an FAA medical examiner or the 24-hour hotline of Brooks AFB's School of Aerospace Medicine.

Scuba diving compounds this problem, for the body absorbs twice the normal nitrogen at only 30 feet down. Before flying to 8,000 feet, a diver should wait at least four hours; above 8,000, wait 24. Another type of decompression sickness is the chokes—a burning in the chest and uncontrollable coughing. Treat this as you would the bends. The central nervous system can be affected by decompression sickness; the symptoms resemble those of hypoxia or pulling positive *g*'s: spots before the eyes, blurred vision, headache, and possibly shock.

Carbon Monoxide Poisoning

Here is a way in which faulty maintenance can kill you. If any elements of your exhaust system are defective, CO can enter the cabin, blown there as ram air directs exhaust gases over the exhaust manifolds. In a typical lightplane heating system, a heat exchanger or metal shroud surrounds the muffler. These elements act as a radiator, absorbing the heat generated by exhaust gases. Turning on the cabin heat channels this heated air into the cabin. CO is a toxic, odorless, colorless gas caused by incomplete combustion of petroleum fuels. A faulty exhaust system, therefore, can be lethal. If smoke enters the cockpit, assume that it contains CO, but smoke isn't necessary for CO to be present.

Carbon monoxide poisoning can induce hypoxia; it can produce death. It has a strong affinity for combining with hemoglobin, the blood substance that transports oxygen to body tissues. Even tiny amounts can prevent oxygen molecules from attaching to hemoglobin, causing a toxic form of hypoxia. Saturations of up to ten percent generally produce no symptoms. At levels between ten and 20 percent, mild symptoms occur: sluggishness, a slight headache, shortness of breath. Saturations above 20 percent produce vertigo, severe headache, a feeling of tightness around the forehead, fatigue, double vision, a sense of constriction in the chest, noises in the ears, and a characteristic red coloring of the blood and skin. A saturation of 40 percent causes convulsions and then coma and death by respiratory arrest.

Exposure to only 600 parts CO per million of air for four hours can mean a 40-percent saturation. Concentrations as small as 200 parts per million can affect one's flying after an hour and a half. Most critical, sudden exposure to high concentrations of

CO can cause death within ten minutes. A prolonged exposure to low CO levels causes a gradual onset of symptoms. A cigarette creates 1 to 1.5-percent hemoglobin saturation.

The higher you fly, the more the atmospheric pressure of oxygen decreases, so that CO in the cabin will more easily prevent oxygen from entering your bloodstream. Even with oxygen therapy, recovery from advanced CO poisoning can take two days.

CO is odorless in its pure state, but the smell of exhaust in the cabin screams its presence. It does not have to be coming through the heat outlets but through cracks, holes, and seams in the firewall. A CO detector is thus a lifesaving item, for it indicates by its color if and how much CO is present (price, less than five dollars). If you suspect CO, immediately:

- Turn off the heat, if it is on.
- Open the fresh-air vents and, if possible, a window.
- Reduce engine power to decrease exhaust gas flow.
- In a pressured airplane, know the proper fume-removal procedures. Many manufacturers recommend depressurization, for a compressor driven by exhaust flow provides cabin pressure.
- Land immediately; get medical help for lasting symptoms.

The best defense is truly preventive maintenance. Inspect the exhaust system on every oil change. Check maintenance records and ADs as well as length of service of exhaust stacks, manifold, and muffler. If they have been welded, they may need early replacement. An exhaust system's environment is highly corrosive, and defects first appear as small cracks and discontinuities undetectable to the naked eye. Regular replacement of even "good looking" components is therefore wise.

Bonds in Bottles

- The pilot was age 56, with commercial, multi-engine, and single-engine sea ratings; total time about 4,500 hours. At Ripley, Mississippi, he visited friends for an hour, was in a good mood and drank nothing. He declined cola and crackers, saying that he had "something in the airplane."

He took off normally, rocking his wings, around 3:45 p.m. and was next seen at 5:15, circling a field. A witness said that the pilot "appeared to be attempting to land. On the first pass, the Cessna 120 was about 200 feet high; on the second pass, he was 250 to 300 feet high; and on the third pass, he was 110 to 125 feet high. Then he started dropping." The pilot was fatally injured when the airplane crashed in a steep nose-low attitude. The weather was clear, with light winds. There was no sign of preimpact engine or control-system anomalies.

The pilot's medical certificate limited him to flight with eyeglasses to correct for distance and near vision. No glasses were found. The airplane reeked of whiskey. In the wreckage were found a portable radio, a box of crackers, and a one-third-full fifth of whiskey. A postmortem examination of the pilot disclosed a blood alcohol level of 160 mg%, at least three drinks worth. The NTSB cited impairment by alcohol as the probable cause of the accident.

In 1982, there were 35 fatal general aviation accidents involving alcoholic impairment. About half occurred as the pilots flew low, buzzed the ground, or performed acrobatic maneuvers. In nine accidents, the pilots lost control of their aircraft. Reported figures form the tip of a grisly iceberg; they don't reflect cases when drunk or hungover pilots endangered innocent people and themselves but managed to avoid crashing. Drunk pilots have been known to barrel into bad weather, exhaust fuel, lose control, and make other fatal and stupid errors.

Alcohol is a depressant that causes a change in the proportion of two neurohormones, norepinephrine and serotonin, which, with intoxication, cause changes in mood, alertness, perception, and judgment. The entire nervous system—from small neural connections controlling fine coordination to the deeper behavioral centers of the brain—is affected. Alcohol spurs hypoxia, and even small amounts of it affect field of vision and night vision. Intoxication causes blurred and double vision, as muscle control is lost with increasing drunkenness. Unable to track each other's movements, the eyes give the brain two images.

FAR Part 91.11 stipulates that pilots must wait a minimum of eight hours after *the consumption* of any alcoholic beverage before flying. Some pilots observe this rule to the letter, however much booze was drunk. In view of the dulling effects of hangovers and detoxification, a more realistic leeway is at least 12 hours after *mild* drinking; the most responsible approach is the airlines' 24-hour-wait policy. For a truly alcoholic pilot, a full day may not prevent the debilitating effects of withdrawal after such "long" abstinence.

In 1985, the FAA added to its rule that no one can act as a crew member while under the influence of alcohol, the criterion being that a blood alcohol level of .04 percent or above by weight while attempting to act as a crew member constitutes a violation.

A normal, healthy liver can detoxify one ounce of alcohol in no less than three hours. Six beers or four mixed drinks require 12½ hours of detoxification, even if food was consumed. This physiological rule is unbreakable. For a person with liver damage, an effect of significant drinking, the process takes longer. Coffee may stimulate the brain somewhat, but it does not sober a person up. It only creates an awake drunk.

A person may be conned by the effects of a small amount of alcohol into a false sense of well-being; he may feel sharp, but his reaction time, judgment, coordination, and memory will be diminished. He will not realize his mistakes and may even feel immune to booze—a rakehell, macho ace. Later, the miseries of a hangover can plague him for hours or days with agitation, irritability, depression, nausea, and other discomforts that can be torture in a cockpit. The NTSB holds that *any* alcohol in a pilot's bloodstream jeopardizes safety.

Compounding Impairment, Plus Going to Pot

• A Gates Learjet 25 landing at Newark International Airport touched down about 500 feet beyond the displaced threshold and then bounced off the runway in a nose-high, right-wing-low attitude. The right wingtip tank and landing gear struck the ground, and the Lear then cartwheeled onto an airport service road and exploded. The captain, who was not wearing his lap belt or shoulder harness, was thrown from the wreckage and died of a massive skull fracture. The co-pilot, pinned by the instrument panel, drowned after some of the wreckage was propelled into a nearby canal.

No satisfactory mechanical explanations could account for the bounce or the pilots' inability to regain control. However, the Learjet had made a very rapid descent, at times by as much as 50 knots faster than the 250-knot legal speed limit below 10,000 feet. It was descending at 1,150 fpm and 180 knots when it turned final about a mile from the runway. It flew a five-degree glidepath, with an average descent rate of 1,000 fpm, at 140 knots indicated—about 15 knots faster than the proper reference speed for its weight and balance. Said the NTSB, "The approach was unstabilized, but a properly trained and experienced pilot, alert and vigilant, should have been able to land safely."

The pilot, 26, was a 5,100-hour ATP, with 1,600 hours in type. The co-pilot, 25, was a 4,122-hour ATP, with 1,488 hours in Learjets. Both pilots were fatigued, having had little rest before their takeoff in Chicago. They were also possibly hypoxic, for tests showed moderate CO concentrations in their blood. They were cigarette smokers. Furthermore, although the pressurization system was set to maintain a cabin altitude of 8,000 feet, the "physiological altitude" of the pilots during most of the flight was about 12,000 feet, high enough to impair the brain's absorption of oxygen to the extent that memory, attention and the ability to make decisions could be affected. Also, phenyl-propanolamine was found in the co-pilot's urine. Contained in cold, allergy, and diet-control medications, this drug can cause nervousness and errors in judgment.

The pilot was subject to considerable stress. Only a month before the accident, he had left one jet courier service under strained circumstances to join another and was known to be worried about job security in the face of keen competition. (The NTSB suggested that job-related pressures may have induced the rapid descent, since a rival company's Learjet was approaching the area.) There also were personal stress-causing factors in his life.

Significantly, careful toxological tests determined that the captain had used marijuana at most 24 hours before the accident. The tests also showed that the co-pilot may have smoked marijuana or had, at least, been exposed to marijuana smoke during the same period. "Passive inhalation," or inadvertently breathing marijuana smoke produced by others, can lead to positive tests for marijuana up to 24 hours after exposure. The pilots were not together during the period until they boarded the airplane at Chicago. The NTSB said that they possibly used marijuana during the flight, though evidence was not conclusive.

The possibility that a professional flight crew smoked pot while operating a high-performance airplane is not as shocking as one might think. Says the NTSB, "The apparent widespread use of illicit drugs, especially marijuana, among the general population suggests that some percentage of pilots in both private and commercial aircraft operations are using such drugs."

There are many myths about marijuana. Chronic users contend that their perception and motor skills are enhanced by the drug. At best, this is a deception similar to the heightened sense of well-being felt by a victim of hypoxia or a drunk just before he falls from his high. More realistic is the NTSB's statement from its report on the Learjet accident: "The documented behavioral effects of marijuana include impaired judgment and concentration, impaired perceptual and motor skills, and reduced short-term memory.'' Among the chemical compounds in pot is delta-9-tetra-hydrocannabinol (THC), which plays havoc with the central nervous system. When marijuana smoke is inhaled, THC is rapidly absorbed into the bloodstream and transported to the brain. Unlike alcohol, nicotine, and caffeine, THC is long retained in fatty tissues and is only slowly eliminated from the body. Marijuana may be active in a person's nervous system well after it can no longer be detected in his blood. And it is addictive. Like alcohol, cocaine (another increasingly popular drug), or any mind-altering substance, it is poison to pilots.

Legal, Prescribed, and Hazardous

Among the monkeys the co-pilot of the crashed Learjet bore on his back was a drug that was legal but may have helped to destroy him. For pilots in flight, prescription and over-the-counter medicines may spell not relief but trouble. They can cause drowsiness, dizziness, headache, nausea, or dry mouth, and these effects can be wider-ranging and more unpredictable at altitude. According to the FAA's Aeromedical Standards Division, a pilot should allow 24 to 48 hours to pass after his last dose of a medicine before undertaking command of an aircraft. If you require medicine, you may not be in shape to command an airplane at all, especially in a crisis.

Ask your physician about *all* the effects—and their duration—of any medicine he prescribes for you. Make sure he knows that you may be considering flying under its influence. If he doesn't know flying, ask if he would recommend driving under the drug. Also consider how much you must take, how often, and how cumulative the effects may be. If you have not used the medicine before, consider that you may be subject to allergic and other side effects that could hit you suddenly and hard.

Over-the-counter drugs also can have side effects that affect flight performance. Furthermore, while a pilot may respect a physician's prescribed dosage, he may be tempted to overdose a patent drug to "knock out the bug." Using an antihistamine while flying, for instance, could clog your mind while clearing your nose. Even aspirin can have bad effects when taken to excess.

If you have doubts about medicine and flying, call your medical examiner. If you suffer aches, pains, or queasiness that have no ready explanation, don't pooh-pooh the strange symptoms while contemplating flying. Don't play doctor with self-diagnoses or rely on patent medicines to dull the symptoms.

The smart, defensive pilot-in-command does not practice self-deception or deny things that are patently wrong. Impairment stems from refusing to confront emotions and their effects, ignoring fatigue, stinting on oxygen, overlooking potential CO sources, pickling or narcotizing the brain, and letting illness threaten safety. Our defenses begin with our own alertness, energy, decisiveness, and ability to execute our decisions. If we ourselves sabotage those faculties, we are left with little armor against other dangers. They are central to our ability to maintain control, remain responsible and exert proper authority. They are the essentials of survival.

"Ahab syndrome," 259–62
Air defense identification zones (ADIZs), 61–62
Airport advisory service (AAS), 19–20
Airport radar service areas (ARSAs), 82–84
Airspeed on landing, 133–35
Airworthiness directives (ADs), 179–80, 181–84
  compliance with, 181
  maintenance or defect reports (MDRs), 182
  service difficulty reports (SDRs), 182
  three types of, 181
Alcoholic impairment, 319–21
Alert areas, 60
A. M. Weather, 217
Annual inspections, 187–89
Area forecasts, 221
ATC control facilities, 91–103
  crash of Aztec 6241 Yankee, 96–103
  visiting, 91
  See also Controlled areas
Autokinetic effect, 41–42
Automatic systems, 270–73
Automatic terminal information service (ATIS), 109–12

Barnicle, Stephan P., 237–40
  on emergency problem solving, 237–40

Barton, Bruce, 122–23
  on night landings, 122–23
Beatty, Edward J., 171–73
  on mechanics' failures, 171–73
Birds, 158–60, 160–62
  at airports, 160–62
  avoiding collisions with, 158–60
  defensive flying and, 161–62
"Blanking," 38–40
"Bligh complex," 262–67
Blind encoders, 38–39
Blind spots, 40–43
  autokinetic effect and, 41–42
  distractions, 42
  glare, 42
  outward scanning activity, 42–43
  relative motion, 42
  visual acuity, 41
Bragg, Don, 233–37
  on sudden weather change, 233–37
Briefing. *See* Weather briefing

Capacitance, 212–13
Carbon monoxide poisoning, 318–19
Chronic fatigue, 310
"Climb, confess, communicate," 240–42
"Combat zones," 57–58
Command, 231–325
  the "Ahab syndrome," 259–62
  authority and responsibility, 250–52

Command (*continued*)
  automatic systems and, 270–73
  the "Bligh complex," 262–67
  checklists and, 266–67
  commuter plane crash in Vieques
    and, 253–56
  control and, 274–99
  co-pilots and, 288–91, 291–95,
    295–99
  decisiveness/flexibility axis and,
    267–70
  ego and, 260–61
  en route decisions, 233–49
  fatigue and, 307–13
  junior pilots and bosses, 283–86
  passenger rights and, 286–88
  pilotage, 242–44
  pilot impairment, 300–25
  proficiency levels and, 256–59
  "self-taught and self-certified pi-
    lots," 261–62
  stress and, 300–305
  temptations and, 249
  threats to authority, 250–52
  two essential principles, 250–51
  "weak links in chain of," 252–56
Common traffic advisory frequency
    (CTAF), 19–20, 25–26
Consistency, 133–34
Constant pressure charts, 222
Contact approach, 87–88
Control by pilot, 274–99
  advice, listening to, 278–83
  ATC controllers and weather,
    274–76, 277–78
  cockpit atmosphere, 274–75
  co-pilots and, 288–91, 291–95,
    295–99
  junior pilots and bosses, 283–86
  passenger rights and, 286–88
  taken by co-pilot, 295–99

Controlled areas, 67–90
  airport radar service areas
    (ARSAs), 82–84
  Boeing 727 and Cessna 172
    N7711G, 68–73
  contact approach, 87–88
  gaining access, 81–82
  ground clutter, 88–90
  high-density terminals, 79–81
  keeping track of position, 86–87
  pilot error, 89–90
  "protection" in, 77–79
  radar vectors, 84–88
  TCA clearance, 81–82
  terminal radar service areas
    (TRSAs), 75–77
  visual separation, 73–75
  See also ATC control facilities
Convective outlook, 227
Co-pilots, 288–99
  control taken by, 295–99
  right-seat perspective, 291–95
Courtesy and cooperation, 10–11
Crises in the Cockpit (Slepyan),
    108, 216
Current conditions, 217–18, 223–25
  GOES imagery, 223
  observed winds aloft, 224
  pilots reports (pireps), 225
  radar summary chart, 224
  remote radar weather display im-
    agery, 224
  sequence reports (SAs), 223

Decisiveness/flexibility axis in com-
    mand, 267–70
Decompression sickness, 317–18
Defensive flying:
  command, 231–325
  maintenance, 163–229

midair avoidance, 1–103
surface conflicts, 105–62
Distractions, 305–306
blunders caused by, 305–306
Diuguid, Randolph S., 296–99
on co-pilot taking control, 296–99
Drugs. *See* Illicit drug use; Medicines
Dundas, Carole K., 157–58
on wake turbulence, 157–58
Duthie, Larry J., 281–83
on "advice," 281–83
Dynamic hydroplaning, 137–38

Ear blockage, 316–17
Electrical quantity gauge, 213
Engine-failure accidents, 190–91
En route decisions, 233–49
"climb, confess, communicate," 240–42
emergency problem solving, 237–40
locating by VOR, 245
pilotage and, 242–44
precautionary landings, 246–69
self-reliance and, 233–37

FAR-based taxi rules, 154–55
Fatigue, 307–13
chronic fatigue, 310
Ferguson, Larry F., 77–79
on TRSAs, 77–79
FM broadcast frequency interference, 112–14
Forecast weather information, 218, 225–29
convective outlook, 227
severe weather outlook chart, 227–28

significant weather prognostic charts ("prog charts"), 227
stability chart, 228
terminal forecasts, 225
winds and temperatures aloft, 226
Forecast winds and temperatures aloft, 226
Freed, James B., 246–49
on safety principles, 246–49
Frequencies and uses (table), 20–21
Fuel contamination, 191–92
Fuel exhaustion accidents, 205–207, 207–208
Fuel gauges, 208–12, 212–13
Fuel mismanagement, 190–213
contamination, 191–92, 192–94, 195
engine-failure accidents, 190–91
extra measures for checking fuel, 198–201
fuel exhaustion accidents, 205–207, 207–208
"fuel starvation," 204–205
gauges and, 208–12, 212–13
jet fuel in nonjet engines, 201–202
pilot's role in avoiding, 203–204
preflight purge routine, 192–94
untopped tanks, 195–98

Gas attacks, 317–18
decompression sickness, 317–18
Gauss, Edward G., 109–12
on IFR approach, 109–12
Go-arounds, 124–25, 131–33
failures to initiate, 124–25
successful, 131–33
GOES imagery, 223
Grass landing fields, 128–31

"Green demon" (military charts), 64–65
  See also Military aircraft
Grosslight, J. H., 289–90
  on co-pilots, 289–90
Ground clutter, 88–90
Greenfield, Lee, 182–84
  on maintenance, 182–84

Handleman, Philip, 128–30
  on grass-field landing, 128–30
Hydroplaning, 135–37, 139–41
Hypoxia, 314–17
  histoxic, 315
  hypemic, 315
  stagnant, 315

Illicit drug use, 322–24
Impairment. *See* Pilot impairment

Jet fuel, 201–202
Junior pilots and bosses, 283–86

Komes, Denny, 294–95
  on co-piloting, 294–95
Krieter, William P., 207–208
  on fuel exhaustion, 207–208

Landing lights and strobes, 16–17
Limited-options landing, 125–26
Lipsky, Dr. William, 307–309
  on fatigue, 307–309

Macomber, Roger, 143–45
  on "X" painted on runway, 143–45
Maintenance, 163–229
  airworthiness directives (ADs) and, 179–80, 181–84
  annual inspections, 187–89
  communicating with mechanics, 187–89
  fuel mismanagement, 190–213

improper maintenance, accidents due to, 165–68
maintenance or defect reports (MDRs), 182
mechanics and, 168–73, 187–89
preliminary troubleshooting by pilot, 185–87
service bulletins, 180
service difficulty reports (SDRs), 182
twenty-seven items for pilots to check, 175–76
weather briefing, 214–29
  See also Fuel mismanagement; Mechanics
Maintenance or defect reports (MDRs), 182
Mansfield, Richard H., 35–36
  on absence of advisories, 35–36
Marijuana use, 322–24
Mark, Robb, 292–93
  on co-piloting, 292–93
Martin, David G., 84–86
  on radar vectors, 84–86
Martin, Rick H., 196–98
  on fuel contamination, 196–98
Mechanics, 168–73, 187–89
  fallibility of, 169–70
  pilot's communication with, 187–89
  training for, 169
  See also Maintenance
Medicines, 324–25
Mellon, Charles W., 145–46
  on landing conditions, 145–46
Meltzer, Herman L., 303–304
  on stress, 303–304
Midair avoidance, 1–103
  ATC control facilities, 91–103
  basic rules for, 26–27
  in controlled areas, 67–90
  military aircraft and, 51–66
  noncontrolled airports and, 3–27

radar contact, loss of, 5–6
radio communication, 17–18
see-and-avoid vigilance, 6–7
seeing to avoid, 28–50
statistics on collisions, 3–4
Military aircraft, 51–66
air defense identification zones
(ADIZs), 61–62
alert areas, 60
"buddies," checking for, 65
"combat zones," 57–58
defensive flying precautions, 64–66
F-4C and Beech Baron, 53–57
"green demon" (charts) and, 63–64
intercept missions, 53–57
military operations areas (MOAs),
59–60
military training routes (MTRs),
62
prohibited areas, 58–59, 60
statistics on midair collisions involving, 52
in terminal airspace, 64–65
warning areas, 61
Military operations areas (MOAs),
59–60
Military training routes (MTRs), 62
Moore, William E., 279–81
on "advice," 279–81

Nesse, Anton S., 177–78
on maintenance, 177–78
Nieman, Steve, 311–13
on sudden illness, 311–13
Night landings, 122–24
Noncontrolled airports, 3–27
AAS and, 19–20
CTAF and, 19–20, 25–26
flexibility at, 25
landing lights and strobes, 16–17

pattern protocol, 12–15
pulse lights, 16–17
radio-effective pilots, 21–23
recommended practices at, 8
reporting around pattern, 23–24
standard instrument approach and
departure, 9
traffic advisory practices, 19

Observed winds aloft, 224
Overshoot accidents, 127–28
Oxygen supply, 313–17
hyperventilation, 316
hypoxia, 314–17

Partnerships. See Maintenance
Passenger rights, 286–88
Pattern protocol, 12–15
Personal problems, 304–305
Pilotage, 242–44
Pilot error, 300
Pilot impairment, 300–25
alcoholic impairment, 319–21
carbon monoxide poisoning, 318–19
chronic fatigue, 310
decompression sickness, 317–18
distractions and blunders, 305–306
ear blockage, 316–17
fatigue, 307–13
gas attacks, 317–18
illicit drug use, 322–24
marijuana use, 322–24
medicines and, 324–25
oxygen supply and, 313–17
personal problems and, 304–305
stress and, 300–305
Valsalva procedure, 316–17
Pilot reports (pireps), 225
Precautionary landings, 246–49
Proficiency levels, 256–59

Puddle jumping, 135–37, 139–41
Pulse lights, 16–17

Radar beacon transponders, 36–37
Radar vectors, 84–88
Radar summary chart, 224
Radio-effective pilots, 21–23
Recorded telephone weather, 222
Remote radar weather display imagery, 224
Reverted-rubber hydroplaning, 137
Roberts, Eugene, 143–49
Ross, Robert M., 209–12
    on fuel gauges, 209–12
Runway(s), 121–22, 143–45, 150–51
    incursions, 150–51
    "unimproved," 143–46
    "X" painted on, 143–45

Scanning, 45–47
Seeing to avoid, 28–50
    absence of advisories, 35–37
    "blanking," 38–40
    blind spots, 40–43
    Cessna and Handley Page collision, 30–35
    dropping one's guard, 47–50
    faulty altimeter or encoder, 37–39
    intermittent or erroneous signal, 39–40
    scanning, 45–47
    structural blinders, 43–44
Sequence reports (SAs), 223
Service bulletins, 180
Service difficulty reports (SDRs), 182
Severe weather outlook chart, 227–28
Significant weather prognostic charts ("prog charts"), 227
Sleep deprivation. *See* Fatigue
Stability chart, 228

Stile, Frank, 91–103
    on crash of Aztec 6241 Yankee, 96–103
Stress, 300–305
    management of, 303–304
    personal problems and, 304–305
    pilot error and, 300
Structural blinders, 43–44
    clearing turns and, 44
    in low-wing aircraft, 44
    in straight-and-level flight, 43–44
Surface charts, 222
Surface conflicts, 105–62
    airspeed on landing, 133–35
    ATIS and, 109–12
    birds and, 158–62
    clearing for approach, 116–20
    consistency and, 133–34
    FM broadcast frequency interference, 112–14
    go-arounds, 124–25, 131–33
    grass-field landings, 128–31
    hydroplaning, 135–37, 139–41
    incursions on runways, 150–51
    limited-options landings, 125–26
    maverick signals, 112–14
    night landings, 122–24
    overshoot accidents, 127–28
    perceptible surface conditions, 143–46
    pilot-controller communications and, 115–16
    runway problems, 121–22, 143–46
    taxi instructions and rules, 153–55
    touchdown zone dangers, 107–108
    traffic adjustment and, 115–16
    "unimproved" runways, 143–46
    verification of clearance, 151–53
    wake turbulence and, 108, 155–58
    "X" on runway, 143–45

Taxi instructions, 153–55
  FAR-based rules, 154–55
TCA clearance, 81–82
Tel-Tail system, 16
Terminal forecasts, 225
Terminal radar service areas
    (TRSAs), 75–79
  pilot on, 77–79
  three stages of, 75–76
Touchdown zone dangers, 107–108

Vaamonde, Manuel, 92, 100
Valsalva procedure, 316–17
Viscous hydroplaning, 136
Visual separation, 73–75
VOR, locating by, 245

Wake turbulence, 108, 155–58
  on takeoff, 155–58
Warner, Robert, 170–71
  on mechanic's failure, 170–71
Warning areas, 61

Water contamination of fuel, 191–95
  three kinds of, 195
Weather briefing, 214–29
  A. M. Weather, 217
  area forecast, 221
  briefers, 219–20
  constant pressure charts, 222
  current conditions, 217–18, 223–25
  forecast weather information, 218, 225–29
  "modernization" of, 216
  pilot's attitudes toward, 215–17
  preflight process, 217–19
  recorded telephone weather, 222
  step-by-step review of, 221–29
  surface charts, 222
  three types of, 219–20
  weather depiction chart, 221–22
Weather depiction chart, 221–22

Yodice, John S., 169–70
  on relying on mechanics, 169–70